J. S. Nicholson

A treatise on money and essays on present monetary problems

J. S. Nicholson

A treatise on money and essays on present monetary problems

ISBN/EAN: 9783744722988

Printed in Europe, USA, Canada, Australia, Japan

Cover: Foto ©Suzi / pixelio.de

More available books at **www.hansebooks.com**

A

TREATISE ON MONEY

AND

ESSAYS ON PRESENT MONETARY PROBLEMS

BY

J. SHIELD NICHOLSON, M.A., D.Sc.

PROFESSOR OF COMMERCIAL AND POLITICAL ECONOMY AND
MERCANTILE LAW IN THE UNIVERSITY OF EDINBURGH ;
EXAMINER IN POLITICAL ECONOMY IN THE
UNIVERSITY OF LONDON

WILLIAM BLACKWOOD AND SONS
EDINBURGH AND LONDON
MDCCCLXXXVIII

PREFACE.

In the spring of 1886, the directors of the *Wholesale Co-operative Society* requested me to write for their annual an essay on Money, suitable for the industrial classes. I gladly took advantage of this request to recast the general principles of monetary science, and I thought the best way to make the theories popular and intelligible was to indicate their bearing upon questions of present interest. In doing so, however, I took the greatest pains to point out where any conflict of opinions arose: my object was not conversion but instruction. This was the original form of the present "Treatise on Money," but many corrections have been made, and the last two chapters have been entirely rewritten.

The second part of the volume consists of a number of essays, differing widely in character, but all dealing with present monetary problems. This description applies even to the essay on "John Law and his

System," for it was never more necessary than at present to show the connection between credit and metallic money, and there has never been a better example in the whole range of financial history than " the system " *par excellence.*

In the paper on " One-Pound Notes for England," a definite scheme for their issue, with the special object of restoring the cold coinage, is proposed.

The essay on " The Effects of Great Discoveries of the Precious Metals " is mainly historical; but the bearing on some aspects of the present controversy is obvious.

Next in order come two addresses in which the subject of " International Bi-metallism " is treated in a somewhat popular manner.

The short paper on the " Stability of the Fixed Ratio " is a statistical illustration of a well-known theory.

The essay on " The Measurement of Variations in the Value of the Monetary Standard " deals with an extremely difficult statistical problem. The general method is original,[1] and the practical form of it may be useful as a supplement to other methods also confessedly imperfect with the statistics at present available.

I venture to call special attention to the last essay

[1] Compare Mr Edgeworth's learned memorandum, presented to the British Association, September 1887.

in the volume, on the " Causes of Movements in General Prices." It was commenced more than two years ago, and has been completed with my examination before the Currency Commission fresh in my mind. The first part contains a brief critical exposition of all the principal causes which have been assigned for the recent fall in .prices, and the conclusion is that several of these causes—*e.g.*, improved methods of production, on which much stress is sometimes laid—are indeterminate in their action, and, at any rate, of minor importance. ·

It is, however, the concluding portion of this essay which will, I hope, provoke most criticism. It contains, I believe, the first complete statement of the various modes in which gold prices, silver prices, and the ratio between gold and silver may theoretically interact, with the consequent effects on international trade. One of these possible modes is of great interest at the present time, as it shows that the fall in gold prices may be the direct effect of the prior depreciation of silver. The general analysis, however, indicates several other possible cases, and only facts can decide whether this particular solution is correct.

J. SHIELD NICHOLSON.

The University,
Edinburgh, *February* 1888.

CONTENTS.

PART I.

A TREATISE ON MONEY.

CHAPTER I.

DIFFICULTIES IN THE STUDY AND PRACTICAL IMPORTANCE OF THE SUBJECT.

CHAPTER II.

FUNCTIONS OF MONEY.

CHAPTER III.

MATERIAL MONEY AND REQUISITES OF GOOD COINAGE.

CHAPTER IV.

GRESHAM'S LAW AND TOKEN COINS.

CHAPTER V.

THE QUANTITY OF MONEY AND GENERAL PRICES.

CHAPTER VI.

EFFECTS OF CREDIT OR "REPRESENTATIVE MONEY" ON PRICES.

CHAPTER VII.

INFLUENCE ON THE GENERAL LEVEL OF PRICES IN ANY ONE COUNTRY OF THE GENERAL LEVEL OF PRICES IN OTHER COUNTRIES.

CHAPTER· VIII.

EFFECTS ON GENERAL PRICES OF THE USE OF BOTH GOLD AND
SILVER AS STANDARD MONEY.

PART II.

ESSAYS ON PRESENT MONETARY PROBLEMS.

PART I.

A TREATISE ON MONEY

ON MONEY.

CHAPTER I.

DIFFICULTIES IN THE STUDY AND PRACTICAL IMPORTANCE OF THE SUBJECT.

§ 1. *The difficulty of getting clear ideas.* — It seems desirable at the outset to warn the reader that, although this treatise on the principles of monetary science is intended to be elementary and introductory, the subject is in its nature difficult, and, in spite of its having been treated by many writers celebrated for their clearness of thought and distinctness of language, has not yet received a form which can be considered easy reading. The difficulties presented are of two kinds.

In the *first* place, there is the difficulty of getting clear ideas and attaching accurate and definite meanings to the words employed. People are apt to imagine that because they are familiar with the use of the words money, pound sterling, exchange, bank-note, &c., they are equally familiar with the things and processes and ideas which the words stand for. As a consequence, they do not think it necessary to strain the attention and couple what seems easy read-ing with hard thinking, and, according to the degree of their self - esteem, they come to the conclusion either that the subject is one which no one can un-derstand with any amount of reading, or one which every one can understand without any reading at all.

§ 2. *The difficulty due to the complexity of facts.*— The *second* difficulty inherent in the subject depends upon matters of fact, and the need for statistics and experience to give body to the abstract ideas and general propositions of the theory.   Even the most zealous student is apt to become bewildered when he finds authorities of equal standing opposed to one another on problems of great practical urgency, and feels inclined to conclude that there are no settled principles in the whole subject.   This conflict of opinions, however, often arises simply from the fact that there is not sufficient evidence on which to base a certain conclusion—just as in medicine the best doctors may disagree, or in war the best generals, although no one would deny the vast progress in modern times of the art of healing or the art of destruction.   It must be remembered, also, that the public only hears of the conflicts between the experts in any subject and of the struggles in making the next advance ; as soon as a controversy is settled it passes from the newspaper or periodical to the text-book.

Only those who take the trouble to compare the monetary policy of successive historical periods can form any idea of the extraordinary progress made in the theory and practice of this branch of finance. This progress, as in other practical sciences, has consisted in overcoming difficulties of both the kinds just noticed. On the one side ideas and general principles have been made clear and intelligible, and on the other large stores of facts and figures have been brought to bear on their practical application. It is to what may be regarded as well established that the following pages will be mainly devoted, and if matters of controversy are introduced, the leading opinions on both sides will be stated, and the reader left, like a British jury, in his own person to form his own conclusions on the facts and opinions advanced.

§ 3. *Importance of general study of money in a country with popular government.*—I have thought it necessary to emphasise and explain the nature of the difficulty of the subject, partly with the view of showing the need for hard thinking in some cases, and a suspension of judgment in others until sufficient evidence has been obtained, but principally on account of its great importance to the industrial classes in a community with popular government. If it is once generally believed that questions of currency can be decided offhand by popular votes, the way becomes open for great national calamities.

At the same time, however, when questions of changes in monetary policy arise, they cannot be left to the decision of a few authorities without appeal to the people. It is hardly possible to make any change of this kind without producing a certain conflict of interests, and all history proves that it is not wise for any class to leave its interests entirely in the hands of representatives drawn from another. In many cases, no doubt, the conflict of interests between capital and labour, for example, or landlords and tenants, or traders and consumers, is more apparent than real; but in some cases of vital importance the divergence of interests is fundamental.

In the exchange of services and commodities, as a rule, both parties to the exchange gain, but in mere monetary changes what one gains another must lose. If, for instance, owing to a change in the currency, there is a general rise in prices, debtors will gain at the expense of creditors; a farmer with a long lease at a fixed rent will gain from a rise in prices and the landlord will lose—the one will obtain a greater and the other a less share than before in the general wealth of the community.

§ 4. *Enormous power for evil in currency regula-*

*tions possessed by Governments, illustrated from English
history.* — The enormous power for evil which a
Government possesses in effecting changes in currency
has received more than one startling illustration in
our own history. "It may be doubted," says Mac-
aulay, speaking of the state of things which rendered
necessary the re-coinage of 1696, "whether all the
misery which had been inflicted on the nation in a
quarter of a century, by bad kings, bad parliaments,
and bad judges, was equal to the misery caused in a
single year by bad crowns and bad shillings. The
evil was felt daily, and almost hourly, in almost
every place and by almost every class; in the dairy
and on the threshing-floor, by the anvil and by the
loom, on the billows of the ocean and in the depths
of the mine. Nothing could be purchased without
dispute. Over every counter there was wrangling
from morning to night. The workman and his employer had a quarrel as regularly as the Saturday
came round. No merchant would contract to deliver
goods without making some stipulation about the
quality of the coin in which he was to be paid.
Even men of business were often bewildered by the
confusion into which all pecuniary transactions were
thrown. The simple and the careless were pillaged
without mercy by extortioners whose demands grew
even more rapidly than the money shrank. The
labourer found that the bit of metal which, when he

received it, was called a shilling, would hardly, when he wanted to purchase a pot of beer or a loaf of rye-bread, go so far as sixpence. Where artisans of more than usual intelligence were collected in great numbers, as in the dockyard of Chatham, they were able to make complaints heard and to obtain some redress ; but the ignorant and helpless peasant was cruelly ground between one class which would give money only by tale (counting) and another which would only vote it by weight."

Professor Thorold Rogers, in his interesting work entitled 'Six Centuries of English Work and Wages,' often calls attention to the importance to the industrial classes of a sound system of currency. "The monetary history of all countries," he writes, "is full of instances which illustrate the rapidity with which people fall into the delusion that high prices, due to over-issues of paper, the coinage of an over-valued metal, or to excessive speculation, are evidences of prosperity. Our English Parliament, in the present century, endorsed the follies of Vansittart and repudiated the truths which were announced by the Bullion Committee and Lord King. But the issue of base money is rapidly and irremediably mischievous. It affects all except those who are quick at measuring the exact extent of the fraud, and by turning the base coin into an article of traffic, can trade on the knowledge and skill which they possess.

To the poor, and indeed to all who live by wages and fixed salaries, it is speedily ruinous. The effect of the base money of Henry VIII. and Edward VI., though it lasted only sixteen years, was potent enough to dominate in the history of labour and wages from the sixteenth century to the present time, so enduring are the causes which influence the economical history of a nation."

§ 5. *Evils of bad currency in France during the Revolution.*—Nor must it be supposed that the evils of bad currency have been inflicted on nations only by despots and irresponsible Governments. The most glaring example of the violation of sound principles of currency recorded in history is the issue by the Government of the great French Revolution of the inconvertible notes called *assignats.* " It was constantly urged," says A. D. White in his work on ' Paper Money Inflation in France,' " that if any nation could safely issue paper money France was now that nation ; that she was fully warned by a severe experience ; that she was now a constitutional Government controlled by an enlightened, patriotic people—not, as in the days of the former issue of paper money, an absolute monarchy controlled by politicians and adventurers ; that she was able to secure every franc of her paper money by a virtual mortgage of a landed domain of vastly greater value than the entire issue ; that with men like Bailly,

Mirabeau, and Necker at the head, she could not
commit the financial mistakes and errors from which
France had suffered when at the head stood John
Law and the Regent and Cardinal Dubois." De-
luded by these arguments, the issues were made, with
fatal consequences to French industry. "What the
bigotry of Louis XIV. and the shiftlessness of Louis
XV. could not do in nearly a century, was accomplished by thus tampering with the currency in a
few months. Everything that tariffs and custom-
houses could do was done. Still, the great manu-
factories of Normandy were closed; those of the rest
of the kingdom speedily followed, and vast numbers
of workmen in all parts of the country were thrown
out of employment. In the words of the most
brilliant apologist for French Revolutionary states-
manship — 'Commerce was dead — betting took its
place.'"

§ 6. *Difficulties in radical changes in currency, but
such changes sometimes necessary.*—It would require
many large volumes to describe the magnitude of the
evils which different nations from the earliest times
down to our own day have suffered from ill-regulated
currencies. So much have some Socialist writers
been impressed by these evils and by other difficulties
which arise even in the best monetary systems, that
they have tried to formulate schemes in which the use
of money would be entirely forbidden: with them

money itself is, in the fullest meaning of the expression, the root of all evil.

Other writers, again, who have given much attention to the subject, have been so much impressed with the evil consequences of any disturbance of a nation's system of currency, that they are opposed to all changes if during a moderate length of time the system has worked at all well. In a recent paper, Mr Giffen has endeavoured to show that the functions of Government regarding money should be reduced to a minimum, and he writes in the most despairing tone of human fallibility. " To obtain the action of Governments you have to submit the discussion to tribunals of a very peculiar description,— to Parliaments which are full of people who have no intellectual interest in the subjects, and no qualification of any sort or kind for dealing with them ; and to constituencies electing the members of Parliament who are still more unfit, and who have little conception of the nature of the problems to be discussed, and no means whatsoever of forming practical conclusions upon them—who are, in fact, likely to be bewildered and confused if a Government makes a change of any kind in respect of the standard money."

It may certainly be conceded to Mr Giffen that very strong reasons ought to be adduced before any great change in a monetary system can be recommended; but the conditions of industry have varied so rapidly, such enormous changes have taken place even during the last fifty years, that it is quite possible that a system of currency which acted well enough in former times may at present require some modification. It would certainly be a most remarkable thing if, when economic institutions of every kind have been remodelled, when vital changes have taken place in the production and distribution of wealth, when remote nations have become more closely knit together by commerce than were cities of the same country fifty years ago, when the whole industrial world has been almost revolutionised, no change whatever in currency, which is the very life-blood of industry, should be necessary or desirable.

§ 7. *The subject of money is in its nature difficult, but not obscure or mysterious—it requires, like mathematics, hard thinking and regular advance.*—And if any change is requisite, the scheme proposed ought to be of a nature which can be made intelligible to the people interested. Bare authority will not be accepted in these days; and after all, the fundamental principles of money may be understood by any person of ordinary capacity who will devote a little trouble, and who is not too proud to begin at the beginning. To say that a subject is difficult is not to say that it is obscure, or unintelligible, or mysterious, or demanding some peculiar, rare native gift. Mathematics is a

difficult study—even arithmetic, although now part
of a compulsory education, is not easy; but mathematical reasoning is eminently clear and distinct. So
it is with money: the principles of the subject,
although in one sense the most difficult, are also the
clearest and most intelligible in economic science.
Those who find the practical problems at present
agitating the public mind difficult of comprehension
and apparently insoluble, would look on them with
very different eyes if they had made a systematic
study of the elements of monetary science. "There is
much," says Professor Jevons, "to be learnt about
money before entering upon those abstruse questions
which barely admit of decided answers. In studying
a language, we begin with the grammar before we
try to read or write. In mathematics we practise
ourselves in simple arithmetic before we proceed to
the subtleties of algebra and the differential calculus.
But it is the grave misfortune of the moral and
political sciences that they are continually discussed
by those who have never laboured at the elementary
grammar or the simple arithmetic of the subject.
Hence the extraordinary schemes and fallacies every
now and then put forth."

CHAPTER II.

FUNCTIONS OF MONEY.

§ 1. *Definition of money.* — A good deal of discussion has taken place as to the proper definition of the term "money," and it must not be thought that, because no particular definition has been generally adopted by economists, therefore the discussion has been wasted. The great use of definitions is to lay bare the meanings of the terms employed, to clear up the ideas for which they stand, and thus to get rid of all ambiguities; but it is a matter of comparatively small importance whether different writers use the same word in precisely the same sense when, either from their definition at the outset or from the context, the meaning is plain.

As regards money, for example, some writers may include and some exclude bank-notes, and other forms of credit, but no harm is done provided the functions of notes, cheques, &c., are properly described. There is, however, considerable danger in laying down, at first, hard-and-fast definitions, and then deducing general laws, and applying these laws to particular cases without due consideration.

In the sequel we shall see that by far the most important proposition laid down respecting money is that, other things being the same, its value depends on its quantity—that if the quantity of money is increased, the value of each particular piece is diminished. Now, if we were to lay down at the outset a definition of money which included convertible bank-notes, and were then to argue, in accordance with the proposition just noticed, that an increase of bank-notes would lower the value of money, we might happen to speak the truth, but unless many more circumstances were taken into account we should only speak the truth by accident. Yet reasoning of this kind prevailed in making the most important law ever made affecting the paper currency of this country. As it happens, it is generally admitted that this Act, passed in 1844, has on the whole worked well, or, at any rate, has done no great harm; but it is more satisfactory when Acts of Parliament succeed on the grounds on which they were ostensibly passed, and not for reasons which were not considered. It would be out of place to discuss the Act in question at this stage; I have only mentioned it to show the danger of being misled by words. Opinions are divided on the

real merits of the Act, but no one now will defend
the reasoning by which it was supported by its
promoters.

I shall not attempt to give a short and simple
definition of money, because it seems to me that the
meaning of the term must vary according to circumstances. An illustration will make this quite clear.
What is meant in the money articles of the news-
papers by the supply of money and the demand for
money? Every one knows it is not merely coin or
notes of the Bank of England, but they would have
some difficulty in explaining what else ought to be
included. The important thing, however, for our
present purpose, is not to decide what is the most
appropriate meaning to give to the term "money,"
but to describe certain functions of the industrial
world which are generally briefly spoken of as being
performed by money.

§ 2. *Money as a medium of exchange.*—First of all,
then, let us consider money as *a medium of exchange*,
and its importance in this capacity. "It is easy to
imagine, even in a primitive society, the inconveniences of pure barter. The griefs of the bootmaker
wanting a hat, who found many who had hats but
did not at the time want boots, and many men who
wanted boots badly enough but were quite as ill off,
temporarily or permanently, respecting hats, have
been related by every writer on money."—(Walker.)

But what is not so often attended to is the ever-increasing importance, with the growing complexity of industrial societies, of a universal medium of exchange : it becomes, as division of labour is extended, not merely a convenience in distributing the finished product, but an actual necessary of production. Let any one consider the vast series of operations necessary to provide for the maintenance in our days of the family of an unskilled labourer; or, better still, let him glance over the list of occupations of the people as given in the census reports, in which he will find hundreds of names to which he can attach no meaning whatever.[1] Without some common medium of exchange, it would be absolutely impossible under our present industrial system to carry on the manufactures and commerce of the country. The only conceivable alternative would be governmental control of the most elaborate kind pervading every home, involving in itself an enormous waste of time and labour. Without a complete revolution in the conditions of society, a medium of exchange is indispensable. Production rests on division of labour, and division of labour involves easy and prompt exchange, which, again, involves a common medium. Money in this sense is as essen-

---

[1] The last census report states that it was found necessary, in order to classify the different employments returned, to make a small dictionary.

tial to the interchange of commodities as language to the interchange of ideas, and in the last resort the exchange of commodities is for the most part the exchange of the services through which they are made. Thus money, in the sense of a common medium of exchange, is necessary in order to exchange all kinds of labour, from the highest to the lowest.

In these days we are so familiar with this universal medium, with this alchemist's stone which turns everything into gold—land and labour, the fleeting wealth of the present and the stored wealth from the past—that it is difficult for us to realise the state of a nation in which custom took the place of contract, and the mass of the people lived practically without money. There can be no doubt that during the middle ages the commutation of various services and labour dues into money equivalents was the principal factor in the industrial progress of that period. The break-up of feudalism, the independence of the towns, the abolition of serfdom, and the growth of commerce, are all largely due to the substitution of money payments resting on contracts in place of services founded on law and custom. So far from being an evil, during this period at any rate, the extension of the use of money as a medium of exchange was the means of effecting great social reforms, and there can be little doubt that progress was retarded largely by the deficiency of the precious metals, and especially the dearth of silver.

The Socialists, who look on money as an engine by which the rich torture the poor, will find in many instances that, on the contrary, it has been the greatest benefactor of labour. We have a modern instance of the benefits of money payments in the state of things which led to the passing of the Truck Acts. Every one knows that the worst mode in which a workman can be paid for his labour is in a quantity of the commodity which he makes or assists in making—in cider, for example, as was the custom in some places in England.

§ 3. *Money as a measure of values.*—Necessarily involved in this function of money as a medium of exchange is its function as *a measure of values.* It is useless to convert all things and services into terms of money as a medium of exchange unless this is done at certain rates. What we want to know in any given case is not the bare fact that by means of money exchanges can be effected between one commodity and ten thousand others, but we want some *measure* of the rates of exchange.

Now it is quite possible that the *actual* medium of exchange adopted may not be itself the measure in which values are expressed—it may itself be measured by some other standard. In this country at the present time the standard unit of value is the sovereign, which consists of a definite amount of gold and alloy fixed by Act of Parliament. Consequently all values in this country are measured in pounds and parts of pounds. But although the sovereign is the standard unit, it is by no means the exclusive medium of exchange. We use not only silver and bronze, but paper as the actual medium.

The important point to observe, however, is that all these substances used as actual means of exchange are measured in terms of the sovereign either as multiples or sub-multiples. Wages, according to the quality of the labour, the times of payment, &c., are paid sometimes in pence, sometimes in shillings, sometimes in bank-notes, sometimes in cheques, but the standard measure is the sovereign, and the values of the pence, shillings, notes, or cheques depend on their relation to the sovereign.

It is extremely important to distinguish between the actual medium and the measure of reckoning. In some parts of Scotland the rent paid for land depends on the prices of certain kinds of agricultural produce ; in effect, we may suppose that the rents consist nominally of so much corn. But they would not be actually paid in corn. Instead of the rents depending on the prices of a few agricultural products, they might depend on the prices of a hundred different articles. That would be just as if the farmer stipulated to pay certain quantities of these articles in different proportions. In this way the unit of value would be very complex, but the payment would never be made in all these articles.

We see, then, that the two functions of money already noticed are not necessarily performed by the same thing: we may measure in terms of one thing and pay in terms of another, but the two functions are equally necessary to an industrial society, and are mutually dependent. The medium of exchange would be useless unless measured in terms of the standard, and the measure would be useless unless some common medium of giving effect to it practically is adopted. A person who has something to sell—whether labour, or land, or produce—wants to know not only that his commodity bears a certain proportion in value to the commodities of other sellers—that is, he not only wants his commodity measured as the others are measured—but he wants some medium by which he can make as many purchases of these commodities as his article entitles him to obtain.

§ 4. *Money as a standard for deferred payments.*—So far nothing has been said of the element of *time*. We have spoken of exchanges being effected and the values of commodities being measured without any reference (except by way of illustration) to deferred payments, or payments extending over a long period. It is this consideration, however, which constitutes the greatest difficulty, both practical and theoretical,

in choosing a standard unit of value as the basis of
money. At any particular time, or, rather, to effect
any single set of exchanges, we might measure the
values of all commodities by any one of them—say
corn—write down their values in terms of corn on
bits of paper, and exchange accordingly. In some
Socialistic schemes it has been proposed to issue
labour - tickets against commodities or services, and
everything being expressed in terms of so much
labour, exchanges might be made on this basis. But
a little reflection would show that there would be
much difficulty in taking an hour's labour as the unit
of value over a long period, because all kinds of
changes might occur in the efficiency, or intensity,
or hardship in the labour ; and the same kind of
difficulty arises with whatever standard is chosen.

§ 5. *Contracts for long periods.*—Under our present
system we must find some means of overcoming uncertainty in the interpretation of contracts : the whole
of industry rests on an endless series of contracts,
which ought to admit of a definite interpretation.
Now it is quite easy to lay down that our unit of
value, our chosen standard, shall consist of a certain
weight of a certain specified substance of a certain
quality, and if we only wanted our unit as a measure
of weight or of fineness, no more would be required.

But the difficulty is this : We want our unit to
measure, not weight, or qualities, or capacities, or

colours, but *values*. We may, by choosing any substance whatever, capable of exact measurement and definition, avoid in one sense any uncertainty in the interpretation of contracts; but we do so in a purely artificial and useless manner unless other changes are taken into account.

To discover what these other requisites are, let us take an example of deferred payments. A farmer takes a farm on a nineteen years' lease at so many pounds, say £1000 a-year. There will be no doubt about the meaning of the contract. He must either pay exactly every year the thousand sovereigns, or give some document or other which will enable the receiver to obtain on demand that number of pounds sterling. In making this agreement, supposing the bargain was the result of competition, the farmer would have taken into account not only how much the land would yield of various kinds of produce, but also the prices he would expect on the average to obtain, as also the prices he would have to pay for the various expenses of production for labour, machines, manures, &c. Suppose, now, that at the end of ten years, owing to any cause whatever, the prices of produce have fallen very greatly, and also that the price of labour and the materials of production have not fallen equally, the result would be that he cannot really afford to pay the same rent as before, and he will be inclined to argue that Government should release him from his contract, because it was entered on with the expectation that prices would on the average have remained steady. The example just taken is essentially the case of many farmers at the present time. And they may very plausibly argue that if they are compelled to pay their rents they will be ruined, that the land in the process will be exhausted, that their successors will not have the same experience, and allege other inconveniences to the nation at large. This is not the place to consider whether this plea should be urged on the Government or on the landlords, but of the hardship to the farmers there can be no doubt.

Let us take another example, also of a practical kind. The Indian Government engages the services of a highly trained body of men, and promises to pay them a certain number of rupees. There is no doubt as to the meaning of the rupee in its material shape. It is a certain weight of a certain quality of silver. Suppose at the time the bargain is made ten rupees go to a sovereign, then the savings of Indian servants remitted home will command that rate so long as it lasts; but it is equally clear that if the value of the rupee sinks to a shilling, for purposes of remittance they will lose half the value of their salaries.

One more example on a larger scale. The Government of this country has to pay more than twenty millions sterling of interest on the National Debt.

To do so it must levy taxes. If, reckoned in money, the taxable wealth of the country has become much less, so much more heavy must the taxation be to make these payments.

§ 6. *Importance of comparative stability of value in money.*—It is clear from these examples that "money" is required not only as a medium of exchange and a measure of values, but as a standard for deferred payments. So long as contracts into which time enters as an element are expressed in terms of money, it is necessary that the standard adopted should possess comparative *stability of value.* It is at this point that one of the most serious difficulties of the subject arises, for it is now universally admitted in works on political economy that any such thing as a commodity with absolute stability of value is unattainable. The best way to see this is to consider the causes on which the value of any commodity depends.

§ 7. *Meaning of terms " demand " and " supply."*— Stated in the most general terms and in the form most familiar to the industrial world, value may be said to depend on demand and supply. Both of these words, however, familiar as they are, require some further explanation. What do we really understand by *demand ?* It is quite clear that we do not simply mean desire to possess, for, roughly speaking, it may be said that human desires are insatiable—

that everybody desires everything. It is obviously not in this vague sense that we can properly speak of there being no demand for commodities of various kinds—for food, clothes, houses, and luxuries. There are, at any rate, always " poor about our gates," who not only desire but very urgently need those very things for which the commercial papers tell us there is no demand.

Precisely the same difficulty occurs in regard to *supply*. All manufacturers would be delighted to supply many times as much of their articles as they actually do if they could only find purchasers. The explanation is found in introducing a phrase which must always be understood. Both demand and supply mean demand and supply *at a price*, and the peculiarity of both is, that in general they vary with the price, but in opposite directions. As a general rule it may be laid down that, other things being equal, if the price of an article falls relatively to that of others, the demand increases.

This is a law which has received striking illustration from the history of taxation. Impose a tax of a very onerous amount, and instead of increasing the revenue you may kill the revenue altogether ; whilst, on the other hand, the progressive diminution of a tax, by increasing the demand, may also increase the revenue obtainable.

As regards supply, the general rule is, that if there

is a rise in the price an additional supply will be forthcoming. If, for example, the price of coal rises, a great stimulus is given to coal-mining; labour and capital are directed to this industry, and there is a great increase in the supply.

§ 8. *Law of demand and supply.*—We see, then, that the demand and supply of any article both vary according to price—both depend upon price : how, then, can we say that price depends on demand and supply ? The solution is found in what J. S. Mill called the "equation between demand and supply," which may be expressed in the following form. In any market, competition will take place between sellers on one side and buyers on the other, until such a price is arrived at that the quantity demanded at that price is equal to the quantity offered. Any increase in the competition of buyers will tend to raise the price, and the rise in the price will drive the poorest and least eager of the competitors from the circle of demanders ; whilst, on the other hand, the same rise will tend to induce dealers who had been withholding their stocks to come forward.

It will be seen, then, that everything depends on competition ;[1] and this disposes of an objection

[1] For the purposes of this treatise it was not thought advisable to push the analysis of value further. The writer fully admits the importance of considering the conception of *final utility* and the case of *monopoly* (cf. Note on Value in his edition of the ' Wealth of Nations,' p. 407).

by the late Professor Cairnes, who said that all J. S.
Mill's boasted equation amounted to was, that in
any market the quantity bought at a price was precisely equal to the quantity sold at that price, which
was no doubt quite true, but also quite useless.   But
the point of J. S. Mill's argument is, that competition is the moving force according to which the
price rises and falls, and the quantities offered or
demanded are increased and diminished.

If, now, we push the analysis further, and ask,
On what does competition depend? we have thrust
upon us at once a variety of causes.   Amongst these,
undoubtedly the most important are the various
conditions of supply.   Some things are absolutely
limited, and this class consists by no means simply
of such commodities as are indicated by the stock
example of old pictures.   The land of a whole
country, and equally the areas of particular districts
and towns, are strictly limited.   It must be remembered, also, that many things which could be increased
if only time were allowed, may be wanted immediately.   Take, for example, the food-supplies of any
industrial area.   No doubt this country could raise a
much greater supply of food within its own borders,
but in case of a great war, or other cause of cessation
of imports, there would certainly be famine prices.

There are, however, other commodities which can
be indefinitely increased at very short notice, and no

one would give fancy prices for existing stocks of
cloth if by waiting a few weeks an abundant supply
could be obtained.   It is not necessary for the present
purpose to go into further detail.   The point which
is essential to the argument is, that one important
factor in determining value is the conditions of supply,
and these conditions are subject to variation, as regards most articles, with every change in the methods
of production.

The conditions affecting demand are equally important, and also subject to variation.   A rise in the
price of any article will probably lead to an increase
in the demand for convenient substitutes, and, with
the progress of civilisation, the wants and desires of
people are constantly changing.   Whether, then, we
look to a simple market and temporary prices, or to
the annual consumption of a great nation, we find
abundant reasons for expecting constant changes in
relative values.   It is, then, quite clear that we cannot in strictness say that any single commodity is
capable of possessing stability of value.   For value
means, as the last resort, exchange value ; and any
commodity we like to choose will, in the lapse of a
very short time, fetch more of one article and less of
another.

§ 9. *Is comparative stability of value in money attainable ?*—Are we, then, to suppose that the search
for a kind of money which will possess stability of

value is an idle quest, and that as regards stability of value every article will be equally unsuitable ? This would obviously be unjustifiable. A little reflection will show that, for practical purposes, we may get for a considerable time a much greater comparative stability in some things than in others. In some things the annual production compared with the total amount in use may be small, and the demand may be fairly constant—that is, not subject to sudden changes in fashion or (to express it more generally) in desire. A commodity of this kind would be properly said to be more stable in value than an article in which these qualities were wanting.

Thus, although we cannot find any substance for our standard money a given quantity of which will always possess the same purchasing power over each and every commodity, we may find that one substance will over a term of years have a much more uniform power of purchasing things in general than is the case with other substances. "Things in general" is, of course, a vague and rather uncertain expression, but it is perhaps the best obtainable. For practical purposes, however, we only require a particular class of things. An agricultural labourer, for example, if he wishes to compare the purchasing power of his wages with those in other times and places, will be able to make a tolerably just comparison by taking a very few commodities; and if he can lay by a few

pounds he will be satisfied with the stability of value
of money, provided they enable him to obtain about
the same amount of the articles of his habitual consumption as when he made his saving.

Unless some stability of value of the kind indicated were attainable in money, the world would be
put to very great inconvenience. This has been
illustrated only too often in history by the criminal,
or at best ill - considered, action of Governments in
artificially changing the value of the standard. It
is, at any rate, perfectly certain that a coin of a
uniform weight and fineness is in all respects more
steady in value, or represents a more constant purchasing power, than one which is subjected to wilful
debasement or diminution. And if, instead of metal,
paper is exclusively used for money, and the issues
are not most carefully regulated, the fluctuations in
value will be still greater and more detrimental.

§ 10. *A tabular standard of value.*—We have now
examined the three most important functions of what
is briefly spoken of as money. Every industrial
society requires a common medium of exchange, a
general measure of values, and a standard for deferred payments; and there can be no doubt that it
will be much more convenient if these three requisites
are found united in, or rather conjoined with, the
standard money of a nation. It has, however, already
been pointed out that it is not necessary that the

actual medium of exchange should itself be the
money of account or measure of values, and in the
same way it is not necessary that contracts for long
periods should be made, as they are usually at present, in terms of definite quantities of the standard
money.

This is especially noteworthy at a time when the
general movement in prices is downwards at an uncertain rate.   It may, then, be worth while to describe
briefly what is known as the "tabular standard," of
which the reader will find a more detailed account in
the excellent manual of Professor Jevons on 'Money'
(pp. 327-333), to which reference has already been
made.   The following passages will, perhaps, suffice
to show the essentials of the scheme: "To carry
Lowe's and Scrope's plans (published in 1822 and
1833 respectively) into effect, a permanent Government commission would have to be created, and en-
dowed with a kind of judicial power.   The officers of
the department would collect the current prices of
commodities in all the principal markets of the kingdom, and by a well-defined system of calculations
would compute from their data the average variations
in the purchasing power of gold.   The decisions of
this commission would be published monthly, and
payments would be adjusted in accordance with them.
Thus, suppose that a debt of £100 was incurred upon
the 1st July 1875, and was to be paid back on

1st July 1878; if the commission had decided in June 1878 that the value of gold had fallen in the ratio of 106 to 100 in the intervening years, then the creditor would claim an increase of 6 per cent in the nominal amount of the debt. . . . The difficulties in the way of such a scheme are not considerable. It would no doubt introduce a certain complexity into the relations of debtors and creditors, and disputes might sometimes arise as to the date of the debt whence the calculations must be made. The work of the commission, when once established and directed by Act of Parliament, would be little more than that of accountants acting according to fixed rules. Their decisions would be of a perfectly *bond fide* character, because, in addition to their average results, they would be required to publish periodically the detailed tables of prices upon which their calculations were founded, and thus many persons could sufficiently verify the data and the calculations. Fraud would be out of the question."

It will be observed that, according to this scheme, there would be no change in the actual currency; the only object would be to give a more definite meaning to contracts for deferred payments by taking into account changes in the purchasing power of the sovereign. Recently the plan in question has received strong support from Professor Marshall. I quote from a paper furnished by him to the Royal Commission on the Depression of Trade (Third Report, Appendix C, p. 33) : "A perfectly exact measure of purchasing power is not only unattainable, but even unthinkable [that is, taking into account the varying wants and resources of industrial societies]. The same change of prices affects the purchasing power of money to different persons in different ways. For one who can seldom afford to have meat, a rise of one-fourth in the price of meat, accompanied by a fall of one-fourth in that of bread, means a rise in the purchasing power of money. His wages will go further than before; while to his richer neighbour, who spends twice as much on meat as on bread, the change acts the other way. The Government would, of course, take account only of the total consumption of the whole nation; but even so, it would be troubled by constant changes in the way in which the nation spent its income. The estimate of the importance of different commodities would have to be recast from time to time."

§ 11. *Index numbers.* — The form in which the problem of a general rise or fall in prices is most often presented to the public is in the calculation of what are termed "index numbers"; and, in fact, the tabular standard is simply an official index number. We may take as an example the index numbers which for many years have been adopted in the annual commercial review of the 'Economist' newspaper. According to this method, the average prices of a number of selected articles were determined for a period of six years (1845-50), and each of these prices per unit taken was reckoned at 100. Thus we might get a pound, or a yard, or a gallon, as the original unit, but the price per unit is in every case 100. Now, suppose changes occur in prices, then the corresponding change is marked by the addition to or subtraction from this 100 of the necessary percentages. In general, we find movements in opposite directions, and the resultant or general movement is determined by simple addition of the new index numbers, as they are called. Thus, if, as in the ' Economist,' 22 articles are taken, the addition of the original initial index numbers would be 2200. If at any time the aggregate index numbers amount to more than 2200, a general rise in prices is said to have taken place; if they amount to less, there is a general fall. It is quite clear that the calculation is very rough, and must always be used with caution. For example, if the index numbers showed a general rise, it would not do without further examination to say that the same money wages would purchase less commodities for the use of labourers, for it might happen that the particular articles consumed by labourers had fallen in price on the whole.

§ 12. *Movements in index numbers in recent years.*— It may be interesting to notice the principal move-

ments in the index numbers of the 'Economist' since
their adoption, when, as explained, the total index
number of 22 commodities reckoned at 100 each
was · 2200.   A fluctuating rise, with occasional re-
lapses in particular years, took place up to 1864,
when the index number was 3787.   This is equivalent to saying that on the articles taken there was
an average rise of about 72 per cent.   (It must,
however, be remembered this very high number is
largely due to the exceptional price of cotton, owing
to the American Civil War.)   From 1864 to 1871
there was a fluctuating fall in prices, the index number in the latter year being 2590.   Then a rise took
place, the numbers in 1872-3-4 being respectively
2835, 2947, 2891.   Thus, in these years of inflation, as they are often termed, though there was a
rise of about 31 per cent on the original index number of 1845-50, there was a still greater fall from
the number of 1864.   From 1874 there has been a
steady and rapid decline, until we find, on 1st January
1886, the aggregate index number is only 2023,
which is lower than the original number, and than
that of any subsequent year.[1]

It is this very remarkable fall in prices which is

[1] For a criticism on the general method of index numbers, compare
the Essay on variations in the value of the monetary standard (p.
298).   By far the best monograph on the whole subject is that furnished by Mr F. Y. Edgeworth to the British Association, September
1887.

at present exciting so much attention, and which has been the principal cause of the appointment of the Royal Commission on currency. I have dwelt at some length on this aspect of the subject, because it is not only the most difficult of the functions of money to understand, but has very serious practical consequences. I am not inclined to think that the use of a general official index number, however carefully it was constructed, would be likely, at any rate for many generations, to be commonly adopted as the basis of contracts, even for a long term of years. It is all very well to talk of getting rid of the speculative element, say in rents, but human nature is on the whole so buoyant and confident, that this is precisely the element an enterprising farmer would wish to retain. At the same time, however, I think it must be admitted that the idea is a very fruitful one, and is capable of less perfect but more practical applications in the shape of varieties of the " sliding scale." If there is any likelihood of a fall in prices during the next ten years, being on the same scale as in the last ten, undoubtedly a great many contracts must be readjusted to the change in the purchasing power of the standard money.

CHAPTER III.

MATERIAL MONEY AND REQUISITES OF GOOD COINAGE.

§ 1. *Early forms of money.*—It is necessary, however, before attempting to explain the causes of these movements in general prices, to return to the simple elements of the subject, and to consider what substances are best adapted to serve for money, or to fulfil these various money functions. We are so much accustomed to regard gold and silver as money *par excellence*, that we are apt to forget the number and variety of materials which have been used at different times. If space permitted, a historical survey would show that what are termed the precious metals may be regarded as "survivals of the fittest" in the struggle for existence of a great variety of substances.

"It is entirely," as Professor Jevons says, "a question of degree what commodities will, in any given society, form the most convenient currency." I give a few examples, chiefly derived from this writer's work on 'Money.' In the hunting stage of societies

skins have very commonly been used, and this is the
explanation of the verse in Job (ii. 4): "Skin for
skin; yea, all that a man hath will he give for his
life." The transition from skins to leather was
natural, and leather money is said to have been used
in many ancient nations. Even in quite recent times,
in the trade of the Hudson's Bay Company with the
North American Indians, furs long formed the medium
of exchange. In the pastoral stage, when the principal wealth of the society consisted of herds, we find
cattle used as a measure of value, and it is said that
pecunia, the Latin term for money, is derived from
pecus, cattle.

In the agricultural state corn came into use as
money, and is said still to form the medium of exchange in some remote parts of Europe, whilst at
different times and places olive-oil, tobacco, tea, dried
fish, salt, and straw mats have been used. Iron, tin,
lead, and copper were also tried at a higher stage of
development, but in the great majority of cases all
other materials for standard money have given place
to gold and silver; and during the last twelve years
in the Western world an attempt has been made to
make gold the sole standard.

§ 2. *Qualities of good metallic money.*—An enumeration of the various qualities good metallic money
should possess will explain this gradual exclusive
adoption of gold and silver. The substance should

be generally acceptable on its own account if it is to serve as a medium of exchange, and no metals are more sought after on their own account than these two. There can be no doubt in our own times that the consumption of gold, especially for the arts, has enormously increased, and is one of the most important factors to be taken into account in considering the effects of the "scarcity of gold," of which more will be said presently. It is well known also that one of the best signs of the prosperity of India is a large importation of gold, not for use as money, but as treasure or ornaments.

Other qualities of good metallic money which require little explanation, and which are eminently possessed by gold and silver, are *portability*, which again is closely connected with great value in small bulk; *durability*, so that no deterioration takes place by saving, and a minimum of wear and tear in use; *uniformity* of parts, so that equal weights, however large or small, shall have the same value; *divisibility*, which is implied in the quality just mentioned; and finally, what Professor Jevons calls *cognisability*, or such characteristics that the purity of the metal may be easily recognised, and that it may be conveniently coined. Taking all these qualities together, gold and silver are certainly the best metals for money; and it may be noticed that gold is too valuable in proportion to its weight to be used for very small, just as silver is hardly valuable enough for very large sums.

§ 3. *Connection of these qualities with the functions of money.*—It is hardly necessary to explain the connection between these qualities of money and its primary functions as a measure of value and medium of exchange; but, as has been shown above, in the progress of society, stability of value becomes of more and more importance, and in this respect it is essential that the supply should keep even pace with the demand if that is possible. The great durability of gold and silver, and the care taken of them in consequence of their value, render the supply in the hands of man very large compared with the annual produce of the mines. At present the proportion of the annual to the total supply is probably not much more than one to fifty.[1] As we shall see presently, the greatest sources of fluctuations are on the side of demand. At any rate, there can be no doubt that these metals are, in respect of comparative stability of value, superior to any others.

§ 4. *Coinage of money.* " *What is a pound?* "—In the list of qualities mentioned as desirable in metallic money, it will be remembered that the last was *cognisability.* At first, after gold and silver were generally adopted, the risk of being defrauded by

---

[1] The statistics as to the total amount of gold and silver in the hands of man are of course extremely vague.

inferior quality or adulteration was left entirely to the receiver of the metals; in fact, they circulated between the inhabitants of the country simply as merchandise, just as at present between different countries. Very early, however, it began to be recognised that there would be great convenience if pieces of the metal were certified by authority to be of certain weights and fineness; and accordingly, coinage has always been one of the first industrial functions that Governments have undertaken.

At the time of the Domesday survey in England (1086) every important town had, as part of its privileges, the right to a mint. It is probable, both from the analogy of other cases and the particular evidence to hand, that the profits of the king or feudal lord acted at least as powerfully as the interests and convenience of the subjects in the institution of coinage, and it is certainly noteworthy how surely and steadily the nominal weight diminished in reality. At the same time, however, in the interests of historical truth, it must be observed that in most cases (until the reign of Henry VIII.) the lowering of the weight of the standard coins was only the legal expression of an accomplished fact (through lawful and unlawful wear and tear). The purity of the standard silver was never tampered with except by the first Defender of the Faith.

The following is an interesting passage from a

speech of Sir Robert Peel in the debate on the Bank
Charter Act, May 6, 1844, in which he asked his
famous question—" What is a pound ? "   " What is
the meaning," he said, " of the pound according to the
ancient monetary policy of this country ?   The origin
of the term was this : In the reign of William the
Conqueror a pound weight of silver was also the
pound of account.   The ' pound' represented both
the weight of metal and the denomination of money.
By subsequent debasements of the currency a great
alteration was made, not in the name but in the intrinsic value of the pound sterling; and it was not
until a late period of the reign of Queen Elizabeth
that silver, being then the standard of value, received
that determinate weight which it retained without
variation, with constant refusals to debase the standard of silver, until the year 1816, when gold became
the exclusive standard of value."

It was in this year that the Coinage Act was
passed, which, though since repealed, was in substance
re-enacted by the Coinage Act of 1870.   According
to this Act, the coinage of gold bullion of standard
value is executed in England (nominally) without cost
to the owner, and without limit as to amount.   In
practice, however, it is usual for the owner of gold
bullion to take it to the Bank of England, which is
bound by law to buy any amount of gold at the rate
of £3, 17s. 9d. per ounce of standard gold.   The

bank is authorised to charge £3, 17s. 10½d. per
ounce to the Mint, the difference (1½d. per ounce)
being its remuneration for trouble incurred, while, as
the owner of the bullion is thus able to convert it
immediately into money, he finds the transaction
profitable, as he saves the loss of interest from delay.
The charge on coining gold bullion is thus about ⅛
per cent practically.

§ 5. *The Mint price of gold.*—It will be seen, then,
that what is termed the Mint price of gold is a very
different thing from other prices. In all essentials,
all that is meant by the Mint price is that a certain
amount of gold, mixed with a definite proportion of
alloy to harden it, is coined into a certain number of
gold coins of a given denomination. The old way of
expressing this in the Mint indentures was that
twenty pounds' weight, troy, of standard gold are to
be coined into 934 sovereigns and one half-sovereign.
If, then, any one foolishly complains that the Mint
price of gold is fixed, the real meaning of his complaint is that the weight of the sovereign is fixed.

Sometimes a difficulty is felt in reconciling this
fixity in the price of gold with the constant fluctuations in the value of gold. The difficulty arises from
the fact that the exchange values of all other commodities are reckoned in terms of gold coins, but there
is not even an apparent contradiction in saying that
an ounce of gold will make a fixed number of coins,

whilst these coins will exchange for a variable amount of other commodities.

§ 6. *The value of gold.*—It is important, however, to observe that by business men the phrase "value of gold" is sometimes used, as is always the case in the writings of political economists, in the sense of exchange value or purchasing power, but more often with quite a different meaning—namely, as equivalent to the rate of interest, and especially the Bank of England minimum rate; in other words, they mean by the value of gold, the price paid for the use of a certain sum for a certain period.

At a later stage it will be necessary to explain that the rate of interest—the rate at which traders can discount their bills, or otherwise obtain advances—often has an important effect on the prices of commodities. A very high rate may cause a fall in prices, and a low rate may in some cases cause a rise; but the two things are absolutely distinct, and it is quite possible, and indeed common, to have a low rate of interest with a low level of prices—that is to say, a low value of gold in the sense of interest, and a high value in the sense of purchasing power.

To summarise: The Mint price of gold depends on the weight of the sovereign as fixed by law, whilst the exchange value of gold means its purchasing power over other things; so that, if the general level of prices is low, that means the value of gold is high

—its purchasing power is great; whilst, if the level of prices is high, conversely the value of gold is low.

§ 7. *Possible difference between the Mint price and the market price of gold.*—It is, however, quite possible that, although the Mint price of gold is fixed in the manner described, the market price of that metal might in certain circumstances rise above the Mint price. This could not happen so long as the standard gold money is the actual circulating medium, and also is in reality of the same weight and fineness which by law it ought to be. But if the actual currency, whether by fraud or by the act of the Government, or by natural wear and tear, becomes of less than its nominal value, then the market price of gold reckoned in these inferior coins will rise in proportion to the inferiority.

In the same way, if inconvertible paper money is the actual currency, the market price of gold reckoned in these notes may rise to any height above the Mint price. The nature and magnitude of the evils which result from depreciation of the coinage may be gathered from the passages already quoted in the introduction to this subject. It must be observed that the ultimate result is the same whether the debasement is caused by natural wear and tear, by individuals " garbling " the coins, or by the Government making light issues. It is quite possible, however, that if the coins have gradually become light by ordinary wear and tear, they may for a long time circulate at their nominal value side by side with coins of full weight more recently issued. It is certain, however, that if the deterioration goes on, at some point it will be suddenly recognised ; the good coins will be melted and exported, and the whole of the actual currency will become, and be recognised as, depreciated in value.

§ 8. *Bad state of English gold coinage.*—It is, perhaps, not generally known, though the fact has long been familiar to experts, that the gold currency of England is at present in a very unsatisfactory state, and that, unless something is done in the way of restoration, the depreciation must soon be taken into account practically, with very injurious consequences to the industry of the nation. So long ago as 1869, Professor Jevons ascertained, by a careful and exhaustive inquiry, that $31\frac{1}{2}$ per cent of the sovereigns and nearly one-half of the ten-shilling pieces were below the legal limit. Since that date matters have certainly got much worse, and an attempt was made by Mr Childers, in 1884, to provide a remedy. The urgency of the reform in itself was generally recognised, but the particular scheme announced did not find favour, and was obliged to be withdrawn.

Without going into details, it may be mentioned that the essence of the plan was to withdraw all the light coins, then to make the sovereigns of full weight by abstracting from the half-sovereign a certain amount of gold, this coin being thus reduced to the level of " token " currency, as it is termed. Before giving an account of this species of money, something more must be said of the manner in which the standard coin may become depreciated, and the difficulties in providing a remedy for the evil.

CHAPTER IV.

GRESHAM'S LAW AND TOKEN COINS.

§ 1. *Gresham's Law and defective coins.* — What is now generally known as Gresham's Law, in honour of Sir Thomas Gresham (founder of the London Royal Exchange), who clearly perceived its truth in the reign of Queen Elizabeth, briefly stated, declares that bad money drives good money out of circulation, whilst good money cannot drive out bad. "At first sight," as Professor Jevons remarks, "there seems something paradoxical in the fact that when beautiful new coins of full weight are issued from the Mint the people still continue to circulate in preference the depreciated ones. . . . In all other matters everybody is led by self-interest to choose the better and to reject the worse; but in the case of money, it would seem as if they paradoxically retain the worse and get rid of the better." The solution of the difficulty is found in the fact that the object for which the bad money is used is simply to effect exchanges

D

and to pay debts, and so long as the money is accepted by the payee, the payer has no further care. Indeed it is for the interest of the payer to pay in the cheapest or worst coins obtainable and acceptable.

Suppose that in any country the coinage, which for simplicity may be assumed to consist of gold only, has become to a large extent much below the nominal standard of weight and fineness. Now let the Government issue a large number of new coins of full value. Obviously under these circumstances, unless the old coinage is effectively withdrawn, no debtor, if he is guided solely by what is called " enlightened self-interest," will be so foolish as to pay his debts with new coins when he might sell them to the bullion dealer, for melting or exportation, for a larger number of the old coins, which, so long as they are actual currency, would answer his purpose equally well. Even if all debtors were as sensitive, moral, or fearful as the repentant sinners who send " conscience money " to the Chancellor of the Exchequer for taxes evaded, there would always be a number of criminals who would be only too glad to make a living by picking and culling and garbling the coinage. This is a species of criminality which it is extremely difficult to detect, and experience shows that there is not much use in imposing heavy penalties when detection is uncertain.

§ 2. *How Gresham's Law operates.*—Before making

practical deductions, however, from Gresham's Law, the peculiar manner in which this law operates must be carefully recognised. It is quite possible, as the present state of our gold coinage shows, that the mere force of habit will be sufficient to keep light coins in use at their nominal value.

With a certain level of prices, a certain quantity of currency of some kind is required by the country at large for the purposes of internal trade. The great majority of people have no means of practically testing the coins which they receive, and creditors will, as a rule, take the coin put into their hand, even if it is obviously light, and trust to passing it again, rather than reject it, and wait for payment. Shopkeepers in particular are not likely to refuse " ready money " of a very inferior kind if they imagine it will be taken by some rival.

If the Government were obstinately to refuse to make new issues of gold coins, and the bad money were limited, then, in accordance with a principle which will presently be explained, there is, theoretically, no limit to the actual depreciation, whilst nominally the coins remain at *par* value, and pass as such. Practically, however, in this case, a stimulus would be given to the illicit manufacture of inferior coins. It will be observed to what a large extent the effective operation of Gresham's Law may depend on breaking the laws of the land; but it does not operate entirely in this manner now, because the laws against the exportation of gold coins have been repealed.

§ 3. *History of token coins.*—The proviso noticed above, as to the limitations of issues by the Government, naturally leads to the consideration of " token " coinage. " Token " coins may be defined in a preliminary manner as coins the nominal value of which as money is avowedly greater than their value as metal, even if the cost of coinage is taken into account. They are essentially bank notes of a very low denomination, and generally placed under peculiar restrictions. The subject may be best introduced by a slight historical sketch derived mainly from Boyne's ' Tokens of the Seventeenth Century ' and Burn's account of the London tradesmen's tokens in the ' Beaufoy Cabinet.'

From the earliest times the small coinage of England was of silver. Silver money was coined as low in value as the penny, three-farthings, half-penny, and farthing. A silver three - farthing piece was struck in the reign of Queen Elizabeth (1561), which is interesting as explaining a passage in Shakespeare, though the poet, with his usual disregard of anachronisms in his historical plays, throws back the usage of the coin of Elizabeth to the reign of John. On the coin in question, beside the queen's head is a rose, and in the play—' King John,' act i. scene 1

—Faulconbridge is made to say, satirically, of his brother—

> " My face so thin,
> That in mine ear I durst not stick a rose,
> Lest men should say—' Look, there three-farthings goes ! ' "

It may be added, that in Shakespeare's time there was a custom of putting a natural rose behind the ear or in the head-dress.

These coins were at first standard coins, and it is easy to see that the silver coin of a penny or three-farthings, and still more one of a farthing, would be very inconvenient in size and easily lost. Besides this, these small coins do not seem to have been coined in sufficient abundance for the purposes of trade; and accordingly, the great want of halfpence and farthings in the reign of Elizabeth compelled the almost general use of private " tokens " of lead, tin, and, it is said, of leather. These issues took place, much to the inconvenience of poor people (for the issuers often refused to change the tokens for goods or sterling money), up to the year 1613, when the king (James I.) granted, for a consideration, the monopoly of striking copper farthings to Lord John Harington.

On the accession of Charles I. the patent for the coinage of farthings was renewed. " The privilege was greatly abused by the patentees, who issued them in *unreasonable* quantities, and at a merely nominal intrinsic value. They encouraged the circulation by giving twenty-one shillings in farthings for twenty shillings in silver; by this means many unprincipled persons were induced to purchase them, and would *force five, ten, and even twenty shillings'* worth of them at a time on all with whom they had dealings. In a short time not only the city of London, but the whole kingdom, and especially the counties adjacent to the metropolis, were so burdened with them, that in many places scarcely any silver or gold coin was left, the currency consisting entirely of farthing tokens."

The patentees were not content with the profits obtained in the home country, but forwarded large parcels of their farthing tokens to the American colonies; but the Old Pilgrim Fathers were not to be taken in in this manner, and it is grimly recorded of Massachusetts—" March 4th, 1634, at the General Court at New Town, brass (or copper) farthings were forbidden, and *bullets* were made to pass for farthings." In England, however, the accumulation of the patent farthings in the hands of small tradesmen caused them so great a loss from the refusal of the patentees to exchange them, that in 1644, in consequence of the public demand, they were suppressed by the House of Commons, which ordered that they should be surcharged from money raised on the patentees' estates. It appears that by this Act the royal tokens were suppressed, and at any rate the decapitation of

the king five years later " annulled for ever all disputes between the patentees of the farthing token
and the public." The Crown had throughout been
the greatest delinquent, and had plundered the poor
most mercilessly. The whole affair, to all who were
engaged or named in it, remains one of indelible dis-
grace. After the death of the king, the old practice
of private issues was resorted to—the tokens being
made of lead, brass, and copper. In Mr Boyne's
work detailed descriptions of 9466 tokens are given,
and probably more than twenty thousand different
kinds were in use from 1648-1672.

§ 4. *Abuses of private tokens.*—The necessity for
small change, and the abuses which arise from the
use of private tokens, are graphically described in an
old print of 1671 in the following passages: " The
number of those whose bowels yearn for their daily
bread before they can earn a penny to buy it, do
eminently exceed all the rest of the people in any
nation, and their extreme poverty makes them incapable of paying if trusted, so that to keep them from
farthings, and such small exchanges, were to starve
three-quarters of the people, and withal to break, and
so in fine to starve, all those multitudes of petty
retailers who sell only these poor all necessaries for
life. This necessity enforceth those retailers, for want
of a publique allowed token, to make tokens of pence,
halfpence, and farthings, and therein, as in all else,

to grind the faces of the poor by wholly refusing, or
at best giving but what they please for their own
late-vented tokens." Evelyn, in his Diary, speaks of
the tokens issued by every tavern " passable through
the neighbourhood, though seldom reaching further
than the next street or two." It is easy to see, without further details, that the issue of private tokens,
though at first made to supply a public convenience,
had become a public nuisance.

§ 5. *Principles of good token coinage.*—The historical references just given show, in the first place, that
the attempt by the Crown to make a revenue from
token farthings by issuing, or allowing to be issued,
excessive quantities, had resulted in a great evil; the
sterling full-value coin had been driven from circulation, and the tokens had become practically worthless.
The only quality of good money they possessed was
probably a certain uniformity.

On the suppression of these royal tokens, the issues
by private people had to some extent provided the
small change needed, but only to some extent, because
there was no uniformity, and the circulation only
extended over a very small area—" the next street
or two."

Thus, by sad experience, the people of this country
had forced upon them the true principles of regulating the issues of small change. To secure uniformity,
and to make the medium of exchange general, it was

necessary for Government to undertake the coinage itself. At first, in defiance or in ignorance of Gresham's Law, it was thought sufficient to utter a number of new silver coins of the value of one penny and twopence "for the smaller traffic and commerce," but these coins were hoarded, and the private issues were continued for the vast profit made from them. At last it came to be understood that the proper plan was to make the small coins of nominal value only, to suppress private issues, to strictly limit the issues by Government, and to make them legal tender only for a limited amount.

§ 6. *Present system of token coins in this country.*— Under the system at present in force in this country both the silver and the bronze coins are royal tokens, the former being legal tender up to forty shillings, and the latter to twelve pence. The metallic value of the bronze is not more than one quarter of its nominal value, and at present the silver is at least 30 per cent below its professed value. It must not, however, be thought that this difference between the nominal and real value is an injury to the persons using the coins. So long as the coins pass current for what they profess to be,—so long as a debt of two pounds can be paid by forty shillings, and a debt of one shilling by twelve pennies,—there can be no injury. It is quite true that the Mint makes a profit on the coins actually issued, but it does not attempt to force the issues, and to all intents and purposes the small coins are the same as convertible bank-notes of the same value.

Quite recently an example on a small scale of the injury inflicted by the use of private tokens has been forthcoming in London. Large quantities of French bronze coins, of about the same size and appearance as the English pennies and halfpennies, were put in circulation. Some people took them, and then they found that they could not pass them. No one who in the course of trade would get large quantities could afford to do so. Brewers and others, by an arrangement with the Mint, may return their English coppers, but obviously the English Mint cannot take at their nominal value foreign tokens. If that were possible, in a short time the country would be flooded with foreign bronze, as in the time of Charles I. with token farthings. Accordingly, the importation of these coins has been stringently prohibited.

§ 7. *Shape, &c., of coins.*—It may naturally occur to the reader who is mindful of the cynical view of human nature on which Gresham's Law rests, that a very profitable industry to a clever criminal would be the manufacture of bronze and silver coins, which in weight and quality were exactly like those issued by the Mint. It is to obviate this danger that the coins are made in such a manner as to require the use of elaborate machinery, whilst, of course, at the same

time heavy penalties are imposed in case of detection.
Thus the device and shape of the coins are by no
means matters of indifference. It may be remarked
also, though the observation applies even more to
coins of standard quality than to token coins, that
the shape and device ought to be such as to render
the wear and tear a minimum, and to reveal any
tampering in the way of clipping. The milled edges
on coins are difficult to make uniformly, and prevent
unlawful reduction by paring. It is, however, obvious, that if the token coins are allowed to be in circulation till they are worn quite smooth, fradulent
manufacture will be more easy.

§ 8. *Difficulties of keeping coins at full value.*—We
are now in a position to see more clearly the meaning
of, and the difficulties in the way of, keeping the
standard coin at its full value. Any one, as was
shown above, can get gold coined into sovereigns and
half-sovereigns practically free of charge, and any
gold imported must undoubtedly be coined before it
can be used for currency. If, however, a large quantity
of the coins actually used are much below the standard, the evil will naturally spread, for there is a direct
encouragement to artificially reduce the good coins,
and at any rate they will always be chosen for export.

As the law stands at present, it is illegal either to
give or receive coins below the proper value; but as
Mr Childers pointed out in introducing his scheme,

this would logically involve the carrying about by every person of apparatus to test any coins he may receive. This is clearly impracticable, and the law is in most cases a dead letter. Even the banks have large accumulations of light-weight gold. The Bank of England, however, and Government Offices, only receive the gold coins at their full weight, and cases are on record in which as a consequence people have been mulcted of large sums.

The practical difficulty is to meet the expense of restoring the coinage, and to make the restoration in an equitable way and without encouragement to fraud. Obviously if the Bank of England offered to receive during a lengthy period all coins at their nominal value, giving full-weight coins in return, a great encouragement would be given to "sweating" or otherwise lightening the coins of full weight as they were issued, as well as those which happened to be in circulation.

Again, as regards the expense, it would clearly be unfair to make the last holder responsible, owing to the letter of the law ; and yet, so long as no practical inconvenience is felt, the Chancellor of the Exchequer would have a difficulty in making taxation for the purpose popular, to say nothing of the danger of fraud as just described. I shall return to this subject in connection with one-pound notes, the consideration of which properly comes at a later stage.

CHAPTER V.

THE QUANTITY OF MONEY AND GENERAL PRICES.

§ 1. *Meaning of appreciation and depreciation of gold and silver.*—This examination of money as the mechanism of exchange, may now be left for what constitutes the most difficult and contentious part of the subject—viz., the connection between money and prices; in other words, the causes which determine the value of money, which is the same thing, as we said, as the general level of prices.

I take this opportunity of explaining a term which is often used in a very confusing manner—*the appreciation of gold.* When we speak of the appreciation of gold, what we mean is, that in the countries using gold as the standard money, the general level of prices has become lower; in other words, that a given gold coin or a certain weight of standard gold will purchase more commodities—or conversely, that commodities will bring fewer pieces of gold.

Accordingly, it is unmeaning to speak of the gen-

eral fall in prices being *caused* by the appreciation
of gold; the two expressions in countries with free
mintage of gold currency mean precisely the same
thing.   We often use the term *de*preciation of gold
in two senses.   We may refer to a depreciation, through
loss in weight or purity, of a gold currency; or we
may mean the converse of the appreciation just described—that is, by depreciation we may understand a
fall in the value of gold compared with commodities.

Some light may perhaps be thrown on the expressions by considering the way in which they are properly
used as regards silver.   In countries such as
England, where gold is the standard and silver is
only used in limited quantities as token coinage,
silver has a price just like any other commodity.
For the first seventy years of this century this price
—for reasons afterwards to be given—was about
60d. per ounce troy, but latterly it has fallen as low
as 42d.   This fall in the gold price of silver constitutes the depreciation of silver.

At the same time, it is often pointed out that in
India, where the standard currency is silver, no depreciation, but rather appreciation, of silver relatively
to commodities has taken place.   This is using the
terms in the same sense as when applied to gold.

§ 2. *General and relative prices.*—To pass, however, from the question of words to the question of
facts, our present problem is to explain the causes

which govern *general* movements in prices, or which determine the changes in the exchange value of money. As has already been pointed out in connection with "index numbers," from 1850, to go no further back, great changes have taken place in the general level of prices, and we ought to be able to discover the causes of these changes. More than this, we ought to be able to explain in a general way the causes which must always be in operation.

First of all, in order to avoid a common source of confusion, it may be well to explain that our problem is the determination of *general* prices, and not, as at an earlier stage of this inquiry (chap. ii. § 8), the changes in the *relative* values of commodities reckoned in prices. It is easy to see how, from causes affecting some particular article, that article may have fallen or risen in value; and similarly, through the whole range of commodities, we may discover causes which have made some to rise and others to fall. If, however, we find that, apart from these relative changes, a *general* change in the level has occurred, it is natural to conclude that this is due either to causes primarily affecting the standard by which prices are determined, or to causes of a very wide-reaching character affecting commodities. It cannot be too often insisted on that the real meaning of the value of money is its value as compared with things in general—that is, its value as determined by the general level of prices.

§ 3. *In explaining general prices, it is necessary to begin with a simple case, or a " hypothetical market."*— Now, under the present conditions of industry and exchange, the causes which lead to general movements of prices are exceedingly complex and various, and in order to understand them it is necessary to begin with the simplest case, and then gradually to introduce the less obvious, though equally effective, causes of movement. I would, then, beg the reader to get rid, as far as possible, of all the notions he may have formed of the causes of the actual movements in prices in recent years in the complex industrial world of to-day, and, in order to isolate and examine the most important cause of all, to take up an attitude of observation in what, for fault of a better term, may be called a " hypothetical market."

The phrase is suggestive of unreality, but no more so than the suppositions or hypotheses constantly made in physics and mathematics, of bodies perfectly rigid, smooth, or without weight, or of lines without breadth, or of points without parts or magnitude.

Let the following, then, be assumed as the laws and conditions of our market: (1) No exchanges are to be made unless money (which, to be quite unreal and simple, we may suppose to consist of counters of a certain size made of the bones of the dodo) actually passes from hand to hand at every transaction. If, for example, one merchant has two pipes but no tobacco, and another two ounces of tobacco but no pipe, we cannot allow an exchange of a pipe for an ounce of tobacco unless money is used. Credit and barter are alike unknown. (2) The money is to be regarded as of no use whatever except to effect exchanges, so that it will not be withheld for hoarding ; in other words, it will be actually in circulation. (3) Let it be assumed that there are ten traders, each with one kind of commodity and no money, and one trader with all the money (100 pieces) and no commodities. Further, let this moneyed man place an equal estimation on all the commodities.

Now let the market be opened according to the rules laid down ; then all the money will be offered against all the goods, and every article being assumed of equal value, the price given for each will be ten pieces, and the general level of prices will be ten. It will be observed, in this operation, each piece of money changes hands only once—it passes, namely, from the moneyed man to the respective traders. It is perfectly clear, under these suppositions, that if the amount of money had been 1000 pieces the general level would have been 100 pieces per article, and if only ten pieces the price per article would have been one piece only. Under these very rigid assumptions, then, it is obvious that the value of the money varies exactly and inversely with the

E

quantity put in circulation. If the merchant with the "money" had sacks full of dodo counters, the value of each would be very small reckoned in goods, perhaps not equal to the thousandth part of a pipe of tobacco, for example.

§ 4. *Illustration of the effects of the quantity of money from the French assignats.*—We have in this way isolated a cause which is in the actual world of commerce, though often hidden and overshadowed, always present, and of the greatest consequence. As I am quite aware that the practical man naturally distrusts abstract reasonings, and considers them as impalpable as ghosts which he can see through, I hasten to support with hard facts the position that, at any rate, one most important factor in determining the general level of prices in a country is the quantity of money in circulation.

I will take, first, as the nearest approximation to an unreal state of things such as was assumed, a state of things which ought never to have occurred. I allude to the issues of the *assignats*, or inconvertible notes, of the French Revolution, the general evil consequences of which have already been noticed. I quote a few sentences, taken almost at random, from the work of Mr White. "Towards the end of 1794 there had been issued 7000 millions in *assignats*; by May 1795, 10,000 millions; by the end of July, 16,000 millions; by the beginning of 1796,

45,000 millions, of which 36,000 were in actual circulation." " At last a paper note, professing to be worth £4 sterling, passed current for less than three-pence in money." It is to be noticed that this tre-mendous depreciation took place in spite of the law imposing penalties on those who gave or received the paper at less than its nominal value, at first of six years in irons, then of twenty years, and finally pun-ishing with death investments of capital in foreign countries.

§ 5. *Fallacy of notes " representing " property.*—This is the most glaring but by no means the only ex-ample of the depreciation of inconvertible notes, and it has at last come to be perfectly understood that the only possible way of preventing or lessening the depreciation is to strictly limit the issues. The very meaning of the term inconvertible is that the note cannot be exchanged on demand against standard metallic money, and consequently the only limit to issues is found in the will of the issuers. The French asserted, at first, that since their notes " repre-sented " property, as indeed at first they were supposed to do, being professedly assignments of public land, they could never become depreciated.

Now this argument is only good so far as it im-plies some kind of limitation of the issues. But it would be quite as effective and rational to make the issues " represent " so many stars in the firmament, or the ages of so many ladies, or anything whatever limited in number or amount. If by representation is not meant convertibility on demand into some valuable commodity, the only thing that determines the value is their quantity compared with the work to be done by them. It may, perhaps, be advisable to repeat that, although the depreciation of the notes is usually reckoned as against gold in the standard metallic money, it implies necessarily a general rise in prices of all commodities to the extent of the depreciation.[1]

§ 6. *Illustration from the Bank Restriction in England.*—Another example, though happily of a less startling character than that just noticed, is furnished by the suspension of cash (metallic) payments by the Bank of England during the period known as the Bank restriction—"the dark age of currency." The Government, being engaged in the vast Continental wars in which Napoleon was the ruling spirit, were afraid that all the specie would be drained from the country, and none be left for military operations.

---

[1] The rise in prices would theoretically be greater than is indicated by the depreciation of the notes compared with gold. For as gold is withdrawn from circulation and thrown on the bullion market, it will tend to fall in value—in other words, gold itself will be to some extent depreciated. Conversely, on the resumption of specie payments, the demand for gold may cause a relative appreciation—that is to say, prices will fall to a lower level than was indicated by the premium on gold. Practically, however, both effects are generally not great, owing to gold being an international commodity.

Accordingly, in 1796 the Bank of England was restrained from paying out specie against its notes —that is, the notes became inconvertible. This lasted practically about twenty-three years, and during this period the notes became depreciated. In 1814 the average price of gold reckoned in notes had risen to £5, 4s. instead of £3, 17s. 9d., and general prices had risen accordingly. The Bank of England directors, when examined as to the plan they had adopted in making issues, gave answers which, as Mr Bagehot has said, have become classical by their nonsense. They imagined that the quantity of notes issued had nothing to do with their value provided only that they were issued in the usual course, on good banking securities, at a minimum interest of 5 per cent. By this plan they did indeed, to some extent, limit the issues, but not enough, as the event proved. The only perfectly safe plan with inconvertible issues is to restrict them as soon as ever the market price of bullion rises above the Mint price.

§ 7. *Further illustrations of the effects of the quantity of money.*—Further illustrations of the fundamental importance of the quantity of money in the determination of its value (or the general level of prices) are furnished in the case of the precious metals, though here, as we shall see presently, the operation of the quantity is, in the modern world at least, not so exclusively overpowering. The decline of the Roman empire was largely due to a deficiency of the circulating medium, which was remitted in payment of taxes in large quantities to Rome and the central cities of the empire. As a consequence, whilst in the provinces prices ruled low, and the miserable taxpayer would give any amount of wealth for coins—in the centre of the empire, where money was abundant, prices were high. It is necessary to add, for the benefit of those who may see quotations in historical works of Roman prices, that the Romans had early acquired the art of debasing their money— a method of reducing its value and raising the level of prices next in efficacy and injurious consequences to the excessive issues of inconvertible paper.

We have in the times of the middle ages a constant dearth of the precious metals, and consequently a low level of prices. Under the Tudors a great rise occurred, which illustrates in a twofold manner the effects of increasing the quantity of money. In the first place, under Henry VIII. and Edward VI. the currency was debased, and thus artificially increased in amount, and next it was naturally increased by the great discoveries of the precious metals in America, especially the celebrated silver mines of Potosi. The rise in prices, occurring as it did in an irregular manner, attracted much attention and produced much social disturbance, and even at that time a few keen minds detected the true cause.

Coming to the present century, we find on reference to the index numbers already quoted an uncommon rise in prices between 1850-64, during which period the great discoveries of gold in Australia and California largely increased the supply of that metal; and there can be little doubt that this fall in the value of gold, as indicated by the general rise in prices, was caused mainly by the increase in the quantity of metallic money. The great fall which has since occurred in prices is at any rate coincident with a gradual falling off in the gold supply and the use of gold in place of silver, thus increasing the amount of commodities to be moved or transactions to be effected by gold.

§ 8. *Influence and meaning of rapidity of circulation.*—It is time, however, to abandon this excursion into the realm of historical facts, which was undertaken to give substance to the " airy nothings " of abstract reasoning, and to return to our " hypothetical market," with its dodo counters and one-idea'd traders.

Let us assume as before that no exchanges are possible without money passing, that one merchant has all the money (100 pieces), and that ten have commodities of equal value ; but instead of the merchant with the money wishing for all the commodities equally, let us suppose that he only wants the whole of number one, whilst number one requires that of number two, and so on up to the ninth merchant, who wants the commodity of number ten, who wants the dodos. In this case each article will be exchanged once, but the money will pass from hand to hand ten times, and the price of each article will be 100 instead of 10 as before.

We now see, under these circumstances, with the same quantity of money and the same volume of transactions, the level of prices is ten times as great as before, and the reason is that every piece of money is used ten times instead of once. This frequent use of money is what is generally called rapidity of circulation, but Mill's phrase, " efficiency of money," is perhaps more suggestive of the meaning intended. The whole argument may be put in a sentence which only requires a little thinking out to become quite clear : *The effect on prices must be the same when, in effecting transactions, one piece of money is used ten times, as when ten pieces of money are used once.*

§ 9. *Practical illustration of rapidity of circulation.* —The reader may, perhaps, rebel against this abstract manner of stating the case, but the object, as before, is to isolate one cause and to be sure of having the conditions the same.

But the truth I am anxious to convey may be seen, though not so clearly and forcibly, by taking the common facts of trade. It surely is quite obvious that, with a certain level of prices, ready-money transactions may be carried on with a small amount of money if it circulates rapidly, whilst, if the circulation is sluggish, more will be required. And practically, this is the same thing as saying that prices may be varied either by increasing the quantity of money or by increasing the rapidity of circulation — i.e., the number of times each piece is used. The reason for taking, in this case, a hypothetical market of a simple kind is, that if we take a whole country for a certain period of time (say a year), it is difficult to estimate the rapidity of circulation, and we are misled by considering changes in the volume of trade and the effects of barter and credit, which require, in order to be properly understood, a separate investigation.

§ 10. *Influence on general prices of the volume of trade.*—We are, then, still a long way from an adequate and complete account of the causes affecting general prices in a great industrial country, even after allowing for rapidity of circulation as well as for quantity of money. As regards the number of transactions or the volume of trade, a glance at our supposititious market will show us that an increase in the transactions, or in the work to be done by the money, must have the same effect as a diminution in the quantity of money, the transactions remaining unchanged.

Again, looking to the ordinary course of trade, it ought to be clear that if the commerce and population

of the world are increased, so that the amount of
ready-money transactions is doubled, then so far, unless the quantity of money is equally increased, there
must be a proportionate fall in prices.   This is practically a very important consideration.

There can be no doubt that, after the great discoveries of the precious metals in the sixteenth and
the nineteenth centuries, the rise of prices would have
been much greater but for the enormous increase in
the volume of trade.

It follows, too, from this consideration, that, other
causes affecting prices remaining the same, any increase in the volume of trade by the extension of
commerce to new countries must, in exact opposition
to the popular view, result not in a rise but in a fall
of prices, unless these new countries happen to produce the precious metals in greater abundance than
their commerce requires.

§ 11. *Influence of barter on general prices.*—In the
abstract presentation of the argument, so far, it has
been assumed that money must pass from hand to
hand at every transaction—in other words, that there
is no barter; and it is only on this supposition that
the level of prices is exactly proportioned to the
quantity and rapidity of circulation of the money.
" And this requires us to observe "—I quote from
Professor Walker (' Money,' p. 64)—" that in the
view of those who hold that money acts as a measure

of value, it performs this function in respect of a vast bulk of commodities where it is not called on to become a medium of exchange. It is its use as a medium of exchange which determines its value, yet its value so determined becomes the means of estimating values without reference to actual exchanges. It costs nothing to measure values in this sense; it costs something to exchange them. It requires the actual use of money for a longer or shorter space of time to effect those double exchanges which we call buying and selling, but the prices resulting from such exchanges may be applied to far greater bodies of wealth without the use of money. For example, a farmer sells a cow to be sent to the city for beef. It is only in the actual sale that money is used, but he takes the price—the money value—thus determined as the means of estimating the value of his herd; and so does the Government in taxing him; so, also, do his neighbours in deciding how much of a man he is. . . . It will be observed that every time a barter transaction is substituted for [ready-money] buying and selling, the demand for money is thereby diminished and its value thereby lowered (the supply remaining the same), while the higher prices of commodities which result from the sales actually effected by the use of money are carried over in estimation to the commodities remaining unsold, or to those whose transfer is accomplished by a direct exchange of goods for goods. And conversely, just so far as sales for money are substituted for barter transactions, the demand for money being thereby increased, the value of money rises, and the lower prices which result are carried over in estimation to the commodities directly exchanged or remaining in store."

§ 12. *Influence on general prices of the use of the precious metals for other purposes besides coinage.*— So much, then, for the effects of barter; and omitting for the present the most difficult and intricate inquiry into the effects of credit, we may advance a step nearer the reality of the modern world by taking into account the fact that metallic money—for the present purpose we will say gold money—instead of being counters of dodo's bones or inconvertible paper, is made from a substance which is highly prized for various purposes in the arts and manufactures, and which is only obtained from the mines with a considerable expenditure of capital and labour.

If gold were no longer used for coinage, it would probably still possess a very high value as a commodity. People would still prefer gold ornaments of all kinds to those made of any other metal. I may mention that the ancient Egyptians, as their mummies reveal, used gold for stopping teeth, and since their time numberless new uses have been found for gold. It follows, therefore, that in prac-

tice, instead of " money " being offered as we at first
supposed against commodities regardless of its value
for other purposes, if the value of gold coins became
very low there would be a tendency to melt them
down to use in other ways.

An illustration will make this clear. If five gold
sovereigns would only purchase five small loaves and
two or three fishes, a man would be much more ready
to cause them to be melted for a gold watch than if
they would purchase a house full of luxuries. In
fact, as in other things, a fall in the value of gold as
a commodity increases the quantity demanded. To
take a practical case : Great gold discoveries, by increasing the quantity of gold money, will so far tend
to make prices rise ; but the rise will not be quite as
great as it otherwise would be, because the use of
gold for the arts will be stimulated by its fall in
value, and thus the quantity available for coinage
will be diminished.

It follows, then, that although in some aspects of
the question it is useful to emphasise the function of
money as a mere medium of exchange, because there
has often been a tendency to confuse money with
the wealth which it measures and exchanges, it
would be an error to neglect altogether the use of
gold for other purposes, especially if, in addition to
those indicated, we consider also hoarding.

§ 13. *Influence on general prices of the cost of pro-*

duction of the precious metals.—There is, however, apart from this absorption and diffusion, a much more direct and powerful check on the rise in gold prices to be found in the conditions of supply; for in the value of gold, as in other things, it is necessary to consider supply as much as demand.

Unlike the issues of tokens or inconvertible notes, in which the quantity depends on the will of Governments, the quantity of gold money can only be increased at considerable cost. Mines which are very productive and easily worked only furnish part of the annual supply; and on the other hand, a certain portion is yielded by mines which it only just pays to work, and which, to adopt classical economic language, are on the "margin of cultivation," and yield their supplies under the most unfavourable circumstances.

What, then, speaking generally, are the limiting conditions which determine whether gold-mines of a certain productivity will be worked — omitting, of course, irrational and spasmodic speculation? Clearly, the conditions are to be found in the expenses of working compared with the yield.

These expenses obviously vary with the general level of prices. If prices are high, the wages of labour, the cost of implements and machinery, and the expenses of transport, will also be high, and therefore the gold produced will yield a smaller profit than if prices were low; and if the expenses of working, owing to a further rise in prices, become still greater, the profit must become still smaller— and if the rise of prices continues, must vanish. It follows, then, that every rise in general prices tends to check production from the mines, whilst every fall, by rendering a diminution of expenses possible, tends to increase and extend production. It will thus be seen *that the cost of production of gold only operates on general prices by increasing or diminishing the annual supply, and thus affecting the quantity in use.*

§ 14. *Effects of the durability of the precious metals.* —If, now, it be remembered that the durability of gold is very great, and that of the annual supplies a large part is required for the arts and for simply maintaining and restoring the gold coins actually in circulation, it will be seen that, under present circumstances, when the average annual supply is less than £22,000,000, whilst the gold coinage of the civilised world is estimated (roughly) at £800,000,000, the influence of the yearly fluctuations in production must be very small.[1]

This is a point which requires the strongest emphasis, as even so clear a thinker as J. S. Mill has

---

[1] The statistics, as before observed, are very uncertain, but the argument rests on the annual production *relatively* to the total mass, and there can be little doubt that it is very small.

been led into the error of over-estimating the effects of this element. In one sense, indeed, the cost of production of gold is certainly the most important cause affecting its value, but only in the sense of imposing a limit on a rise in prices, or a fall in the value of the metal. If gold could be produced very cheaply by a kind of alchemy, there would be hardly any limit to the rise in prices; but, seeing that the quantity of gold is only one element in governing prices, and cost of production only one element affecting this quantity, it is a gross error to say, as Mill does, that "the value of gold depends, apart from temporary fluctuations, on its cost of production."

For, to take only one other cause, the volume of trade, it is clear that, although the annual supply of gold was increasing, and the cost of production diminishing, if the volume of trade was increasing at a much greater rate, the value of gold would rise, or, in other words, general prices would fall.

It is easy to see the way in which the error arose. It was observed quite correctly that the value of gold coins must on the average be equal to the value of the same weight of gold bullion. But the next step in the argument was a mistake of effect for cause; for it was supposed that if we only determined the value of the bullion, we should in that way determine the value of the coins into which it could be made. It was then argued that gold bullion was simply a commodity, and that its normal value depended on its cost of production. Herein lay the mistake. Rightly understood, the general level of prices rests on many causes, and this general level of prices determines the exchange value of gold coins — in fact, that is the very meaning of their value — whilst the value of the coins determines the value of the bullion.

Cost of production can only affect the value of any article through supply, and its effect is very different in case of a durable commodity like gold, which is only slowly worn by being used, and in the case of one such as corn, of which the greater part of the annual supply is consumed in a year, though, of course, it may be allowed that so far the difference is only one of degree.

F

CHAPTER VI.

§ 1. *Great use of credit substitutes for money in England.*—It is, however, at the stage of the inquiry
now reached, in which it becomes necessary to examine the effect of credit on prices, that the greatest
difficulties in connection with the value of money
arise. The importance of this element may, perhaps,
be best seen by considering what would be the effect
on prices if, in a country such as modern England,
the conditions first assumed in our "hypothetical
market" actually prevailed, and if money in the shape
of coins were necessary in every transaction. It is
almost impossible to picture to the mind what would
be the extent of the fall in prices, but some idea may
be formed by taking into account a few well-known
facts.

In the first place, it is very unusual for coin to be
used at all in wholesale transactions. In the ' Statisti-

cal Journal ' for September 1865, Sir John Lubbock
published some particulars concerning the business
of his bank during the last few days of 1864.
Transactions to the extent of £23,000,000 were
effected by the use of credit documents and coin, and
the proportions per cent were as follows: Cheques
and bills of exchange, 94·1 ; Bank of England notes,
5·0 ; country bank notes, ·3 ; and actual coin only
·6. That is to say, of business transactions to the
amount of £23,000,000, a very little more than ½
per cent were effected by means of coin, and only a
little above 5 per cent by credit documents, which
are supposed to represent coin directly.

The "clearings" of the Banker's Clearing House
in London, in which the reciprocal obligations of the
banks are balanced, exceed £6,000,000,000 sterling
per annum, and these form part only of the total
payments of the whole country, whilst it has been
calculated that the whole value of the metals employed in the currency is less than £140,000,000.

§ 2. *Influence of credit on general prices shown by
reference to commercial crises.*—The way in which
changes in credit at once produce changes in general
prices is illustrated by the phenomena which precede
and follow commercial crises. We get, as a rule,
in the first place, an excessive use of credit instruments of various kinds, accompanied by a great rise
in prices. All sorts of paper, which in less confident

times would not be looked at, are used as a basis of buying and selling. But the competition of those who buy on credit, so long as that credit is accepted, obviously affects the demand for commodities, and raises prices just as much as when ready money is offered. A person whose cheque will be taken in payment can bid as effectively as one who brings a bag of money, and in times of inflation and confidence the banks will advance directly or indirectly on all kinds of securities.

Thus, in the period of the culmination of a commercial fever, the amount of "representative money" is largely increased, and with this increase there is an inflation of prices. As soon, however, as the contraction of credit sets in, the bankers make wry faces over credit documents not of the first class, and there is a sudden diminution in the representative money and a great fall in prices. So great is the effect of credit, even in the dullest times, that there is a tendency for people to rush to the other extreme in estimating the influence of the precious metals, and to consider the quantity of metallic money as of the very slightest effect in governing general prices, and thus the exchange value of money.

§ 3. *All credit ultimately rests on a metallic basis.*— It seems at first sight that, just as there is no limit to the rise in prices due to the issue of inconvertible paper, except the will of the Government in limiting the issues, so, also, there is no limit to the creation of credit substitutes for coin, except the will of bankers, traders, and merchants. It is well, then, to state, in the most emphatic manner, that the whole of this vast superstructure of credit must rest on a metallic basis, and if this basis is cut away, the whole structure would fall.

Let us consider the way in which, in England, this metallic basis imposes a limit — though an elastic one—on the rise in prices. In the first place, the banks themselves are built up on gold foundations. It has been said that if all the banks at the same moment were obliged to meet their obligations in actual coin, they would just be able to pay 4d. in the £ ; but if this is true, it is equally true to say that, small as 4d. seems, still if, as a body, they only kept 2d. per £ in reserve, they would be unable to conduct their business.

In this country, more than in any country, the economy in the use of gold has reached a marvellous development. Every bank is obliged to keep a small amount of " till " money, but its real reserve is usually lodged with the Bank of England. We have, as a matter of fact, as Mr Bagehot's ' Lombard Street ' shows in the most forcible manner, a *one - reserve* system.

A banker who has a sufficient balance at the Bank of England to meet any drain at all likely to be made upon his bank thinks, and thinks rightly, that he has his reserve quite safe, and yet, as a rule, there is not gold enough in the Bank of England available to meet these bankers' balances if all drawn at once, for the Bank of England itself, being a bank, lends its deposits. But the directors of the bank are fully aware of the limits imposed upon them by the necessities of having a sufficient reserve, and they speedily check these advances, and take steps for attracting gold from abroad when the gold at their disposal falls below a certain point.

In order to understand the nature of the credit institutions of this country, it is most important to form a clear idea of the position and functions of the Bank of England, which is the heart of the circulating system. These functions, rights, and obligations may be described as partly legal and partly customary. The governor and directors of the Bank are, in the world of commerce, like the Prime Minister and his Cabinet in the world of politics—they have to observe the letter of the law and the spirit of the constitution.

§ 4. *The Bank Charter Act of* 1844.—So far as the law is concerned, it is practically settled by the famous Bank Charter Act of 1844. Seeing that many miles of print have been devoted to the merits and demerits of this Act, it may be thought impossible to discuss it profitably in a few lines. As my object, however, is mainly descriptive, and not critical, the task is not hopeless.

In the first place, it must be observed that the Act says nothing, paradoxical as it may seem, of what is generally understood by banking—nothing, for example, as to the kind of securities on which advances may be made, of the proportion of reserve to liabilities, of the method of fixing the rate of interest, or of the kind of business which the Bank may undertake. In fact, the Act may be best described as is done by Macculloch. " In dealing with the Bank of England, Sir Robert Peel adopted the proposal previously made by Lord Overstone, for effecting a complete separation between the issuing and banking departments of that establishment, and giving the directors full liberty to manage the latter at discretion, while they should have no power whatever over the other."

Thus the main object of the Act was to regulate the issues of bank-notes, and the plan adopted was as follows:[1] " The notes of the Bank of England in circulation for some years previously to 1844 rarely amounted to £20,000,000, or sunk so low as £16,000,000.   And such being the case, Sir Robert Peel was justified in assuming that the circulation of the Bank could not in any ordinary condition of society, or under any mere commercial vicissitudes, be reduced below £14,000,000.   And the Act of 1844

[1] 'Macculloch's Commercial Dictionary'—Article " Bank."

allows the Bank to issue this amount upon securities of which the £11,015,000 she has lent to the public is the most important item. Inasmuch, however, as the issues of the provincial banks were at the same time limited in amount [also determined by their average circulation during three months before the passing of the Act], and confined to certain existing banks, it was further provided, in the event of any of these banks ceasing to issue notes, that the Bank of England might be empowered by order in council to issue upon securities two-thirds and no more of the notes which such banks had been authorised to issue. [Under this condition the total secured issue of the Bank has been increased to £15,750,000.[1]] *But for every other note which the issue department may at any time issue over and above the maximum amount* (£15,750,000) *issued on securities, an equal amount of coin or bullion must be paid into its coffers.* And hence, under this system, the notes of the Bank of England are rendered really and truly equivalent to gold, while their immediate conversion into that metal no longer depends, as it previously did, on the good faith, the skill, and the prudence of the directors."

The position of the Bank in respect of its note issues is well described by a former governor as fol-

---

[1] This amount has recently been still further increased to £16,200,000.

lows: "The issue department is out of our hands altogether. We are mere trustees under the Act of Parliament to see that these securities are placed there and kept up to that amount; and in no case can any (ordinary) creditor of the Bank touch that which is reserved for a note-holder. We are in that respect merely administrative; we are trustees to hold that amount in the issue department, and our banking department has a totally separate function, which has no relation whatever to the issue department."

§ 5. *Practical illustration of the working of the Bank Act.*—The practical effect of these regulations may be illustrated by an example which happily is historically purely fictitious. Suppose the directors of the Bank of England had used the deposits of the public or of other banks with them in an imprudent manner, and locked them up in securities of various kinds which had become unrealisable on demand. Suppose next that the depositors draw to an unusual amount on the Bank, and the Bank has not a sufficient reserve to meet these demands in the banking department.

Now, although the depositors might be perfectly willing to accept Bank of England notes in payment of their claims—and for all internal trade, at least, they would answer the purpose equally well—the Bank has no power to issue these notes. It may be that £20,000,000 of gold is lying idle in the issue department against notes already in circulation : the Bank cannot use this gold to pay away nor as a foundation of further issues. The example is fictitious so far as the management of the deposits of the Bank of England is concerned, but in three great commercial crises since the Act was passed it has been suspended.

This suspension of the Act requires a word of explanation. It did not mean that the notes were rendered inconvertible, as was the case at the begining of the century during the period of the bank restriction already alluded to, for although the Act was suspended, any one who wished could take notes to the Bank and get gold in exchange : it simply meant that in case of need the banking department might issue additional notes to its customers on security. It is worth noticing that the principle of this Act has recently been adopted to regulate the Imperial Bank of Germany, with a modification suggested by the experience of England in commercial crises.

The German Bank may issue notes not backed by gold to a certain fixed amount, and in case of need it may issue notes on securities beyond this sum, on payment to Government of a tax of 5 per cent on the additional issues. The Act is thus self-suspensory, instead of requiring, as in England, the

direct intervention of the Government, which afterwards receives Parliamentary sanction.

§ 6. *Bank of England notes are simply a convenient
form of currency.*—Bank of England notes are thus,
in ordinary circumstances, simply and solely a
convenient form of currency, the gold which they
represent being in the vaults of the Bank instead of
in the pockets of the people. But this gold is held
solely against the notes, and cannot be used for
ordinary banking purposes. Every week the Bank
of England issues an account in which the affairs of
the two departments are kept distinct. Any one who
refers to one of these accounts, as published in the
'Economist,' for instance, will see that the reserve in
the banking department is for the most part held in
notes. The account, for example, for the week ending December 14, 1887, states that the total value
of the notes issued was £35,401,930, of which
£16,200,000 were issued in the manner described
above against Government debt and other securities,
and the remainder, £19,201,930, against gold bullion.
In the banking department we have as assets Government and other securities to the extent of about
£33,000,000, notes to the amount of about
£12,000,000, and gold and silver coin about
£1,250,000. This last sum must be considered as
" till " money in coin, but coin for the Bank of England notes would be obtained from the issue department.

§ 7. *One-pound notes used in Scotland and Ireland, and recommended for England.*—Under the present law, no bank in England can issue notes for sums under £5, whilst in Scotland and Ireland notes for £1 may be issued by the authorised banks, under similar restrictions as to holding gold for issues above a certain amount. The fact that these £1 notes, although strictly convertible, have to a large extent supplanted gold sovereigns as currency, seems to show that, in the opinion of the people of Ireland and Scotland, they are found to be a more convenient form of currency. One way, then, of restoring and maintaining the gold coinage in England would be to issue £1 notes, and to allow the Bank of England to issue a sufficient amount *not* against gold to pay for re-coining the old sovereigns and half-sovereigns. This plan would leave untouched the principle of the Act of 1844, except by changing the limit of issues not against gold from £16,200,000, as at present, to, say, £20,000,000. All the gold withdrawn from circulation would be kept in reserve against the notes in the issue department, but it would be reckoned at its full weight value. Space will not allow me to give further details of the scheme.[1]

§ 8. *Not only bank-notes but all forms of credit substitutes rest on a gold basis.*—The brief examination

---

[1] I give full details of this scheme in a paper read before the British Association at Birmingham, September 1886. See page 177.

of the Bank Act of 1844 just made shows clearly enough that at any rate the bank-notes rest on a gold basis definitely fixed by law ; but in the exchange of commodities in all wholesale transactions, and even to a large extent in the retail trade, other forms of representative money play an important part, and in these cases the connection with gold is neither so definite nor so obvious.

Any explanation of an adequate kind would involve a more complete account of banking and the money market than can be attempted in this place, but the reader who wishes for a lucid, popular, and sound exposition of the subject may be confidently recommended to read Mr Bagehot's 'Lombard Street : A Description of the Money Market.' He will there find ample illustration of the general proposition laid down above, that all credit in this country rests on gold, and ultimately on the gold held in the issue department of the Bank of England against the notes held in the banking department.

" In consequence," says Mr Bagehot, after a preliminary survey of the system, " all our credit system depends on the Bank of England for its security. On the wisdom of the directors of that one joint-stock company it depends whether England shall be *solvent or insolvent*. This may seem too strong, but it is not. All banks depend on the Bank of England, and all merchants depend on some banker. If a merchant have £10,000 at his banker's, and wants to pay it to some one in Germany, he will not be able to pay it unless his banker can pay him, and the banker will not be able to pay him if the Bank of England should be in difficulties and cannot produce his reserve."

One other passage may be quoted: "We see, then, that the banking reserve of the Bank of England— some ten millions on an average of years now, and formerly much less—is all which is held against the liabilities of Lombard Street; and if that were all, we might well be amazed at the immense development of our credit system—in plain English, at the immense amount of our debts payable on demand, and the smallness of the sum of actual money which we keep to pay them if demanded. But there is more to come. Lombard Street is not only a place requiring to keep a reserve—it is itself a place where reserves are kept. All country bankers keep their reserve in London. They only retain in each county town the minimum of cash necessary to the transaction of the current business of that county town. Long experience has told them to a nicety how much this is, and they do not waste capital and lose profit by keeping more idle. They send the money to London, invest a part of it in securities, and keep the rest with the London bankers and the bill-brokers. The habit of Scotch and Irish bankers is much the same. All their spare money is in London, and is invested as all other London money now is; and, *therefore, the reserve in the banking department of the Bank of England is the banking reserve not only of the Bank of England, but of all London; and not only of all London, but of all England, Ireland, and Scotland too.*"

§ 9. *Further limit to the effects of credit by the necessity for cash payments in some cases.*—We have now progressed a long way from our " hypothetical market," and made a corresponding advance towards the many-sided actuality of the practical world. Before proceeding further, however, it must be observed, in considering the limits imposed on a rise in prices due to the expansion of credit, that, however much the use of credit instruments may be extended, there are always a large number of payments which can only be effected by means of " cash."

In England generally, and in Scotland and Ireland, for all sums below £1, wages must be paid in actual coin, and a considerable amount of retail transactions can only be conducted by the same means. Wholesale transactions might all be ultimately settled, so far as our country is concerned, by simple transfers on the banking accounts of the different merchants, but smaller payments cannot be met so readily. Accordingly, if wholesale prices rise, owing to an expansion of credit, they will soon find a check in the increased payments which must be made to the working classes, and the increased demands for currency on the retail trades.

We are thus, again, brought back to the effect on the bank reserves as the immediate cause of the check to the rise in prices. So long as employers of labour can obtain supplies of currency from the banks, wholesale prices, and with them wages, may continue to rise; but as the reserves of the banks are dispersed, a rise in the rate of interest at which advances can be made must take place, and a check will be put on the rise in prices.

CHAPTER VII.

INFLUENCE ON THE GENERAL LEVEL OF PRICES IN ANY
ONE COUNTRY OF THE GENERAL LEVEL OF PRICES
IN OTHER COUNTRIES.

§ 1. *The general fall of prices in England during
recent years cannot be accounted for by any scarcity of
gold in this country.*—It might, perhaps, be thought
that this investigation of the connection between
money and prices is at length complete. But it is
not so; and a practical problem which is at present
exciting much attention, and to which, in another
connection, reference has already been made, furnishes
a striking illustration of the incompleteness of our
survey. We have already seen that, according to
the 'Economist' index numbers, general prices in
England have fallen more than 30 per cent during
the last twelve years; and since Mr Goschen gave
the authority of his name to the explanation, it has
been very commonly said that the fall is due to the
relative scarcity of gold. We should expect, from the

G

causes already examined, that if the production of gold had fallen off whilst the demand for gold had at any rate not diminished, a fall in general prices would take place.

But this general argument is met very plausibly in the following manner. I give, as an example, a passage from the statement to the Royal Commission on Trade by Mr Luke Hansard : " If the fall in prices in this country is caused by gold itself, that fall must arise from a scarcity of the metal in circulation and a scarcity of gold currency for carrying on our daily transactions, either internally as coin or externally for export, when it becomes a mere commodity used as barter the same as any other commodity. Is there any evidence of a want of metallic currency in this country, of an insufficient paper currency, or of gold for export ? I think not."

The answer is supported by statistics. First, as regards the national circulation—the currency used in cash transactions—it is pointed out that whilst in the five years 1870-74 there was a coinage of gold at the Mint exceeding £32,000,000, in the two succeeding periods of the same length the coinage was, from 1875-79, a little over £8,000,000, and from 1880-84 a little under that figure. It is further stated that " it used formerly to be customary for one banker to solicit other bankers to take surplus coin by courtesy, rather than run the risk of having some few sovereigns cut by paying it into the Bank of England. [The gold coins are taken by the Bank of England only by weight.]   This still, to some extent, holds good.   But so little demand is there for gold coin in the country for internal circulation that it is not uncommon, and is becoming necessary, to pay a premium or accept a discount from those who have facilities for paying away large sums.   This, I contend, would not be the case were there any deficient supply of gold, or were there any such want of it for currency purposes.   This difficulty in forcing the coin into circulation again is not to be attributed solely to the defective state of the coinage, as many of the coins are of the standard weight."

Again, it is urged that the alleged scarcity has not operated through the banking reserves of the Bank of England—the ultimate reserve, as we have seen, of the country ; for, it is said, had this been the case— had an unusual demand arisen through a foreign drain—the rate of interest would have been raised in order to check the export and induce importation. But we learn that " our rates for advances have been so low as to offer, if anything, an inducement for other countries to take gold had they wanted it; " and it is found, as a matter of fact, that from 1874-84 on balance, the imports of gold into the United Kingdom have exceeded the exports by about £9,500,000. " From this fact," the writer states, "and from the bank rate of discount not showing any markedly adverse state of the foreign exchanges, I am forced to the conclusion that there is no scarcity of gold with us. Hence it has no agency in causing the recent fall in prices."

§ 2. *We must look for an explanation of the fall to foreign countries.*—It will be remarked that throughout this argument, as to the facts of which there will be no dispute, the question is constantly regarded from the point of view of this country alone; and the answer is, that in the close intercommunication of markets in these days, this limited view is entirely insufficient. Without entering into the details of the theory of foreign trade, it is quite clear that if for any reason prices had fallen in other countries with which this country has commercial relations, the fall must have been reflected to our home markets. It would plainly be impossible—to take an example of a particular commodity—to explain the fall in the price of wheat, without considering the rates ruling in foreign markets—from America in the West to India in the East. And in precisely the same way, if general prices have fallen in other countries owing to the comparative pressure on gold, there will be a corresponding fall in this country.

§ 3. *General prices will always be adjusted until there is sufficient currency to effect transactions.*—There is thus no contradiction whatever between this apparent abundance of gold in this country and a fall in prices due to the scarcity of that metal. To make this quite plain, it is only necessary to reflect on the connection between gold as an actual means of exchange and as a measure of values, to which at an earlier stage of the inquiry attention was directed ; and the general law there indicated may now be stated in a more formal and complete manner as follows :—

The measure of values or the general level of prices throughout the world will be so adjusted that the metals used as currency, or as the basis of substitutes for currency, will be just sufficient for the purpose. We see, then, that the value of gold is determined in precisely the same manner as that of any other commodity, according to the equation between demand and supply. Competition will go on between those who hold the metal on the one side and those who wish to obtain it on the other, until such a general level of prices is reached that the quantity demanded at that level is equal to the quantity offered.

Strictly speaking, then, and after making allowance for the temporary difficulties of readjustment, there must always be a sufficiency of gold. If there is not enough to keep prices at one level, prices will fall until there is enough for the new level. It seems probable, for reasons which I have given in another publication, that the process of readjustment to a new level began in the new or undeveloped countries, where the effect of a contraction of currency, credit being in a rudimentary stage, is brought about more rapidly and directly.

§ 4. *Two ways in which prices in any one country are directly affected by the monetary conditions of other countries.*—There are, then, to resume the general argument, two modes in which prices in any particular country depend on the monetary conditions of the rest of the world. *In the first place*, the world requires to keep up a certain level of prices, a certain amount of gold as actual circulating medium, and if there is not enough in any area, prices must fall in that area. But in these days the fall would be at once telegraphed, and other markets would be influenced.

Secondly, the great national banks require, in order to support the credit superstructure of their respective countries, a certain proportion of metallic reserve to liabilities. The proportion, as Mr Bagehot has so well explained, varies according to circumstances, but there is a minimum which may be regarded as the danger point. If, for example, the Bank of England finds its reserve rapidly diminishing, and there seems a probability of further and possibly uncertain calls, it at once raises its rate of discount. Those who wish to get accommodation from the Bank can only do so at this higher rate. As a consequence they will, in the first place, try other banks, but under our one-reserve system any such pressure caused by foreign demands must fall on the Bank of England, and in the last resort the market rate must follow the Bank rate.

These high rates in a country where the margin of profits is very small, and where the discount of bills is carried on to an enormous extent, must act as a break upon trade, and prices will fall. We might find then that prices in England fell below the level of prices in other countries owing to scarcity of gold in this form, due, in the first place, to foreign demands.

In whatever manner the subject is regarded, it thus becomes clear that the general level of prices in any one country depends on causes beyond the power of that country to control, and a fall in prices cannot be explained without a wide survey. Those who assert that the relative scarcity in gold, the falling off in its production, and the exceptional demands for currency purposes, and similar causes, cannot have caused a fall in prices in this country, because here there is abundance of gold for the existing level of prices, are guilty of the same kind of fallacy as a man who should suppose that the ship cannot sink because there is no leak in the particular cabin in which he happens to sleep. To change the simile—in these days one body politic may catch low prices from another, as readily as one body physical may catch fever.[1]

---

[1] For an elaboration of the argument in this chapter, see the essay on the "Causes of Movements in General Prices," p. 332.

CHAPTER VIII.

EFFECTS ON GENERAL PRICES OF THE USE OF BOTH GOLD AND SILVER AS STANDARD MONEY.

§ 1. *Warning to the reader of differences of opinion on the Silver Question.*[1]—It is time now to complete, so far as the limits of this inquiry allow, the enumeration of the causes affecting general prices, by taking into account one more circumstance which, for the sake of simplicity in the argument, has hitherto been omitted. I have spoken sometimes of the precious metals and sometimes of gold, and I propose at this point to consider the effects of the fact that for standard currency—that is, for their unlimited legal tender—some nations use gold, some silver, and some both. I have elsewhere given my views on what is termed the silver question, in its practical and political aspects, and in this place I am only concerned to explain the general theory of this subject in such a manner as to make the controversy intelligible.

[1] For some useful estimated statistics and facts, see Appendix A.

§ 2. *The meaning of bi-metallism.*—In any country or group of countries forming a monetary union,
bi-metallism implies that both as regards coinage
and legal tender, gold and silver are on precisely the
same footing.   It is not the mere use of both metals
for currency, but the use of both as standard money,
which constitutes the essence of bi-metallism.   It
can only lead to confusion to say that bi-metallism
exists *de facto* everywhere, on the ground that in all
countries silver is used at any rate for token money.
For the relations of token money and standard money
to prices are essentially different, and the difference
may be expressed in the following general principle :
*The quantity of standard money, other things remain-
ing the same, determines the general level of prices,
whilst, on the other hand, the quantity of token-money
is determined by the general level of prices.*   The quali-
fying phrase, "other things remaining the same," refers
to the various conditions already enumerated which
also operate on general prices.   The difference may
also be expressed by saying that a standard metal
is coined in unlimited quantities when brought to
the mint, but that token money is issued only in
limited quantities, according to the wants of the community, at the discretion of the authorities.   There
is, for example, no reason why very great discoveries
of silver should cause the issue of one extra sixpence in this country, but similar discoveries of gold

would be sure to cause an increase in the amount of gold coined.

§ 3. *The necessity of a fixed ratio between gold and silver in a bi-metallic system.*—It is conceivable that a Government might coin both metals on the same conditions, receive both on equal terms in payment of taxes, and constitute both equally legal tender, and yet at the same time allow the ratio of one metal to the other to vary according to the market price of the two metals, or according to proclamation from time to time. When, however, it is remembered that cash payments are effected not in bullion but in coins, it will be apparent that much inconvenience would arise if the relative value of the gold and silver coins were constantly changing. Consider, for example, the common case of getting change for a sovereign, or, still better, the frauds to which the poor and ignorant would be liable. Accordingly, nations which have adopted bi-metallism practically have always issued their coins at a ratio which was intended to be fixed and unalterable.

§ 4. *Consequences of the adoption of fixed ratio bi-metallism by one country.*— Suppose, for the sake of illustration, that England alone were to adopt bi-metallism at such a ratio of gold to silver that the gold in a sovereign was precisely equal in value to the silver in twenty shillings. Under this supposition silver could be minted to any extent, and used for the payment of debts in the same way as gold at present. But now assume that, owing to some change in the demand for, or the supply of, silver abroad, the market ratio varied from the legal ratio in such a manner that the silver in twenty shillings was no longer equal in value to the gold in a sovereign. In these circumstances Gresham's law (cf. chap. iv.) would at once come into operation. No one would be willing to pay his debts in gold when, by first selling his gold for silver, he could obtain more than twenty shillings for his sovereign. Thus either the silver would actually drive the gold from circulation, or else the gold would command an *agio* (or premium), just as it does compared with depreciated inconvertible notes. It follows, then, that either the country would become really mono-metallic on a silver basis, or else that practically, in all large operations at any rate; the ratio would become variable.

It must be observed also, in the case assumed, that other nations would be likely to send their silver to this country. So long as the bi-metallism existed in full operation, any depreciation of silver abroad would cause it to be sent to its best market. It is not true to say that silver could be taken to the bi-metallic mints and directly exchanged against gold, but it is easy to see that so long as the bi-metallic country possessed any gold and acted on bi-metallic principles, silver could always indirectly obtain gold at the fixed ratio price. For a foreigner could send silver (say) to London, and draw against his remittances, and sell his bill for gold.

At the same time, however, it may be suggested that the mere existence of bi-metallism in any great country would have a steadying effect on the gold price of silver in other places, just as the London quotations of many stocks and commodities govern quotations in other markets. Such is alleged to have been the effect of the existence of bi-metallism in France for a period of seventy years in this century; and certainly, as a matter of fact, the market ratio fluctuated within very narrow limits in spite of the enormous gold discoveries about 1850 and a number of other important commercial and financial changes.

The steadiness in the price of silver during this long period need not, however, be ascribed wholly to the existence of partial bi-metallism, for so long as some nations used gold and some silver, and preserved their respective standards, the ratio would clearly remain more steady than could be the case when suddenly the mintage of silver as standard money was abandoned by several countries.

§ 5. *International bi-metallism.*—If, however, it be granted that one country alone could not effectively maintain a fixed ratio between gold and silver, and keep both metals in circulation as standard money, it may still be maintained that, if the principal commercial nations were to simultaneously adopt bi-metallism at the same fixed ratio, no disturbance of that ratio could take place. I have in another place [1] elaborated this argument, and need only state here the principal positions. It rests essentially on what is known as the *compensatory action* of the double or (to adopt a better term) the joint standard. To illustrate this theory, suppose that all the great commercial nations have adopted bi-metallism in the manner suggested; and next suppose, if it is possible, that silver, for example, suddenly becomes cheaper, reckoned in gold, than it ought to be according to the ratio. This would, as explained in the last section, at once bring into play Gresham's law, and the silver would tend to drive the gold from circulation. But then the crucial question arises: Whither would this gold go, and whence would the silver be obtained to take its place? It is maintained that as the gold was thrown upon, and the silver withdrawn from, the bullion market, the former would fall and the latter rise in value, and thus that the ratio would be restored. In fact, it is argued by those who rely most on this compensatory action of the double or joint standard, that the ratio never

---

[1] Essay on the "Stability of a Fixed Ratio between Gold and Silver under International Bi-metallism," p. 288.

could be disturbed, and the argument is really a *reductio ad absurdum.*

On the other side it is maintained, following the contention of Lord Liverpool, that all rich nations naturally prefer gold as their standard. Consequently, if all the great commercial nations adopted bi-metallism, and yet at the same time they really preferred gold as the principal money, it may be thought that a premium on gold would arise. In support of this view, it has been urged that no bank would, in the light of recent experience, and merely in reliance on the *theory* of international bi-metallism, run the risk of keeping a large reserve of silver. Again, it is said that Government would prefer gold to silver for their war chests, and also that gold would be hoarded or converted into plate, rather than be passed at what might appear too low a value compared with silver.

Sometimes, however, the objections to international bi-metallism are based (as for example by Professor Nasse)[1] on the dangers which the banks, and consequently the Governments of the bi-metallic nations, would undergo, from the fact that the discredited and disliked silver would be paid into the banks and would not be withdrawn, and thus that

---

[1] See Essay in 'Schönberg's Handbuch,' vol. i. p. 279. This essay is, perhaps, the best statement yet made on the mono-metallic side and well deserves translation.

the whole credit system of the civilised world would rest on an insecure foundation.

Finally, it is objected that with conventional bi-metallism, in which silver was presumably over-valued, a stimulus would be given to the production of silver, and relatively a check placed on the production of gold.   Such a stimulus and check, however, could operate but very slightly on mines which yielded any rent (for it may be assumed that they are worked at full pressure), and the difference in the annual supply due to this cause would thus be very small in amount compared with the total stock.

I shall not attempt in this place to decide on the relative merits of these conflicting arguments.   It may not, however, be out of place to observe that the logical conclusion to the argument that all the more highly civilised nations naturally prefer gold, would seem to be that they will all attempt to adopt the gold standard.   If the argument has any force at all, it certainly applies with far greater cogency to the United States or France at the present day than to England at the time when Lord Liverpool wrote. But the probable consequences of any attempt to make the gold standard universal may be expressed in the words of Mr Goschen, at the Conference at Paris in 1878.   "If, however, other States were to carry on a propaganda in favour of a gold standard and of the demonetisation of silver, the Indian Government would be obliged to reconsider its position, and might be forced by events to take measures similar to those taken elsewhere. *In that case the scramble to get rid of silver might provoke one of the gravest crises ever undergone by commerce."*

§ 6. *The effects of changes in the relative value of gold and silver on the general level of prices in gold-using and silver - using countries respectively.* — The sentence just quoted from so eminent a financial authority as Mr Goschen, naturally leads to an inquiry as to the manner in which such a grave crisis could arise. Since Adam Smith destroyed the mercantile system, with its fetish of a favourable monetary balance, popular opinion, which is ever liable to run from one extreme to the other, has been inclined to exaggerate the position that money is in general not the end but the medium of exchange. No one now will deny the truth so clearly stated by John Law, nearly a century before the ' Wealth of Nations ' became famous, in the words : " Money is not the value for which goods are exchanged, but the value by which they are exchanged ; " but, at the same time, it is equally false to imagine that changes in money values only produce nominal effects.

Suppose that, owing to " a scramble for gold " by Western countries, silver becomes depreciated relatively to gold, the question arises : What (if any) will be the effect on general prices in gold-using and silver-using countries respectively? The answer depends upon two lines of argument. In the *first* place, it can hardly be disputed that, when allowance is made for the cost of carriage and the remittance of payment, the price of any commodity reckoned in either standard, except in the case of transitory market influences, must be the same in both gold- and silver-using countries (say) in England and India. This adjustment of prices to practical equality has of late become much more ready than formerly, since now most wholesale business is transacted by telegraph. It follows then that, other things remaining the same, if silver falls in value relatively to gold, either silver prices must rise or gold prices must fall, or a movement in both directions must take place. To take an extreme case, assume that silver falls suddenly to half its former value, reckoned in gold. Obviously if Eastern produce were to command the same gold price in London as before, that would mean twice as much silver; and conversely, if Manchester goods were to obtain only the same silver price in Calcutta as before, that would mean only half as much gold. But if the general level of prices in both countries remained the same, Eastern goods would be exported to England in great quantities, whilst the Eastern markets would remain practically closed to English wares. As a natural consequence, the gold price of Eastern goods would tend to fall, owing to the abundant supply, whilst the silver price of English goods would tend to rise, owing to the bareness of the markets. Thus, in time, the two sets of prices must be adjusted, so that the amount of silver which any article of commerce obtains in the East becomes— allowance being made for carriage, &c.—of the same value as the gold which it obtains in the West.

Now, suppose that the adjustment is made entirely by an operation on gold prices—in other words, that the rupee price of Manchester goods, for example, does not rise, and that the gold price of Indian exports falls. In this case there will be no disturbance of relative prices in India, everything selling, after allowing for charges in cost and the like, for the same silver as before. So far no difference to Indian interests will arise. The Indian Government, however, to meet its obligations in gold on this side, will have to transmit the value of twice as much silver as before, which will involve twice as much taxation, other things remaining the same.

In gold-using countries, on the other hand, taking England as the type, we have supposed that all the articles of Eastern trade have fallen in their gold price proportionately to the fall in silver. In this case, either wages, and all the other elements in the cost of production of exports to the East, must fall in proportion, or the exportation must cease. Similarly, as regards articles which compete with exports from the East (wheat, for example), unless the English cost of production is lessened, a check will be placed on production.

If, however, in all the industries which supply Eastern markets, and in all which compete with Eastern produce, a fall of prices sets in, and this fall in turn operates on the various items in the cost of production (fixed capital, profits, wages, raw material, &c.), it is necessary, according to the general principles of industrial competition, that other branches of production should also be affected. In this way, under the supposition made as to the nature of the adjustment, a fall in the price of silver, reckoned in gold, may cause a proportionate fall in the general level of gold prices. This, however, is only one supposition—for, by parity of reasoning, the adjustment may take place by a rise in silver prices to the full extent of the depreciation, or by a rise in silver prices and a fall in gold prices coincidently. It is, then, of the utmost importance to discover which method of adjustment is most probable.

§ 7. *The general level of gold prices more unstable than that of silver prices.*—It has often been observed by economists, especially since attention has been directed to the recurrence of decennial cycles in trade, that in a highly civilised community—England, for example—the amount of gold used, both for reserve and for circulation, does not vary exactly with the rise or fall in prices,—in other words, that the same quantity of gold will, within certain limits, sustain very different systems of general prices. A reference to the argument in previous chapters on the causes which determine the general level of prices, will at once show that there are several other variable elements besides the quantity of gold. In the same way, in countries in which silver is the standard, we have to consider other elements besides the quantity of silver. Apparently, so long as the general conditions of production and distribution remain the same, the most important of these variable influences is the elasticity of credit; and no demonstration is needed to show that the development of credit is carried to a far higher degree in the gold-using than in the silver-using countries. It follows, then, that so far the level of gold prices is more unstable than that of silver prices.

Again, although there is a tendency to exaggerate the influence of custom in fixing prices in the East, there can be little doubt that custom operates to a much greater extent there than is the case in the West, so that a diminution of supply which, in the West, might cause a rapid and great rise in prices, might in the East have a much less effect. To take a concrete example, it would be much more easy to raise the price of shirts in this country than of dhooties in India, in response to a rise in raw material.

It thus appears that general prices can only rise over the vast areas of silver-using countries by an actual increase of the circulating medium sufficient to force up the customary rates ; and it follows that if silver falls relatively to gold, it is much more probable that gold prices will be forced down than silver prices raised to make the necessary adjustment. It must be remembered that in the East gold is simply a commodity, and, to the native mind, there is no reason why a rise in the silver price of gold should cause a rise in the price of cotton goods or wheat.

Now it is well known that since 1874 a great fall has occurred in the value of silver compared with gold. Without entering into the causes of this fall, it may be said that some adjustment, in the manner described, of gold and silver prices became necessary. Apparently silver prices have not risen, and gold prices have fallen, as might have been expected, seeing that no great increase in the shipments of silver to the East seems to have taken place. On the question of fact, however, the report of the present Commission will, it may be hoped, speak with authority.

§ 8. *Causes of disturbance in the relative value of gold and silver.*—Seeing, then, that the disturbance in the relative values of the two metals are of such consequence, it is important to discover the principal causes of a possible variation. Stated generally, variations can only arise from changes in the conditions of supply and demand. Silver, in the markets of gold-using countries, has a price which will vary with the supply and demand, and a fall in price may arise from an unusual excess of supply or a falling off in demand. A great increase in supply may take place either from great discoveries (or improved processes in working the mines and ores), or from the release of hoards, or from a Government selling silver which it intends to replace with gold. Conversely, a falling off in demand may arise either because Governments require less for their coinage, or because less is required for export. The only element which presents any difficulty is the last. For the demand for export will depend on the balance of indebtedness, which cannot be met except by the actual transmission of silver (that is to say, the balance which remains after other means of remittance are exhausted). Obviously, however, this balance, so far as dependent on commercial transactions, will itself depend partly on the quantities of exports and imports, and partly on the state of prices. But, as was shown above, the state of prices must depend partly on the relative value of gold and silver, and we thus seem to be led into an argument in a circle. If, however, the greater immobility of silver prices be admitted, we escape from the vicious circle, and, in any case, the demand for export is only one element in the demand, and the price of silver may vary from other changes in demand or from changes in supply.

We thus arrive at the position that if silver and gold are left to market influences alone, variations in their relative values are liable to occur, with consequent effects upon prices and commercial transactions. The secondary effects seem of more importance than the mere inconveniences of a fluctuating exchange, though, no doubt, to those actually engaged in trade with silver countries this is a source of annoyance.

§ 9. *Money a proper subject for international agreement.*—It appears, then, that the consideration of this additional factor—namely, the use of both gold and silver as standard money by different countries—has strengthened the conclusion of the last chapter, that the causes of movements in the general level of prices in any one country cannot be explained without a survey which embraces the whole commercial world. Any nation may, of course, choose the metals for its money, and may vary or not the weights and the purity and the denominations of its coins as it pleases, but no nation can be independent of the rest of the world as regards the most important quality of a good system of money—namely, stability of value. Thus, so long as gold and silver form the principal bases on which contracts are made and exchanges take place, every particular nation must consider the monetary conditions of other nations, and a formal definite recognition of this mutual dependence seems the natural outcome of commercial development. Since, however, in this essay I wish to avoid even the appearance of controversy, I will conclude by saying that, if it could be effected, every one would rejoice in a stable international agreement, but that to some the initial difficulties and the possible evil consequences seem to outweigh the probable advantages.

APPENDIX A.

Statistics used in the argument on the Silver Question.—The principal statistics and facts relating to the depreciation of silver are as follows :—A summary of the Mint regulations of the principal countries of the world, prepared as an appendix (B¹) to the Third Report of the Royal Commission on the Depression of Trade, by Mr R. H. Inglis Palgrave, formerly editor of the 'Economist,' and one of the commissioners, shows—(*a*) "That down to the year 1871 silver was a principal standard of value in Europe, and that the demonetisation of silver by Germany in that year was followed by the closing of the Mints of the Latin Union against silver in 1874. The Latin Union (comprising France, Belgium, Switzerland, Italy, Greece, and Roumania) continued in force about seven years and a half, from 1st August 1866 to 30th January 1874. (*b*) That at the present time the only important Mints open to silver *without restriction* are those of British India and Mexico. The United States, also, coins a considerable quantity of silver ; of this, however, a large portion cannot, even taking the silver certificates into account, be said to be in circulation. The other coinages of silver are only of 'token' coins."

Currency Regulations of France.—"The present (nominal) monetary arrangements of France date from 1785, when the declaration of Louis XVI. fixed the value of gold

---

¹ This is a most valuable document, containing a vast quantity of information relative to the "silver question."

and silver in the proportion of one mark of gold to fifteen and a half of silver. This principle was continued by the law of 1803, gold coin and silver in five-franc pieces being equally legal tender for any amounts. The mintage of both gold and silver was unlimited in amount; the charge for coinage was to be borne by the coiner of the bullion at the rate, in 1803, of nine francs per kilogramme of gold and three francs per kilogramme of silver. Some alterations in the mint charges have occurred since, but the principle of the unrestricted mintage of both gold and·silver was maintained till 30th January 1874. After this date the coinage of silver was restricted."

Currency Regulations of the United States.—"The Congress of the Confederation established the double standard in 1786 with the ratio 1 : 15·25, altered in 1792 to 1 : 15, in 1834 to 1 : 16·002, in 1837 to 1 : 15·988. The law of 1873 made the gold dollar the unit of value, gold coin being unlimited legal tender, and silver coins up to five dollars. The law of 1878 (the Bland Act) directed a limited coinage of silver dollars (2,000,000 at least per month, 4,000,000 at most), and gave them full paying power, except in cases where it is strictly stipulated otherwise in the contract. Specie payments were suspended in the United States in 1862 and resumed 1st Jan. 1879."

The Price of Silver in London, reckoned in pence per ounce, taking periods of ten years, from 1801 to 1850, oscillated between $60\frac{13}{16}$d. as a maximum and $59\frac{5}{8}$d. as a minimum, and from 1851 to 1875, taking periods of five years, between $61\frac{5}{8}$d. as a maximum and $59\frac{1}{16}$d. as a minimum. Between 1876-80 the average price was $52\frac{11}{16}$d., and between 1881-84 it was $51\frac{1}{8}$d. Since then a still further fall has occurred, and it has been quoted as low as 42d. per ounce.

General Prices in India.—Prices generally reckoned in silver have fallen, though not in the same degree as prices reckoned in gold, during the same period. The price of silver, reckoned in gold, in London has dropped more than the prices of commodities in India have fallen.

General Prices in Gold-using Countries.—The movements in these prices have already been pointed out in connection with the explanation of "index numbers." It will be sufficient to remind the reader that since 1874 a continuous fall has taken place, until the general level is lower than at any time during the last forty years.

Production of the Precious Metals.—Estimating the value of gold to silver on the rate of $15\frac{1}{2}$: 1, the following figures are interesting. Taking periods of five years, the production of gold, 1851-55, was about £27,500,000, of silver about £8,000,000 per annum; 1856-60, gold, £28,750,000, silver a little over £8,000,000 : since these years the production of gold has diminished and that of silver increased, until we find, 1876-80, gold £24,000,000, and silver £22,000,000; for the year 1883, gold about £20,000,000, silver about £26,000,000; and for 1884 the figures are estimated as—gold, £19,500,000, silver, £25,750,000.

Estimated stock of gold in money and hoarded in the principal civilised countries (United Kingdom and Colonies, United States, and Europe) in the following years:—1850, about £167,500,000; 1860, £395,000,000; 1870, £535,000,000; 1880, £638,000,000; 1884, £654,500,000.

Corresponding Estimates of Silver. — In 1850, £481,500,000; 1860, £441,000,000; 1870, £409,000,000; 1880, £420,000,000; 1884, £437,500,000.

Coinages of Gold and Silver by the same Countries.—It must be noticed that the following estimates include recoinages from old materials. Taking periods of five years we find :—

		Gold.	Silver.
1851-55	. .	£166,500,000	£23,000,000
1856-60	. .	£179,000,000	£46,000,000
1861-65	. .	£156,500,000	£35,000,000
1866-70	. .	£130,000,000	£58,000,000
1871-75	. .	£189,500,000	£69,000,000
1876-80	. .	£194,000,000	£87,000,000
1881-84	. .	£120,750,000	£47,750,000

The importance of considering the element of re-coinage is shown by another calculation of Mr Palgrave, that even in *silver* the production falls short of the coinage from 1871-75 by 17 per cent, and from 1876-80 by 28 per cent, though from 1881-84 it has exceeded the coinage by 10 per cent. In this calculation the coinage of India and Mexico have been taken into account in addition to the civilised countries.

Imports of Gold and Silver into India.—As regards silver, I may refer to a table prepared by Mr Barbour, Financial Secretary to the Government of India, and a member of the recently appointed Royal Commission on Currency. The table gives millions of rupees [at the rate of $15\frac{1}{2}:1$, about 10 rupees = £1 sterling], and is so constructed as to show the amounts due to borrowings in various forms, and the amounts due to the ordinary course of trade, found by deducting the borrowings from the total net imports. ('Theory of Bi-metallism,' p. 110.) "It will be seen," the writer says, "that from 1856-66 India imported annually 108,000,000 of rupees; but that if we deduct the borrowings, India imported only 45,000,000 of rupees annually during this period, notwithstanding the special impulse given to imports of silver by the American war" (owing to the great increase in exports of cotton at a high price). From 1866-76 India imported very little silver indeed, except what she borrowed. From 1876-85 India imported, apart from borrowings, about 55,000,000 annually, the borrowings being about 17,000,000 on the average annually.

The imports of gold into India (p. 147 of work cited) from 1873-80 averaged annually a little more than 3,000,000 of rupees, whilst from 1880-85 the average has been nearly 7,000,000.

PART II.

ESSAYS ON MONETARY PROBLEMS.

JOHN LAW OF LAURISTON:

AND

THE GREATEST SPECULATIVE MANIA ON RECORD.[1]

*ADDRESS TO THE EDINBURGH PHILOSOPHICAL
INSTITUTE, JANUARY 24, 1888.*[2]

In the invigorating address[3] with which Mr Morley opened the course of lectures for the present Session, the most remarkable feature to my mind was the way in which the most brilliant, ingenious, and witty aphorisms of the cynical man of the world were made to appear stale and flat compared with the wisdom of those whose "great thoughts come from the heart." At any rate, all who listened to the address must have been impressed with the fact that, however

---

[1] I have been much indebted to 'Recherches historiques sur le Système de Law,' by E. Levasseur; 'Histoire de Law,' by Thiers; Wood's 'Memorials of Cramond' and 'Life of Law'; the 'Memoires de la Vie privée de Louis XV'; the account of Law's system in Sir James Steuart's 'Political Economy'; and various minor works of Montesquieu and Defoe.

[2] Some parts were omitted in delivery for want of time.

[3] On Aphorisms.

coldly and impartially history is written in these days, the heart still warms to the good man struggling with adversity, and pays but listless attention to the brilliant achievements of energy without moral purpose, and intellect without soul.

For my own part, I soon became painfully afraid that, in taking for the subject of my lecture John Law of Lauriston, I had, in one important respect at least, chosen a most uninteresting theme. For, as his earliest biographer puts it, " to his moral character, I am sorry to say, no compliments can be paid ; " and in support of this statement he quotes the remark of a contemporary that, even before he attained his majority, " he was nicely expert in all manner of debaucheries."

A few facts from his early life will justify and partly explain this judgment.

John Law was born in Edinburgh in April 1671. His father was a goldsmith, an occupation which in those days was more that of a banker of a primitive kind than a craftsman. He amassed a sufficient fortune to buy the estate of Lauriston, but died the next year (1684), and left his son, at the age of fourteen, heir to his estate, and committed to the charge of a prudent but too indulgent mother. The boy was gifted with a handsome person, and became accomplished in all the arts and amusements of society, including tennis and fencing.

Freed from control, he soon began to waste his substance in riotous living. He went up to London about the age of twenty, and celebrated his coming of age by making over the estate of Lauriston to his mother, so as to provide funds for his debts. His next exploit was, at the age of twenty-three, to kill in a duel another man of fashion with whom he had some hot words relating to a married lady. For this affair, after a three days' trial, he was convicted of murder and sentenced to death. On a representation of the case to the Crown, however, he obtained a pardon; but as the relatives of the man who was killed made an appeal, Law was put into prison, and apparently thought it safer to bribe his jailers and escape to the Continent.

He remained abroad about six years, providing the means for his extravagance and pleasures chiefly by gambling.

So far, John Law appears simply as a man of the world, as the world was at the beginning of the eighteenth century. He set off a fine person with handsome dress, and won the hearts of men and women by his brilliant wit and pleasant manner. We have the authority of no less a person than the Professor of Anatomy in the University of Edinburgh of the time, that Mr Law was one of the easiest, most affable, and best behaved men he had ever seen; and

I

the professor is supported by a crowd of dukes and
duchesses.   John Law was by no means a needy ad-
venturer, as is too commonly supposed.   He was of
good family : his father was great-grandson of James
Law, Archbishop of Glasgow, and his mother was
connected with a branch of the ducal house of Argyll.
After his hurried departure to the Continent, as a
natural precaution against the possible success of the
appeal against him, he was soon appointed Secretary
to the British Resident in Holland ; and some years
before he attained his great celebrity, he married
Lady Catherine Knollys, daughter of Nicholas, third
Earl of Banbury.

Thus John Law had every right to rank as a man
of fashion and a man of honour, which is not indeed
saying very much, comparing our standard with the
standard of his day, but which is saying enough to
show that he was not a cardsharper and swindler, or,
as the French called him after his fall, the " eldest
son of Satan."

But whatever judgment be passed on Law's moral
character—and the popular judgment has certainly
been far too harsh—there can be no two opinions as
to his great financial genius.   Having regard to the
circumstances of the time, to the rudimentary condition of monetary science, and to the want of national
experience in credit transactions, he displayed both
wonderful originality and wonderful soundness.   It

is not just to test a man's ability by the mere event
of success or failure, which may be largely due to the
action of others beyond his control. John Law's system certainly ended in the most tremendous financial
collapse on record. But in spite of this catastrophe,
John Law may have been an excellent financier, just
as Napoleon was a great soldier in spite of Waterloo,
and the man who lost his soul to the devil at a game
of chess may have been an excellent chess-player.

The Bank of England was founded in the year in
which John Law killed Mr Wilson and fled the
country, and the Bank of Scotland was founded in
the next year.

Perhaps the most effective way of bringing before
you the rudimentary state of banking at the time, is
not simply to mention the fact that Bank of England
notes fell considerably below par, but to recall the
main features of a caricature, published after the
failure of Law's great Mississippi Scheme, about
twenty-five years after the foundation of the Bank
of England. The "Goddess of Shares" is seated in a
beautiful car drawn by the Goddess of Folly. Lest
the car should not roll fast enough, the agents of four
great companies, who are known by their long fox-
tails and cunning looks, turn round the spokes of the
wheels, upon which are marked the names of the
several stocks and their value, sometimes high and

sometimes low, according to the turns of the wheel. Upon the ground are the merchandise, day-books and ledgers of legitimate commerce, crushed under the chariot of Folly. All this is simple and natural; but the most startling thing is to find that those who are drawing this car of Folly are representatives of great financial schemes, and that the Bank of England, though a quarter of a century old at the time, is placed in the same yoke with the South Sea Bubble. Imagine the state of credit in which the Directors of the Bank of England could be represented as foxes with cunning looks and long tails, and that noble institution as trampling upon legitimate commerce !

For the sake of a convenient illustration, I have abandoned chronology; but at the time the Bank of England, the first regular bank in the kingdom, was founded, John Law was forced to retire to Holland, and in Amsterdam he founded a bank that had been in a flourishing state for nearly a century. The banking, however, which it performed was of the simplest possible kind. Holland was the centre of the world's trade, and it was by trade that she amassed her wealth and became the richest country in Europe. The Dutch traders, however, were much troubled with the defective state of their own coinage, and still more by the circulation of a mass of foreign coins of uncertain value. No merchant could tell exactly what a bill payable in Holland would realise.

The Bank of Amsterdam was instituted to remedy this evil. It would lead me too far from the path of my narrative if I were to describe in any detail the principles on which this bank was founded, and I will confine myself to the idea which so much impressed John Law.

Avoiding technicalities, the essence of the institution may be explained in very few words. The merchants took all sorts of coins to the bank, and the bank gave them credit for the real and not for the nominal value. It is just as if in England the gold coins became so light that the banks were afraid to take them at full value, and only allowed the value by weight. The bank locked up the money, and practically gave the merchants bank-notes representing the money.[1]

These bank-notes were bought and sold in order to settle bills, for every one knew that the bank-note represented a certain number of perfect coins. The most curious thing was, that the notes were so much valued that they actually sold for a little more than their nominal value.

---

[1] The Bank of Amsterdam did not actually issue bank-notes in the way practised at present. The precise method of dealing with the bank-credits and bullion, however, is too intricate for consideration in this place. Compare Adam Smith's 'Wealth of Nations,' Bk. iv. chap. iii., and Sir James Steuart's 'Principles of Political Economy,' Bk. iv. Part ii. chaps. xxxvii.-xxxix.

It may seem paradoxical to say that a bank-note should ever be worth more than the gold it represents; but again, let me refer to our own light gold coinage for illustration.

Suppose that our banks decide to take the gold only by weight, what would be more natural than for a trader to say, when offered a bag of suspicious-looking coins in payment of a bill, Pay me in notes which the banks must meet in coins of full value; I cannot weigh and test all those coins?

But if many merchants did that at once, and the notes were limited, for a time they would command a premium. People would pay for the extra convenience of a note as they pay now for a post-office order.

To return to the Bank of Amsterdam. It was seen at the time, and it has always been admitted since, that the bank-notes issued by it were in every respect better money than the actual gold and silver coins in circulation. Obviously, so long as the bank retained all its gold, and made no advances at all, so long as it kept to its primary object, its notes were absolutely safe—safer, indeed, than the coin in the possession of the merchant, and in every way they were far more convenient; that is to say, paper money, under certain conditions, was better than metallic money.

It was in Holland that John Law may be said to

have matured the leading ideas of his system; and undoubtedly, if not originally due to, they were largely influenced by, his experience in that country. He contrasted Scotland and England with Holland, and found that, whilst all the natural advantages were in favour of the former countries, the trade and wealth of Holland were far superior. The only reason, he thought, must be in the different treatment of industry by Government. So much was he convinced of this, that he wrote: " If Spain, France, or Britain, or any one of them, had applied to trade as early, and upon the same measures, as Holland did, Holland would not have been inhabited."

What, then, were the essential points of difference ?

In the answer to this question John Law discovered the elements of his system.

In the first place, he observed that, owing to its banking system, there was in Holland an abundance of money to drive trade, and that credit lent the support of capital to new undertakings, at a very moderate return. In Scotland, on the contrary, trade was fettered, and the development of industry checked, because there was not enough money and credit to give free scope to enterprise.

Accordingly, he thought one of the principal needs of the time was to supply the nation with sufficient money; and as a consequence he has been accused of holding all the errors of the inflationists, and of believing that it was only necessary to flood the country with " counters " (metallic or paper) to bring about prosperity.

There is nothing more dangerous to clear reasoning than to push an analogy to an extreme, and the analogy of " counters " has in recent days probably done much more harm than good.   Money is certainly a medium of exchange, and may thus be compared to " counters," but a metaphor does not exhaust all the functions of money and credit.

We shall approach much nearer to the idea in John Law's mind if we suppose, not that he could not distinguish between the real and the nominal wealth of a country, but that he appreciated the difference between a country or city, or even village, with and without a banking system.   If it were proposed to establish a branch bank in a new district, it would not savour of practical wisdom to object that money was only " counters "; and it is about as sensible to write down John Law's system as false, under the impression that he did not understand that elementary fragment of monetary science.   At any rate, he understood it sufficiently well to write, " Money is not the value for which goods are exchanged, but the value by which they are exchanged ; the use of money is to buy goods and silver, whilst money is of no other use ; " and Adam Smith himself could not better express this " counters " theory of money.

Next as regards money, John Law observed that in Holland, not only was the paper money better than gold or silver, but that, owing to the preference of people for the paper, the precious metals which it represented remained locked up in the bank and were never demanded. What, then, more natural than to suppose that a paper-money, or at any rate an extensive credit system, might be formed with some other real security, such as land, at its back? And in modern times, is not every advance by a bank upon securities of various kinds an example of what Sir James Steuart called the melting down of wealth into bank-money?

But apart from the superiority of its monetary system, John Law imagined that Holland had an advantage over other countries, because she understood much better the general industrial functions of government, both by way of freedom and by way of control. Accordingly, we shall find that Law's system, when fully developed, was, on the one hand, an anticipation of free trade in the widest sense of the term, involving the abolition of monopolies and petty restraints and the repeal of oppressive taxes; whilst, on the other, it imposed on the State certain large duties in industrial organisation, the neglect of which in modern times has been the principal encouragement to Socialism.

It was with the view, in the first place, of benefiting his country, by placing the relations of government to industry on a sounder basis, that, soon after he returned to Scotland, he published his proposal for a Council of Trade.

The Council of Trade was to have under its control the whole of the king's revenues, charitable endowments, tithes, and certain specified duties. This enormous income, after a certain portion had been handed over for the use of royalty, was to be employed for the promotion of industry. Scotland was then swarming with beggars, and they were to be compelled to work; monopolies of various kinds were to be prohibited; duties on imports and exports were to be repealed or reduced; fraudulent bankrupts were to be punished and honest debtors liberated; and in short, the Council of Trade was to carry out a complete scheme of industrial and mercantile reform, on what was a very liberal basis, considering the circumstances of the country at the time.

This proposal, however, came to nothing; and five years later, when about thirty-five years of age, John Law tried to carry out the less ambitious project for the reform of the currency and the extension of credit. With this object in view he published his principal work on ' Money and Trade.'

The treatise is written in a vigorous style, and is strictly argumentative. The reasoning is perfectly clear, but often so briefly stated as to be difficult to follow. The design was evidently struck off by the writer at white heat, and under the full conviction that it was perfectly practicable and of the highest national importance. There is not a trace of the prospectus-monger who, to promote his own interest, professes to trade for the public good. Any one who imagines that John Law was simply a projector who deceived a credulous public by flattering, glowing hopes, which he himself knew to be false, cannot do better than glance over the little book on ' Money and Trade.' It is from beginning to end a pure piece of political arithmetic, and has no more of the gorgeous visions of speculation than one of Ricardo's tracts on " Currency." In fact, to a person not well versed in economic reasoning, it will be about as entertaining as to a non - mathematical reader a treatise on the differential calculus.

As the scheme was not approved by Parliament, I do not propose to discuss it in detail. The leading idea was to issue bank-notes upon landed security, the amount issued being strictly limited, and the whole management being of the most public character. The reason given was, that at the time there was not sufficient currency in the country to develop its resources, and that the money in use was subject to great and uncertain variations in value. Whether the scheme could ever have worked practically is more than doubtful; but as a piece of theory it is interesting and instructive.

As soon as he found that his proposals for the improvement of the national finance and industry were not likely to be carried out, John Law resumed his old life on the Continent. He visited many of the principal cities in Europe, especially in Italy, and everywhere studied banking and finance, and indulged in gambling and speculation. He first visited Paris in 1708, and became notorious for his high play. It is said that he always took with him to the gambling-table two bags containing gold to the value of several thousand pounds sterling, and was accustomed to play for such high stakes that he used counters to represent his money, to save the trouble of handling the large sums,—the counters always being duly honoured at the close of the evening. It was on this occasion that he met the prince who later, as Regent and Duke of Orleans, gave him a field for the development of his system. He made enemies, however, was compelled to leave Paris, and resumed his rambles over Europe.

By a rare combination of skill and good fortune, he amassed considerable wealth; and soon after the death of Louis XIV., in September 1715, and the assumption of the Regency by the Duke of Orleans, he returned to Paris, bringing with him more than £100,000 sterling.

Between the middle of 1716 and the end of 1720 occurred a series of events of the most astonishing character, which for a time made John Law the most powerful man in France and the most celebrated man in the world.

To understand this extraordinary drama, it is necessary to grasp both the character of the man and the state of affairs in France.   As for the man, he may be known by the deeds already noticed.   He had studied finance amongst the phlegmatic Dutch and the crafty Italians, and had lived a life of pleasure in the most corrupt courts and cities of Europe. His manners were pleasing and even enticing, yet he was quick to resent an injury.   Full of resource and untiring in energy, he commanded the respect always accorded to superior intellectual activity.   Thoroughly convinced of the truth of his own theories, he infected others with his own enthusiasm.   He dazzled the world with his bold cool-headed gambling, and yet wrote like a philosopher on the mysteries of value and money.   He had large statesmanlike views on the industrial policy of nations; but at the same time he altogether underrated practical difficulties, as if life were only a game of chance and skill; and he was prepared to reorganise the industry of a nation or of the world in less time than other men have taken to describe in a book an ideal Utopia.

Such was the man, and by a strange fatality

France afforded him a field exactly adapted for the
display of his peculiar genius.

France, at the death of Louis XIV., was on the
verge of national bankruptcy. The heavy expenditure of the closing years of his reign had only been
met by loans contracted at ruinous rates of interest,
and by the most burdensome methods of taxation.
Every device for raising money had been tried.
When no more could be obtained from the people by
force, the king resorted to the sale of patents of
nobility and of all kinds of offices and monopolies,
until Paris was filled with royal officers whose fantastic titles provoked the ridicule of the people.
Even public lotteries were practised to such an extent, that at last they ceased to be productive. The
people became too poor or too hopeless to invest
a shilling for the sake of a fortune. About five
years before the death of the king, a tenth of the
property of every one, from the Dauphin downwards,
was exacted; but gradually exemptions crept in, and
this new tithe became practically a tax on agriculture
and commerce. The coinage was called in, in order
that the Government might abstract a certain portion
and reissue at the same nominal value. By an operation of this kind in 1709, the king gained about 23
per cent—that is to say, he practically reduced the
weight of each coin by that amount. But the evils
caused by the discredit attached to the debased coin-

age were so great, that in 1713 an edict was passed
to bring it up to the value at which it had been for
nearly fifty years of the flourishing part of his reign.
Large amounts of promissory-notes on the part of the
State (*billets d'état*) were issued, most of which did
not pass for a quarter of their nominal value, and
some were hardly worth a tenth.

Thus Louis XIV. left to his successor (his great-
grandson), a child of five years, a total debt of $3\frac{1}{2}$
milliards of livres (or about 250 millions sterling at
the proper rate of conversion), a mass of accounts
hopelessly entangled, an empty treasury, a ruined
credit, a people crushed with new taxes that became every year more unproductive, and a growing
expenditure.

All the real power of the State fell into the hands
of the Regent, the Duke of Orleans. The Parliament
attempted to assert some power, but was speedily and
roughly crushed, and the Duke was, for all practical
purposes, an absolute ruler. His court became so
hopelessly corrupt, that the satirists of the time could
only find fitting parallels in the worst scenes of the
Roman Empire. The Regent himself indulged in the
grossest debaucheries; and the day after some of his
Saturnalia, in which the very footmen joined, he was
incapable for hours of attending to any serious
business. One of his mistresses was moved to
say that God had made man's body out of clay,

and with some mud left over, the souls of princes and lacqueys.

Yet even in the muddy soul of the Regent some grains of pride and honour were left, and he refused to assent to a complete national bankruptcy. A Commission was appointed to examine critically the obligations of the late king, and to divide them into classes. In the end the national debt was reduced by about one-half, on which interest of 4 per cent was promised. In order to raise funds for present expenses, however, the coinage was again suddenly reduced in real value, in spite of the warnings of experience. The coins which the late king had brought up to their old level were called in and re-stamped with the new child-king's effigy, and nearly 30 per cent abstracted. It is needless to say that the people, at least the money-dealers, exported their full-weight coins to Holland and other places where they could get them re-coined at a cheaper rate.

Such was the state of France when John Law came to Paris to renew his acquaintance with the Regent, who was of course prepared to regard with favour any project that seemed likely to yield money. Law had only to persuade this one man of the probable success of his schemes to ensure full scope for their development, and he lost no time in commencing his work.

In the first act of this great national drama, the

principal characters appear in a most favourable light. John Law gives the Regent elementary lessons in banking, and points to the great success of the banks which had already been established in the most flourishing cities of Europe. The Regent learns with a will, and approves of the project for a great national bank ; but new to banking and despotism, he takes advice from his counsellors, who, being for the most part of the Polonius order, naturally advise against the scheme.

After much discussion, however, Law was at last allowed to establish a private bank at his own risk— the letters patent being dated 2d May 1716 ; and having first, at the humble request of the Parliament, been naturalised, he commenced operations about June.

The bank was established and conducted on the soundest principles, and its services soon began to be appreciated, and John Law proved that bank-notes representing a fixed amount of gold are far better than coins, the value of which is being constantly changed by the Government. His notes were promises to pay so many crowns (*écus de banque*) of the value of the day on which they were issued ; and thus they always represented the same amount of fine silver, whatever change was made in the coins. So far, indeed, he simply carried out a system of banking which had been practised with success in

K

Amsterdam for a century, and in other places for
shorter periods.   It was allowed on all sides that
the bank was a great success.   "If," says Thiers,
"Law had confined himself to this establishment, he
would be considered one of the benefactors of the
country, and the creator of a superb system of
credit."

We are so familiar with banks, and so unfamiliar
with the evils of a fluctuating coinage, that we are
apt to underrate this great improvement effected by
Law.   The success of the bank, however, was so great,
that it gradually became in reality a national or royal
bank.   The collectors of taxes were ordered to make
their remittances in its notes, and these notes, like
those of Amsterdam, bore a premium.   The formal
conversion, however, of Law's private bank into a
royal bank took place in December 1718, and was
marked by a change of vital importance.

The notes issued were now simply promises to pay
so many current coins (*livres tournois*), and were thus
subject to change in real value with every fluctuation
in the coin.   At the same time, the first step was
taken towards making the notes really inconvertible
—for all payments above a certain amount were to
be made either in gold or notes, not silver; and as
there was very little gold in the country, this practically amounted to a forced circulation of the notes.

Law was so much impressed with the superiority

of paper money, that he apparently thought that to compel people to use it by a little pressure was only to promote their own interests against their will; but he overlooked the fact that the essence of all credit is the voluntary action of the contracting parties.

So long as the notes were freely taken as convenient substitutes for metal, they were of advantage to the country; but when they obtained a preference in payments, simply by force of law, the way was open for great abuses.

In the meantime, however, John Law had begun to apply the other leading ideas which he had in vain tried to induce Scotland to put in practice— namely, to promote the national industry by measures of a wide-reaching character.

At that time, in nearly every country in Europe the principal part of the maritime commerce was in the hands of privileged companies. Thus the English East India Company had for more than a century been extending its branches and preparing the way for the ultimate creation of an Indian empire. Holland, also, had a similar company in the same region; and no doubt John Law not only appreciated fully the success already achieved, but anticipated still greater success in the future. The French, too, under Richelieu had started companies for the development of certain portions of America; and their West India

Company was intended as the counterpart of the
Dutch and English East India Companies. The partial colonisation of Canada by the French took place
in this manner. But the French companies seemed
to possess no vitality; and when John Law turned
his attention to the development of the foreign trade
of France, they were all dead or dying.

He did not think the principle wrong, but ascribed
the failure to a bad selection of country and bad
methods of administration. About the time of Law's
birth two Frenchmen, penetrating the wilds from the
Canadian possessions of France, had discovered and
explored a large part of the basin of the Mississippi,
and had in the name of Louis XIV. taken possession
of the vast tracts which were afterwards to form some
of the most fertile and wealthy of the United States.
The whole region had been christened Louisiana, in
honour of the king; a few forts had been erected, but
beyond this nothing had been done for the development of the country.

It occurred to Law that with sufficient capital and
vigorous management on a large scale, this territory
might be made to rival or excel the East India of
England; and accordingly, in 1717, he promoted the
Company of the West—which was the beginning of
the famous Mississippi Scheme. The privileges granted
to the new Company were of the most unlimited kind

—and, in fact, it was entrusted with sovereign power over the whole territory.

It is important to observe that this Mississippi Scheme was no more a fraudulent projector's bubble than was the English East India Company; and an impartial observer at the time might well have thought that France had a better chance of establishing magnificent colonies in the fertile and almost unoccupied lands of America, than Britain of bringing under her sway the millions of India who had already made great advances in war and civilisation. John Law was, as events abundantly proved, perfectly right in supposing that the Mississippi basin was capable of extraordinary commercial and industrial development. But he failed to observe that, for success, both a very large capital and a considerable length of time were necessary. He was a man of excellent theories, but, probably owing to his gambling habits, he was apt to underrate all practical difficulties.

It is true that the capital nominally created was for the time very large, but the real value obtained by the Company was far too small. The Company did not obtain its privileges for nothing—in fact, the subscriptions for its shares were mainly used for reducing the national debt and providing for the immediate extravagance of the Regency. The Company only received the interest—the capital was lent·

to the Government. Had John Law been free to act according to his own judgment—had he not been compelled to purchase every privilege at an extravagant price, and to consult a despotic ruler whose natural abilities had been ruined by excesses, and whose court was a whirlpool of extravagance,—he might have relieved France from her burdens and given her new life by providing freedom for expansion. But the Regent's insatiable extravagance, and Law's boundless confidence, from the first made success more than doubtful, and a new force was soon to come into play which rendered failure inevitable. This was the most unbridled frenzy of speculation which the world has ever witnessed.

It would be hopeless to attempt to condense into a few sentences the details of the development of John Law's extensive schemes. Suffice it to say, that in less than two years from the establishment of the Company of the West, he had merged it in a new company, styled the Company of the Indies, the powers and privileges of which must have surpassed his most extravagant dreams.

This Company was primarily a commercial company which absorbed all the old companies, and thus practically monopolised the whole of the trade of France with new countries. But step by step it acquired new privileges and assumed new functions. Most of the important taxes in France were levied

by a pernicious system of "farming." The privilege
of collection was sold for a lump sum, just as till
lately in this country was the case with the tolls.
The Company of the West had already acquired the
monopoly of tobacco; and the new Company of the
Indies, created in May 1719, had obtained in a few
months the management of all the taxes levied under
the farming system.

For this privilege Law undertook a great and novel
scheme for the conversion of the whole national debt.
He proposed to lend the Government at 3 per cent
sufficient money to pay off all the old creditors,
which, as the debt was paying 4 per cent, would
really relieve the Government of a fourth of the
burden. If successful, the operation would thus be
a gain to the country as a whole; and, as Law said,
although the creditors of the State (*rentiers*) did not
like it, the principal part of the State is composed of
workmen and merchants in towns, and peasants and
labourers in the country, who are the real source of its
wealth. At the same time, however, he did not propose to make the conversion compulsory, but to offer
sufficient inducement to the owners of *rentes* to accept
the capital sum due. This inducement was the privilege of buying shares in the new company; and how
great this attraction was, will soon be made apparent.
Thus in effect the operation consisted in the Company
buying up the whole national debt with a great

issue of shares. This vast operation was in a fair
way of completion before the end of 1719, when
John Law attained the height of his power. He had
now only to assume the title and office of Comptroller-
General to be in name, as in reality, the Prime Minister of France.

A strong light is thrown on the morality of the
times by a preliminary step which was necessary.

To start his bank, the foundation of his system,
Law had to become a naturalised French citizen;
and to become Comptroller-General — to place the
last ornament on the summit of the edifice—he was
obliged to become a Catholic. The task of conversion was committed to the Abbé Tençin, the
peculiar infamy of whose character was sufficient,
even in such an age, to arouse popular detestation,
and to give an entirely commercial complexion to
Law's change of faith. The conversion, such as
it was, was rapidly completed, and the Abbé received for payment shares to the nominal value of
about £10,000.

The system of Law, during the few months in
which it dazzled the world, was a strange mixture of
prudence and recklessness, of the soundest finance
and the wildest gambling, of favourite theories
abandoned and forgotten, and of others carried to
impossible extremes.

The good intentions of the system may be noted

first, as in the nature of things they have been more
readily forgotten than the evil effects.

First of all, then, the burden of taxation was
lessened.   Under Law's organisation the people paid
far less, and yet the State received far more.   Not
only was the national debt consolidated, and the
rate of interest greatly reduced, but a multitude of
imposts and monopolies which had strangled commerce were annulled, and legitimate trade began to
flourish.   He regarded his system simply as providing and ensuring the fundamental principles of industrial organisation as the natural duty of an orderly
government ; but apart from this, he may be regarded
as a thoroughly practical exponent of the principles
of Free Trade and natural liberty.   He considered
the interests of the common people as of primary importance.   For example, when the butchers of Paris,
for plausible but fictitious reasons, raised the price of
meat, Law told them plainly that if they could not
distribute meat at a fair price he would soon find
others who could.   As an experiment, he bought two
oxen, and after a careful calculation of all the expenses, and allowing for profits, he found he could
sell for nearly half the price charged by the butchers,
and thus compelled them to lower their prices.

He did his best to develop the internal commerce
of France.   His bank advanced to manufacturers
immense sums at 2 per cent ; a great number of

people imprisoned for debt were liberated; money
unjustly confiscated by the tribunals was restored;
and the artisans who had been driven from France
in the time of her distresses were recalled, the State
paying their passage.   Throughout France many
vast improvements were commenced—roads, canals,
bridges, and useful and magnificent buildings were
the first-fruits of the new system.   Under the genius
of the Comptroller-General, industrial France vibrated
again with new life, like the earth at the approach of
spring.

Not content merely with the development of the
commerce of the towns, he turned his attention to
the country.   He relieved the peasants from their
most oppressive taxes; he tried to break up the large
estates held in mortmain by corporations; he established a sound system of poor relief for the impov-
erished peasantry; and bought up and extinguished
all kinds of unjust and prejudicial monopolies which
had sprung up through the sale by Louis XIV. of
fragments of his sovereign rights.   Unfortunately for
France, most of these reforms were nipped in the
bud, so that we must judge of their value rather
from the intention than the deed.   But on the whole,
the industrial reforms which John Law attempted in
his short term of office and power, may be fairly
compared with the reforms effected in this country
during the present century by a series of great

statesmen, who have worked on the same lines in the simplification of taxation, the abolition of monopolies, and the extension of the freedom of industry.

The system of John Law, viewed merely as a system of finance and industrial organisation, was a work of genius; and had it not been vitiated by the growth of a malignant principle, opposed to its very essence, it would have conferred upon his adopted country inestimable benefits.

But in order to obtain funds for the completion of his schemes, Law had always viewed with favour, and even encouraged, a rise in the value of the shares already issued. He thus called up a spirit of evil which, like the genius of an Eastern tale, placed at his disposal endless wealth, only to make it disappear still more suddenly.

This demon of speculation, at first the slave of John Law's system, soon became its master and destroyer.

Without entering into details, it is easy to see the progress of the enchantment. A trading company was started, with very fair prospects, by a man who had already proved himself an excellent banker, and who had obtained the confidence of the despotic ruler of the country. In spite of its advantages, however, its shares were for nearly two years below

par. Gradually other schemes were amalgamated
with the original plan (*e.g.*, the farm of the tobacco
duties), and these schemes found more favour. But
the new shares (*les filles*) were only issued to those
who already held old shares (*les mères*), and consequently the demand for the new shares raised the
value of the old in a way that is perfectly familiar
to the present race of directors and shareholders.
The magnitude which the Company of the Indies
attained, on the completion of its privileges, may be
judged from the fact that its actual profits were, at
the end of 1719, estimated at more than four million pounds sterling per annum. It is easy to
imagine how the gradual issue of shares corresponding to such a vast real revenue would, in the nature
of things, encourage speculation. The most ignorant
and blind could observe the rapid rise in the value
of the old shares, and could see how, merely by the
sale of documents, enormous fortunes were made in
a few weeks.

Consequently, on a new issue, a rush was made to
subscribe, and when the speculation had reached its
height, the dividend fixed a few months before was
not sufficient to pay $\frac{1}{2}$ per cent on the market value
of the shares.

Shares of the nominal value of 500 livres had
been issued at 1500, and through speculation had
been raised to 12,000 livres in December 1719.

Consequently, the dividend fixed before at 12 per cent on the original share value, would really pay on the 12,000 only ½ per cent. But every one, in these days, knows that this is a position of extremely unstable equilibrium, and that if the interest does not rise, the value of the shares must fall.

Had Law acted with prudence, instead of with excessive hopefulness, he would have allowed the shares to have fallen in the ordinary course of things, and only have used his influence to prevent the fall being too rapid. But his system was not yet complete, the conversion of the debt was only partially accomplished, and apparently he was afraid that a rapid fall in the value of the shares would injure the wider prospects of the Company.

Accordingly he set himself, during the early part of 1720, to bolster up the shares. He declared that the Company would pay a dividend of 40 per cent instead of 12. Yet with the shares of 500 livres at 12,000, even this dividend, which was the utmost that could possibly be paid in the most sanguine estimate, only yielded less than 2 per cent, and a heavy fall was certain to take place.

In most cases a speculation involving millions would be checked, owing to the impossibility of finding coin or credit for further extension; but the Company of the Indies was, from the first, under the same guidance as the Royal Bank — Law was the moving spirit of both, and the bank had the power of issuing unlimited quantities of notes. Then, again, through its control of the Mint and the coinage, which it had acquired soon after its foundation, the Company had the power of giving a preference to the notes by arbitrary changes in the coins. John Law had truly remarked that notes were better than a fluctuating currency; but it was carrying the doctrine to a dangerous and immoral extreme, to make the currency fluctuate in order to stimulate the demand for notes.

Yet in his anxiety to keep up the use and credit of the notes he resorted to this expedient, and deliberately made rapid changes in the value of the coin, at the same time proclaiming that no change would be made in the nominal value of the notes. By inducing people to believe that gold and silver would be made to pass for less than the corresponding notes, in a few days large sums were drawn to the bank.

Imagine what a run there would be for £1 notes if it were announced that after next Monday a sovereign would, in the payment of debts, be considered only as fifteen shillings, whilst before that date the banks would give a note for every sovereign, the note to be always worth for the payment of debts the full pound !

Practically, by these measures, notes became the

real standard, and very little more was required to make them inconvertible. But Law not only tried to attract specie to the bank by this unworthy device, but he used his political power, no less than his financial authority, and, in contradiction to all his own better principles, absolutely prohibited the use of gold and silver as money, or even the possession of it beyond a certain limited amount. Finally, in the belief that the Company was stronger than the bank under these conditions, he endeavoured to support his notes by joining the two institutions. The creation of notes, in spite of promises to the contrary, went on in alarming quantities. Even at the end of 1719 it was found necessary to simply print the notes without signature by hand as was at first the case, and the printing-presses were worked day and night.

It was therefore this power of the creation of money to an unlimited extent which enabled the speculation to attain a height that would otherwise have been impossible. Every one tried to obtain notes to buy shares, in order simply to sell and pocket the difference. No one knew what the real value of the shares ought to be, and at first even the most prudent and cautious were enticed by the rapidity of the rise.

Yet even in yielding to these imprudent excesses, John Law probably acted in good faith, although

with great imprudence.   His confidence in the ultimate success of his vast schemes was boundless.   The
commercial and financial business of the Company
and the Bank was indeed so enormous, that exaggeration of the value of the shares was natural, if not
pardonable.   Again, the constant issues of notes, and
the advances made by the bank for all kinds of purposes, had lessened the rate of interest, and of course
every fall in the rate of interest caused a corresponding rise in the nominal value of the capital.   There
was also plausibility in the notion that his notes
could not be issued in excess if they simply took the
place of the coin, and if they were issued to meet a
corresponding demand.   The national debt was, for
example, intended to be bought up with notes, and
the receivers of the notes were expected to use them
to take shares in the new company ; and thus it may
be said there was a demand for the notes.

And in justice to Law, it must be remembered
that he had to make decisions on the spur of the
moment, on questions of credit and finance, which
even now are not thoroughly settled.   The directors
of the Bank of England, during the suspension of
cash payments at the beginning of this century, acted
on Law's idea that notes could not be depreciated if
they were always issued against a genuine demand.
Again, the Government of France, during the great
Revolution, based the issues of their *assignats* on a

gross exaggeration of the principle which John Law had proposed as the basis of his land bank. Surely no better proof could be given of the plausibility of the banking part of the system than this exaggerated imitation by the very country which professed to hold the author up to detestation as an. impostor.

And as regards the wider aspects of the system and its ambitious projects for the development of industry, history has shown that Law discovered, with wonderful foresight, the way in which, in the modern world, credit would become the life-breath of industry.

The great mistake which he made was the attempt to force the growth of generations into months with the vapour and heat of speculation. He admitted as much after his fall, when he wrote: "If I had the work to do again, I would go more slowly but more surely, and I would not expose the State to the dangers which must accompany the derangement of an old-established system."

When we reflect on the unparalleled excitement of those few months—on the sudden elevation of a foreigner and unknown commoner to the highest power and dignity of a great nation—on the opening to an enthusiastic theorist of an unlimited field for the conversion of his ideas into facts—on the gross adulation bestowed by all the aristocracy of Europe on a man already familiar, in a humbler capacity, with

L

the pleasures of fashion and society,—the wonder is, not that John Law made mistakes, but that he kept his reason sufficiently to make any application of his principles. And yet, had it not been for the fierce frenzy of speculation that burst out in Paris, it is not improbable that, in spite of his errors, he would have succeeded in placing his system on a sound basis. Thoroughly to understand the causes of his failure, we must attempt to realise the nature and extent of this national madness.

Milliards and millions, especially when expressed in an unfamiliar currency, only create a vague sense of wonder; and it would be of little use to quote the swollen values of the shares and notes as estimated in French livres. A few concrete facts will probably give a better idea than a mere aggregate of inconceivable figures.

A milliner happened to come to Paris about a lawsuit; she was successful, and invested the proceeds in speculation, and she amassed in a few months a sum which, converted into our currency, represents nearly £5,000,000 sterling. Amongst other millionaires, we have coachmen, cooks, and waiters, as well as representatives of all the nobility of Europe. We are told that, in the closing weeks of 1719, more than 35,000 strangers flocked to Paris to take part in the speculation,—that all the means of transport from the other large cities were exhausted,—and that in Marseilles and other places there was a lively speculation for seats in the coaches. No class of the community escaped the infection. Two of the ablest scholars of France are reported to have deplored the madness of the times at one interview, only to find themselves at their next meeting bidding for shares with the greatest excitement. The scene of operations was a narrow street called Quincampoix, and the demand for accommodation may be judged of from the fact that a house which before yielded about £40 a-year, now brought in more than £800 a - month. A cobbler made about £10 a-day by letting out a few chairs in his stall; and a hunchback, who is celebrated in the prints of the time, acquired in a few days more than £7000 sterling by letting out his hump to the street-brokers as a writing-desk.

In every social circle throughout the city the only conversation was on the rise and fall of *actions* (shares). A doctor is said to have nearly frightened a lady to death by muttering to himself, as he felt her pulse, "Alas! good God! it falls, it falls," alluding, of course, to the price of his stock.

The central figure in these scenes of excitement was John Law, who held levees which were more crowded by distinguished guests than any Court in Europe. Extraordinary devices were resorted to, even to see or hear the famous man. One lady ordered her coachman to upset her carriage on Law's approach, that he might rescue her from the wreckage ; whilst another shrieked beneath his window during a dinner-party that the house was on fire.

Nor was the power and influence of Law only celebrated amongst the Parisians. His native city of Edinburgh, proud of having produced so great a man, transmitted to him the freedom thereof, in a gold box of the value of £300 sterling, the diploma being dated 5th August 1719.

But the most remarkable proof of Law's influence is shown by the recall of Lord Stair, the British Ambassador at Paris. This nobleman, apparently with the utmost good faith, had warned his Government that Law was a dangerous enemy ; but the only result was that he himself was recalled. He was replaced by Earl Stanhope, and writing to a friend some time after, Lord Stair said : "I shall readily agree with you that if his Lordship (*i.e.*, the new ambassador) has gained Mr Law and made him lay aside his ill-will and ill designs against this country, he did very right to make all sorts of advances to him—to promise his son a regiment; to engage to bring Lord Banbury (his brother-in-law) into the House of Lords ; and to sacrifice the king's ambassador to him. *If I had thought Mr Law to be gained, I should very readily have advised to do all these things, and a great deal more.*"

We find also from this and other correspondence

that Law was regarded as the real Prime Minister of France; and good authorities state that at the time his power was greater than that of the great Richelieu a century before.

A terrible example of his imperious determination is recorded. Robbery, accompanied by violence, and even by murder, had become frequent during this delirium of money-getting. A young Flemish nobleman, Count Horn, who, though only twenty-two years of age, had plunged into the worst excesses, planned and carried out with two associates the murder of a rich stock-jobber. They were taken red-handed. Count Horn was connected with the noblest families in Europe; he was allied to several sovereign houses; he was even related to the Duke of Orleans himself. The strongest pressure was used to prevent his execution, but John Law was determined to make a striking example; and according to the letter of the sentence the unfortunate man was broken on the wheel. We ought to blame the cruelty of the law, not of its administrator; for had the criminal not been a nobleman, not a voice would have been raised against the execution.

Another example of Law's power is worth quoting, because it shows that he made every effort to render his Mississippi Scheme a commercial success. He scattered press-gangs through France, with instructions to seize and ship to America all who could not prove they were earning an honest living. The intention was no doubt good, for France was crowded with paupers, and the new colony only needed hands. But in the end the refuse of the streets and prisons was exported, to the disgust of the earliest colonists; whilst a shock of horror passed through France on the discovery that several young men and women of good family and honourable life had been seized for the plantations, that the abductors might get their reward.

But in both respects Law's agents alone were to blame. He himself arranged, in the most careful manner, although, of course, the worst side of French raillery was stirred by it, for the emigration of some young women brought up in charitable institutions; and many of them in the sequel were honourably married, and became the founders of some of the best families in New Orleans, which was one of the few tangible remnants of the system.

But Law's power, great as it undoubtedly was, was destined to be short-lived, and the catastrophe was in keeping with the rest of the drama. The dangers of the outrageous speculation, and of the excessive issues of notes, had already been foreseen by the more prudent speculators in the early part of 1720, and cautiously and silently they began to convert their paper into gold and silver or other forms of real wealth. At first Law tried to counteract these sinister influences, but he soon became convinced that a heavy fall was inevitable, and that his whole system was threatened. The great mass of people, however, had no more idea of the collapse of the system than the inhabitants of Pompeii of the eruption of Vesuvius. Thus the edict of the 21st of May 1720 caused sudden and universal consternation. Its professed object was to reduce the nominal value of the shares and notes to what was supposed to be their fair commercial value, but the result was—not to restore reason, but to hopelessly shatter confidence.

The essence of the edict was, that by gradual stages, but in a very short time, both shares and notes were to be reduced to about half the nominal value at which they stood when the decree was issued. The natural question people asked was—If the paper is forced down one half by the edict of to-day, how much will it be worth after the edict of to-morrow ? Thus a panic ensued, from which the system never recovered. "On the day following the edict," says Sir James Steuart, "any one might have starved with 100 millions of paper in his pocket."

There can be no reasonable doubt that John Law himself was responsible for this fatal edict, although attempts have been made to ascribe it to his enemies. It has been said that he would have foreseen the result, and would never have consented willingly to

the ruin of his plans. But the most striking
characteristic of his genius was the bold way in
which, regardless of time, place, or circumstance, he
applied his theories to practice. And some time
before he had certainly become fully aware of the
necessity of reducing the inflation. Early in March
he had caused a decree to be issued to suppress
speculative bargains; and a little later the street
where the gamblers were wont to congregate was
closed, and all dealings in paper prohibited except
directly with the Bank or the Company. But laws
and decrees were powerless over the popular delirium, and the speculation went on as keenly as
ever in new quarters.

Again he had made vain attempts to reduce the
issues of notes, and place them on a more sure
foundation. This, indeed, was the primary object of
the union of the Bank with the Company. The
excessive issues had in the natural course of things
caused a general rise of prices, the poor began to
suffer severely, and some remedy was urgently
needed. In some parts of France the notes had
already been refused.

Thus the decree of the 21st of May was a desper-
ate attempt to avert the threatened catastrophe when
milder measures had failed. And nothing is more
natural than that John Law should have seen that
his magnificent system was endangered by the fury of

speculation, and that, in the height of his power, he should have relied on his own strength to govern the fall, as he had apparently governed the rise. The best proof, however, that he really suggested the decree is, that in spite of the immediately disastrous consequences, he strenuously opposed its withdrawal; and the actual circumstances of its promulgation, as well as the peculiar style of the preamble, confirm this view. In a few days, however, the edict was annulled; but it had already done its work, and notes and shares fell of their own accord more rapidly than had been ordained by compulsion.

There is a popular impression that the whole system collapsed immediately after this official recognition of the necessity of checking the inflation; and Sir James Steuart even writes as if John Law was at once banished from France.

As a matter of fact, however, he remained in Paris more than six months, striving with the utmost coolness and pertinacity to regain the field, or at least to convert the rout into an orderly retreat. He tried every expedient to restore the credit of the Bank, and to promote the commercial prosperity of the Company. However much we may condemn the man for his criminal imprudence in leading astray a whole people, it is impossible not to admire the courageous honesty with which he laboured, under the most depressing circumstances, to restore the

really sound part of his system, by getting rid of the
abuses.

Unfortunately, just at the time when firm resolute
guidance was necessary to avert the worst consequences of the crisis, his authority was broken. A
few days after the fatal decree, he was deprived of his
office of Comptroller-General, and for two days he
was actually placed under arrest.

The influence, however, of his friends restored the
original confidence of the Regent in his ability, and
he was allowed to devise new schemes. " These ingenious combinations," says Levasseur, " prove that
in the midst of his peril Law preserved all his pres-
ence of mind, and that his genius, fruitful in resources,
was not yet exhausted."

The interest of the drama, however, at this point
consists not in following the stages of the hopeless
retreat, but in observing the consequences of the
collapse on the French people, and the character of
John Law when struggling with adversity.

As regards the effects on the nation, they were
such as almost to alienate all sympathy from the
man. If the blow had only fallen on the Missis-
sippians, and had taken away their ill-gotten gains,
the people at large might even have rejoiced, for large
as was the number of speculators, they did not embrace
the great mass of the real workers of the country.

But the actual currency of the country consisted entirely of these discredited notes, and thus the discredit, like a pestilence, affected the good and evil alike. The bank had very little real reserve; but to relieve the popular distress, attempts were made to redeem the smaller notes.

A few weeks before, the streets were crowded with throngs of people eager to obtain new issues of shares and indulge in the wildest speculation. Money was abundant, and the consumption of wealth most extravagant.

Now the approaches to the bank were packed with people driven by hunger and misery to try to exchange their bits of paper, often the reward of hard work, for money with which they might obtain the means of life. Day after day, and night after night, for months, they waited for the chance of making the exchange, and were only kept in order by military force. When the doors of the bank were opened, the pressure was often so great that men and women were crushed to death.

On one occasion, on a hot dark night in July, about 15,000 people were wedged in the narrow streets about the bank, trying to get to the front, like drowning men to the shore, and filling the air with tumultuous cries and savage imprecations. When day broke, it was found that fifteen persons had been crushed to death and trampled upon. As the news spread, the crowd was silenced with horror; then, after hasty indignant consultations, some rushed to the palace of the Regent, whilst a large body carried the corpse of a woman to place before the windows of the young king, and urged him, with furious threats, to hang both Law and the Regent.

This scene, dreadful as it is, perhaps hardly strikes the imagination with such horror as the discovery, in the middle of December, of a house in which the husband had killed his wife and children and hanged himself through destitution, whilst in the very room was found, with two or three halfpence, 200,000 livres of bank-notes, which at one time would have been worth £10,000 sterling.

Yet in the midst of these appalling scenes the courage of John Law no more faltered than that of Napoleon on the retreat from Moscow. The miserable besotted Regent, when the crowd tried to burst open his palace gates on that famous July morning, at first implored his servants to say that he was not there; and when the military had been smuggled in in disguise, he appeared, white as a sheet, and "did not know what he asked for."

Very different was the conduct of John Law. As soon as he heard of the tumult, he hurried to the palace: he was recognised, his carriage was surrounded, and he was at once assailed with fierce

threats. A woman shook her fist at him and cried,
" If there were only two or three more like me, you
would be torn to pieces."

It seems marvellous, when we remember what a
Parisian mob is capable of, that Law escaped, and he
certainly did so only by his courage. He leaped
through the door of his carriage, and in a tone of
contempt thundered, " Vous êtes des canailles ! " and
the mob, always respectful to audacity, allowed the
carriage to pass.

It is worth recording that when it came out, and
the coachman tried to use his master's authority, the
carriage was at once smashed, and the man only
escaped with his life.

Again, on the 15th December 1720, when Law
knew that the Regent had been pressed to assent to his
arrest, and that his very life was in danger, he calmly
went to the opera, affected the utmost security, and
treated with contemptuous silence the hisses and
threats of the people. And during all these months,
from June to December, in spite of the machinations
of his enemies, the vacillating imbecility of the
Regent, and the hatred of the people, he laboured
night and day to restore confidence and prosperity.

If the educated mind is now growing too peaceful
to profess to admire personal courage, there is another
side of Law's character shining out with pleasing
lustre at the close of his romantic career, which can

hardly fail to command respect. "Virtue!" said
Dirk Hatteraick, when upbraided by the sheriff,—
"Donner! I was always faithful to my ship-owners—
always accounted for cargo to the last stiver." And
those who most condemn John Law must allow him
a large share of this kind of virtue.   In the midst
of his power he accumulated far less wealth than
hundreds of ordinary speculators, and he did not invest one farthing of it beyond the frontiers of France.
He entered Paris with £100,000 sterling, and he
left the whole of it there.   He refused even to accept
money on retiring from France.

Whatever his faults and failings, he believed in his
system, and staked his whole life and fortune upon
it; and as in ability so also in virtue, he would serve
as an example to many directors of the present day.

He did not long survive his fall.   He obtained his
full pardon from the English Government for the
technical crime for which he had first fled the country, and an interesting debate took place in the
House of Lords because an admiral had taken upon
himself to bring over the celebrated financier in a
man-of-war, as if he were still a person of great
importance.

The last we hear of him is from Montesquieu, who
found him at Venice, shortly before his death, still
involved in all kinds of schemes and projects,—the
same man as of old.

His remains rest in the Church of St Moses, where they were placed in 1808 by the dutiful affection of a descendant, who was a celebrated soldier and a marshal of France.

As the judgment, implied rather than expressed, in my account of John Law, may seem to some too favourable, I will quote, in conclusion, the opinion of Levasseur, who has exhausted research for material, and has shown in the treatment of his subject the utmost impartiality, and who is besides a native of that country which Law is supposed to have ruined for his own purposes.

" If John Law," he writes, as the closing sentence of his work, " was too absolute in his ideas, and too violent in his means, he was at any rate animated by the desire of doing good, steadfast in the principles which he believed to be true, and honest in his conduct : his system rested on a false principle, which was, however, only the exaggeration of a truth. By cleaving to this principle Law perished, but he made valuable contributions to economic theory, and would have rendered great services to commerce if a more prudent reserve had kept him within more narrow limits."

I shall not attempt to add to this judgment, nor to point the many morals which spring up from all parts of the narrative. I shall be well satisfied if I have brushed away some of the dust of oblivion and the mire of calumny from the name of a man who, in power and determination and sheer ability, was one of the strongest men Scotland has produced, and who crowded into two or three years of his life a series of events which find no parallel out of the tales of Eastern imagination.

ONE-POUND NOTES.

*READ BEFORE THE BRITISH ASSOCIATION AT
BIRMINGHAM, SEPTEMBER 1886.*

To discuss profitably within the limits assigned to
this paper the advantages and disadvantages of a
system of £1 notes, it is absolutely necessary to
make the question as definite and precise as possible. For there is scarcely any argument usually
advanced on either side which, if examined critically
in all its aspects, may not lead to disputes on the
fundamental principles of banking, credit, currency,
and even the proper functions of government. It is,
however, much more easy to point out in general
terms the necessity of limiting the field of inquiry
than to put a ring-fence round a definite space; and
in attempting this operation I am quite aware, from
the difficulty I have experienced myself, that the
limitation I have assigned as best may not appear

M

reasonable to others interested in the question.   The
temptation is certainly great to take up, first of all,
the general principles of the regulation of a convertible paper currency, and to apply these principles to
the special case of £1 notes ; but in this way I am
afraid that the sermon would be so long that we should
never arrive at the practical application.

It is, however, primarily as a practical problem in
our England of to-day that I would consider the subject, and in currency, as in other matters, for a long
time to come, we must recognise that the actual will
fall short of the ideal, and the less revolutionary any
change proposed, the more likelihood there is of its
being carried.   We can only take thought for the
morrow in so far as to choose, of possible paths, that
which seems to lead in the direction of our ideal, or
at any rate does not lead us backwards.

Briefly stated, then, the problem which I wish to
attack is this : What would be the effect of introducing, with as little disturbance as possible, into our
present system of currency £1 notes ?

It follows at once, from this limitation of the inquiry, that many topics often discussed under the
title of this paper must be excluded.   For example,
the wisdom of the principles and the benefits derived
from the operation of the Bank Act of 1844 have
been questioned, and the repeal of the Act, or at least
great reforms in the direction of freedom of issues,

have been advocated, and, *inter alia*, it has been proposed that the issue of £1 notes should be left entirely to the discretion of individual competing banks.

For the present, however, these large reforms must be left on one side, and the attention must be confined to the effects which might be expected to follow if that Act were amended in the comparatively small particular of the alteration of the minimum denomination of bank-notes issued under the Act, from £5 to £1. A change of this nature would leave the general principles of the Act unaffected. Briefly stated, the principal provisions are as follows:—

A certain amount of notes, at present about £16,000,000, may be issued by the Bank of England against Government securities, and for any issues beyond that amount there must be gold (for the possible use of a certain amount of silver may be left out of consideration) in the issue department. The issue department is thus practically purely automatic. The banking department cannot, within the terms of the Act, even in the case of a foreign drain which threatens to exhaust its resources, make use of this gold except so far as it can offer in exchange notes to that amount held by it as a banking reserve. The reserve stored to secure the convertibility of the notes issued is absolutely independent. Accordingly, when we take into account the fact that the profits on the

issues of the greater part of the £16,000,000 of notes
not issued against gold are appropriated by Government, whilst the profits on the remainder are supposed
to be equivalent to the expenses of management, it
will be seen that as a banking institution, compared
with other banks which do not issue notes, the Bank
of England has no peculiar advantages. The country
banks which had the right of issue at the time of the
passing of the Act, retained that right only in so far
that the maximum of their issues was, for the future,
never to exceed the average of a certain time before
the passing of the Act. They did not acquire the
right, which was in the corresponding Act of 1845
for Scotland, of increasing their issues beyond this
amount, even against gold held by them. Accordingly, the issue of bank-notes in England, beyond a
certain amount absolutely fixed, depends entirely on
the amount of gold brought to the issue department
to be exchanged against notes.

It follows, then, according to the main principle
of the Act, with the exception noted, that in England
bank-notes are not regarded as a form of banker's
credit, but simply and solely as a convenient kind of
currency. Any one who prefers it can carry about
with him, instead of five or fifty sovereigns, a £5 or
£50 note, and these notes will be equally legal
tender. But, on the other hand, a person who prefers a £1 note to a sovereign, or four such notes to

four sovereigns, whilst he would have the option in Ireland and Scotland, has no choice in England.

It may, I think, be fairly argued, from the experience of Scotland, that if the present banks of issue in England were entitled to issue £1 notes, these notes would very soon, to a considerable extent, replace sovereigns in the currency.

It must be remembered that the use of notes, which are really convertible, in preference to gold, must depend entirely on the convenience and inclinations of those who have the option; and the people of Scotland being proverbially cautious and far-sighted in money matters, would certainly not make a general use of £1 notes unless in their opinion the advantages and conveniences were considerable.

I wish to avoid carefully any appearance of resting too much on the experience of Scotland, and I am quite willing to admit that the use of these small notes is partly due to the way in which, for a long period, they have been intimately connected with the credit system of the country, and to the interest of the banks in putting them into circulation. But, under present circumstances, the interest of the banks in increasing the circulation is by no means either of the degree or the precise kind that is imagined in England.

According to the Act of 1845, the banks are obliged to have gold against all notes in circulation above

the authorised amount.   This is about £2,750,000,
whilst the actual issues are about £6,000,000,
of which £4,000,000 are in £1 notes.   On this excessive issue, then, there is no direct gain, but, considering the expense involved, a certain loss.

The gain to the bank consists, first and principally,
in the power of over-issue, if necessary, which enables
them to keep notes as till-money; and secondly,
there is often some advantage owing to the fact that
the gold held must be against the average monthly
circulation; and in some cases notes may remain
out but a very short time—*e.g.*, on term-days notes
may be issued in excess, but returned the same day.
The power of over-issue (against gold) has certainly
enabled the Scotch banks to establish branches when
otherwise they could not have done so; but still
the general proposition I have stated remains true
—neither directly nor indirectly can the banks force
their issue on the public.   The conclusion, then,
seems inevitable, that the use of these notes in preference to sovereigns is founded on real and solid
advantages, and that if their use were permitted in
England, they would in time, to a large extent, replace sovereigns.   It must, however, be admitted that,
in matters affecting currency, the maxim *quieta non
movere* is always held to apply with much force.
English people are familiar with sovereigns, and the
bulk of the population consisting of wage-earners,

have never, unfortunately, use for notes of such a large amount as five pounds, and accordingly know nothing practically of bank-notes. At first, then, there might be a prejudice against £1 notes, and it is possible that, even if they were put into circulation, an unreasonable panic might occur which would cause indirectly, by the disturbance created, some loss. So that many authorities, as for example the late Mr Bagehot, although acknowledging the advantages theoretically of £1 notes, speak doubtfully of the expediency of their practical adoption, and in effect they say we should leave well alone. Unfortunately, however, for this argument, the present state of the gold currency is far from well, and one of the strongest practical arguments in favour of £1 notes is the facilities their adoption would afford for the rehabilitation and maintenance of the gold currency.

There can be no doubt that something must be done to restore the gold coinage to its nominal value. No one disputed the urgency of the proposed reforms of Mr Childers—the only doubt expressed was on the method he advocated — and there is no need to waste time in proving that matters cannot be allowed to go on as at present. The inevitable result would be that at no distant date the gold coins would cease to circulate at their nominal value, and we should be thrown back on all the uncertainties and inconveniences of a rudimentary currency by weight.

The principal difficulty to be overcome, if the present system is to continue, is one of expense, and although it is plausible to argue that the advantages of a sound currency are so great that the expense of restoration ought never to be considered by a wealthy country, that is not the way in which it strikes the Chancellor of the Exchequer. As the law stands at present, the person technically responsible for a lightweight gold coin is the holder of it, and in many cases the holders are large and wealthy banks, but in others they are people of the poorer sort, and both classes would appeal to the sense of justice.

The banks, by breaking the letter of the law, have spared the public, and no one would dream of practically taxing the poorer classes for the benefit of the community. If the sum necessary is to be raised from general taxation, the Chancellor of the Exchequer has to face additional expenditure with, it is to be feared, a declining revenue. He must also devise some method of a more efficient character than that adopted in the Coinage Act, which is at present supposed to be in force to secure the coinage for the future. It is not unnatural that in Scotland, at any rate, the plan which seems most plausible is the adoption by England of £1 notes. It would certainly be unfair to tax Scotland for the wear and tear of coins which it does not use, and Ireland has of late had a good deal of practice in formulating grievances, and would no doubt object to pay for restoring coins mainly worn down by England. If £1 notes become as popular in England as in the sister countries, for the future the wear and tear of coins would be greatly lessened, and there would be far greater facilities for withdrawing them when necessary from circulation. As regards the immediate expense of restoration, the adoption of £1 notes, with a slight alteration in the provisions of the Bank Act, would meet what was required, in a way which seems unobjectionable. Without going into details, a scheme on the following lines may be suggested.

In the first place, let the Government call in all the gold coins, and issue in their place notes promising to give gold in exchange on demand after a certain date, a sufficient time being allowed for the collection and restoration.   At the same time it must be made clear that those who refuse to give up their gold will be made liable for any defect — in fact, that the existing, or some more efficient, law will be put in force.

This ought to be a sufficient inducement to make the calling in of the coins effective.

On the date fixed, those who wished could obtain gold for their £1 notes, and unless it were also thought advisable to keep in circulation the notes of ten shillings, they would be gradually cancelled. It is hardly conceivable that all the £1 notes would be offered for gold, and it might be assumed that from the beginning a considerable number would be retained in circulation. The Government could then quite fairly, and with full confidence, reckon on making up the expenses of the restoration from the gold corresponding to the notes which would remain permanently in circulation. The only change necessary in the Bank Act would be that the Bank of England would be allowed to issue notes to the value (suppose) of £20,000,000 instead of £16,200,000 as at present, without having corresponding gold in its vaults. It would be absurd to suppose that the convertibility of the note would not be absolutely secured. If it was safe in 1844 to assume that £15,000,000 of Bank of England notes would, in any case, remain in circulation, surely there can be no doubt, with the great increase in wealth, population, and security since that date, that a somewhat higher limit could now be reckoned on. And if the reasoning advanced above in reference to Scotland is sound, we may assume that every year a larger amount of £1 notes would be issued, and consequently the danger of a drain of gold become continually less and less. At present about £18,000,000 of Bank of England notes are issued against gold, and there is no reasonable doubt that that amount of gold would support, with perfect safety, a larger circulation of notes.

According to the scheme suggested, the whole of the gold obtained from circulation would be retained on security against the new notes; but the gold would be reckoned as equivalent to its real and not to its nominal value, and besides this the expense of the restoration would have to be met.

There is no suggestion to make a financial gain to the Treasury. All that the proposal amounts to is the restoration of the currency to its full value by substituting notes for a part of it.

An alternative plan on practically the same lines would be for Government to issue £1 notes to the extent of the estimated loss of restoration, and call in the worn coins and substitute others directly. The advantage of the first scheme is that the mass of the people would become familiar, for a limited time, with the note issues.

It is necessary to notice, in conclusion, some of the principal arguments advanced against the adoption by England of £1 notes, even on the basis of the Bank Act of 1844 amended as proposed. 1. It is said, that if the substitution of £1 notes for sovereigns were as thorough in England as it has been in Scotland, that at least £50,000,000, and possibly more than £80,000,000, of gold, in addition to that already held, would be locked up in the issue department.

This would offer, it is urged, an irresistible temptation to the Government at a time of expenditure and increasing burdens.   If year after year such a mass of gold remains untouched, the feeling will arise that much less would answer the purpose quite as effectively.   Then, the process of abstraction once begun, the reserve will soon pass from an absurdly large to a dangerously small amount.   As a consequence, the money market will become extremely sensitive, and trade will suffer.   There would, under these circumstances, even be a possibility, it may be said, of a foreign drain, perhaps instituted for speculative purposes, exhausting gold at such a rate that the notes will become temporarily depreciated, or at any rate really inconvertible and liable to depreciation. And in support of this view, it may be plausibly argued that Governments have generally shown themselves ready to take advantage of sinking funds and other reserves without much pressure ; and that to borrow money with millions lying not only idle, but apparently useless, would at some time or other appear to some strong-minded Chancellor of the Exchequer the most puerile conservatism.   It must be remembered also, in reference to the danger of a small reserve and the chance of a foreign drain, that convertibility of notes is a very different thing from solvency of the issues.   A strictly convertible note is convertible on demand — it is not a promise to pay, even with full interest on a liberal scale, at some future date.   Every commercial crisis shows us the ruin of concerns which can ultimately pay twenty shillings in the pound, and in international payments the importance of bullion may become paramount.

I have tried to put the objections of this class as strongly as possible, because, strong as they are, I do not think they are insuperable.   The practical question is: Should we, under the scheme proposed, be worse off in the matter of security than we are at present?   It is no doubt quite true that, so long as the people of England use gold as actual circulating medium, there is in appearance a great gold national reserve; but under the existing law it is so in appearance only.

There is no method by which, if the banking department of the Bank of England were threatened by a foreign drain, it could obtain supplies from this source.   On the contrary, a time of panic would be a time in which all history shows there would be a tendency to hoard gold.

I do not mean to assert that it is at all probable that gold would be hoarded in this country to any great extent.   My point is this—that, under our present system, the ultimate banking reserve is the gold and notes (mainly notes) in the banking department: these notes can be exchanged for gold in the issue department, but the rest of the gold in the issue department, and *a fortiori* the gold in the hands of the public, are absolutely, so long as the Bank Act holds, unavailable for banking purposes. If in an emergency the Bank Act is suspended, that only enables the bank to issue more notes against its existing stock of gold ; and if there were a persistent foreign drain, as soon as that stock was exhausted the notes would be inconvertible, and gold would rise to a premium. The bank could not obtain the gold from the actual circulation. Now under the system proposed, if effectively carried out, the gold in the issue department would be increased by a large amount, and then a suspension of the Act would make the gold available in case of need. The whole strength of the opposing case rests on the assumption that the Bank Act would be broken without cause, and that insufficient reserves would be held against the note issues. But assuming that no further changes are made in the law than are suggested in this paper, and that the law is never suspended, except in extreme cases as formerly, the position of the Bank of England would be strengthened.

2. An objection may also be raised from the possibility of an internal drain arising at the same time as a foreign drain. But, in the first place, the experience of Scotland lends very small probability to this supposition. £1 notes are not of such a low denomina-

tion as to be held in large quantities by the mass of the people, who are quite unfamiliar with credit, and who might be liable to a sudden panic. And, secondly, if there were a corresponding reserve in the issue department, the convertibility of the notes would never be in danger. The foreign drain could only operate through the notes.

3. As regards the danger of forgery, it is a curious fact that in Scotland spurious sovereigns are more frequently met with than forged £1 notes, and the art of engraving notes has made much progress since England had £1 notes in circulation [1] (1826).

The limits of this paper will not allow me to notice the wider aspects of the question. I have supposed throughout the minimum of change in our currency regulations. I will only say in conclusion that the change suggested is, in my opinion, so far a step towards a system more in harmony with the requirements of the country.

These more fundamental questions, however, it would be useless merely to mention cursorily at the conclusion of a paper written from a much lower standpoint.

I will repeat, that the question to which I think

---

[1] It may be said that in Scotland the notes come back more rapidly to the bank issuing them than would be the case in England under the plan proposed ; but, on the other hand, the notes would be uniform, and this would assist the general public. Reissues of notes must be permitted on the ground of expense.

the discussion, if it is to be practical, must be at present confined is this: What would be the effect of the introduction of £1 notes without contravening the principles of the Act of 1844, which has since that date formed the basis of our currency?

THE EFFECTS OF GREAT DISCOVERIES OF THE PRECIOUS METALS.

READ BEFORE THE
CHARTERED ACCOUNTANTS STUDENTS' SOCIETY
OF EDINBURGH, DECEMBER 1, 1886.

MANY circumstances combine at the present time to direct public attention to the subject on which I have to address you this evening.   In the first place, there is an idea generally prevalent that we are on the eve of an enormous increase in the production of gold.   As to the soundness of this belief I am quite unable to give an opinion, but I may perhaps remind you that, just as a very small amount of gold in the vaults of the Bank of England supports a gigantic system of banking and credit, so a very tiny amount of gold discovered in some new region seems able to support a most extraordinary amount of speculation, hopefulness, and credulity.   But of the interest aroused by these reported new discoveries there

N

can be no doubt, and I hope some share of this
interest may be directed to the more general aspects
of the question.

In the mean time, however, we are feeling the
effects of a contraction in the supply of gold relatively to the demand made upon it, and one of the
best methods of obtaining an accurate view of these
effects is to study carefully the converse case. The
key to the present controversy on the connection between the currency and the fall in prices is found in
the dependence of prices on the quantity of standard
metallic money. Those who experience a difficulty
in tracing this great and general fall largely to currency causes, may find that difficulty much lessened
by considering the way in which, at previous times,
a rise in prices has undoubtedly been connected with
an increase in the supplies from the mines.

But, apart from this fundamental difficulty, there
is a difficulty of a more special character, connected
with the fact that there are two precious metals used
as standard money in the currencies of the world.
The principal point that arises in the controversy as
to the possibility of bi-metallism, is the effect on the
relative values of gold and silver, of variations in
the production of either of them, and it will be instructive to notice the changes which have occurred
in previous times.

I shall then, in the first part of this essay, examine the effects of great discoveries of the precious metals, with special reference to the influence on prices of an increase in standard metallic money; and, in the second part, I shall consider the changes which have occurred in their relative values, when great changes in production have taken place.

It will be most convenient to give in outline the general theory applicable in the first case, and afterwards to bring in the special historical illustrations.

Suppose, then, that in some distant country there are suddenly made great discoveries of gold, and assume that gold is the standard money of the country in question, which implies that any amount of the metal can be taken to the mint and converted into coins.

Before the discoveries are announced, we may suppose that the labour and capital of the country were devoted to a variety of industries, and that all of these industries were in an average condition, furnishing steady supplies to regular demands. We may suppose further, that, owing to the *comparative* difficulty of producing some things, and the comparative ease of producing others, a foreign trade existed, in which the former class of commodities was imported, and the latter exported.

In any new country, for example, labour and capital devoted to the production of raw materials would obtain, through their exportation, a larger amount of manufactures than if they were directly devoted to this form of production. It is this comparative advantage in one form of industry, and relative disadvantage in others, which is the primary cause of all foreign trade.

It is, however, in terms of prices that movements of trade are generally expressed; and as we are concerned mainly with prices, this theory of comparative cost may be put in that form.

Let us assume, then, that in the country taken as our example there is a certain general rate of wages, reckoned in money, differing in different employments according to well-known causes of difference, such as the skill required, the hardships involved, &c.; and further, let us make the same assumptions as regards profits.

If, then, at these money rates, the cost of producing any article is greater than the price at which it could be imported, it will naturally be imported; and, similarly, an article which can be produced more cheaply (including carriage) will be exported. All this, no doubt, seems simple and obvious enough, but the difficulty really arises at an earlier stage.

What is it that determines the general level of prices in the country? The only answer is, that it must depend on the quantity of money in circulation, including, of course, that part which is held as the basis of the credit system. For suppose that, compared with other countries, the general level of prices is very high, what would happen? Obviously, imports would be stimulated—every foreigner would wish to sell in such a favourable market; and, similarly, there would be a corresponding check on purchases. As a consequence, the aggregate value of the imports would exceed that of the exports, and it would be necessary to export gold; and, apart from the influence of debts, or other monetary obligations, this export of gold would go on until, at the average level of prices, the exports just balanced the imports. But this is really the same thing as saying that prices would fall through the diminution of the quantity of money in circulation. And, in fact, we cannot proceed a single step in any argument on general prices without assuming their dependence on the quantity of money.

We must then assume in the country which we have taken as the example that, when the gold discoveries are made, prices are at such a level (owing to the quantity of money) that the balance of trade is even. Observe now what will naturally happen on the discoveries. Labour and capital will be drawn from other industries to be devoted to mining, and the consequent shortness of supply will tend to raise prices, including, of course, the price of labour and the rate of profit. This change in the level of prices would of itself tend to check exports and in-

crease imports, and unless gold is furnished from the
mines, the consequent exportation of the metal would
again reduce prices, the only real difference being
(unless foreign capital is imported) that the country,
owing to the diversion of part of its labour and
capital to unproductive mining, has a less amount of
wealth to consume.

Suppose, however, that the mines are successful,
then it is quite possible for the high level of prices
to be maintained, or to rise still higher.   The more
abundant the supplies from the mines, so much more
will labour and capital be attracted from other industries to mining ; and so much higher can the level
of prices rise, because the new gold being exported,
corrects of itself what otherwise would be an adverse
balance of trade.   So far, then, as the gold-producing
country is concerned, what we should naturally expect, first of all, is a great rise in prices, accompanied
by a corresponding increase in imports, a check to exports except gold, and a falling off in the production
of everything except gold.   Such would be the immediate results ; but we must advance a step further.

Another circumstance must be taken into account,
still considering the effects in the gold-producing
country—namely, the influx of foreign capital and
labour which is certain to take place.   This may be,
and probably will be, more than sufficient to replace
the withdrawal to the mines ; and if only sufficient

supplies are forthcoming of gold, in spite of the increase in production through foreign importations of the means of production, the high level of prices will be unimpaired, and the development of the country will go on at an enormous rate, always accompanied by great importations. In fact, the very operation of sending capital from abroad to the mining country will, as is well known, increase the importations—any loan at the time it is made rendering the adverse balance due to a falling off in exports so much less. Such, in brief outline, is the theory of the effects of great discoveries of gold on the gold-producing country.

Now let us take a practical illustration, and for the present purpose, the gold discoveries in Victoria in 1851 is a good example. I quote a few sentences from a shrewd observer who wrote in 1855. "When," he says, "the gold fever set in, towards the end of 1851 to the middle of 1852, every necessary except beef and mutton, and every luxury except the precious metal itself, had to be imported for the sustentation and convenience of the teeming myriads who poured into the colony. As a natural consequence of the demand being greater than the supply, the prices of all commodities rose immensely."

Perhaps, however, we see the stimulus given to importation even better from the statement by the same writer, that at one time there were lying at the docks in Melbourne a three-legged iron pot and a camp stove for every man, woman, and child in the colony —the importation under the stimulus of high prices having naturally been overdone. I may quote also a few prices of articles of consumption in Melbourne. Eggs, which in January 1851 had been 1s. the dozen, rose to 6s. in 1853, and to 10s. in July 1854. A pair of ducks which in 1851 sold for 5s., in 1854 cost £1, 4s.; and cabbages rose from 2d. to 5s. These articles might of course be considered luxuries, so that it is worth noticing that between the same dates the price of flour was doubled, and the 4 lb. loaf in 1854 sold at 1s. 9d. It is also noteworthy, that amongst the imports we find large quantities of butter, timber, and other articles which would in the ordinary course of things be produced in the colony, or even exported. Timber abounded in all parts of the colony, but the price for cutting it was more than the expense of bringing it from America or Norway, whilst Ireland, Scotland, and America supplied most of the butter and cheese, although dairy produce could be easily raised in Victoria. As regards exports, with the exception of wool, and, of course, gold, they became almost nominal in amount. The rise in wages may be judged of from an extract from the 'Argus' newspaper, October 28, 1854: "The state of the labour market may be ascertained from the following *Wanteds* which have appeared within these few days in the local papers—500 pick and shovel men at 10s. to 12s. per day, tents, tools, wood, and water being provided; 500 stone-breakers at 6s. to 10s. per yard, it being possible for any tolerable workman to break from two to three yards a-day." When the least skilled and most simple kinds of labour were paid at these high rates, it is easy to understand how joiners and masons earned from £6 to £7, 10s. per week.

The growth of population is shown by the fact that it had risen from about 33,000 in 1846, and 77,000 in 1851, to 236,000 in 1854; whilst, as regards the wealth of the colony, we are told that the sudden and unexampled rise and prosperity of the city of Melbourne had, in a few years, produced effects which it takes centuries to accomplish in the settled countries of Europe. The writer from whom I have already quoted says—observe it is only three or four years after the gold discoveries,—"If I could tell a tenth part of the wonders of Australian wealth, the statement would appear so exaggerated that few at home would believe my statements. Men with incomes of £5000 to £50,000 per annum are as common in Victoria as bakers' boys in London—you meet them in every street." Thus we find every point in the theory practically illustrated in the experience of Victoria — a great rise in prices, a stimulus to importation, large exports of gold, and a rapid development of all kinds of commercial prosperity. The gold obtained from the mines was partly used to support the enormous increase of transactions within the colony at a higher level of prices, and partly exported to pay for the imports which, in spite of the flow of capital to the country, were still so great as to leave an adverse balance.

It is time now to examine the effects of large exportations of gold from the gold-producing countries on the rest of the world, and for this purpose it will be necessary to extend our view; but before turning to practical illustrations, some attention must again be given to the theory of the subject.

For the sake of simplicity, and in order to lay bare what is always the fundamental principle, however much it may be concealed, it is best to assume, first of all, that there is little or no credit; and accordingly, that the new supplies of the precious metals can only raise prices in any particular country, or industrial area, or city, or town, or village, by actually getting into circulation. If the gold or silver is obtained in exchange for commodities, these commodities will naturally rise in price — in fact, such a rise is necessary to attract them to the mining country; then the money wages and profits of the producers or traders in these articles being raised, they in turn can demand more of other articles, and in this way the rise in prices will be transmitted from one industry to another. According to this view, then, the great trading centres, and the great highways of commerce, will be the first to feel the influence of the new treasure; and out-of-the-way places and regions, with little commerce, will only gradually and slowly be affected. Even if the treasure is obtained in the first place by plunder, as was generally the case in the sixteenth century, the effects will be similar as soon as the precious metals begin to be dispersed; and a tyrannical Government, with piratical subordinates, is generally a very rapid distributor of money. Such is the general principle of the distribution of additions to the world's stock of precious metals, and we find apposite illustrations in commercial history.

In the sixteenth century the new supplies of the precious metals were obtained by Spain, through her discoveries and military successes in America, and were largely squandered in ambitious political schemes in Europe; but, in the natural course of things, they soon found their way into the great channels of trade.

At that time the Netherlands held the commercial supremacy of the world, and Antwerp was the Queen of the Netherlands. It was almost entirely by trade that the Dutch amassed their wealth. The celebrated description of Holland, written about the middle of the seventeenth century, is equally true of the sixteenth. "Never any country traded so much and consumed so little; they buy infinitely, but it is to sell again. . . . In short, they furnish infinite luxury which they never practise, and traffic in pleasures which they never taste." It was, then, through the great cities of the Netherlands, with their wide-spreading trade connections, that the treasure of Mexico and Peru was diffused over the world, and no one is surprised to hear that Antwerp was the dearest city in Europe.

It would, however, be a great mistake to suppose that, even in the sixteenth century, when credit was comparatively, and, according to our notions, quite undeveloped, this distribution of the new supplies of the precious metals took place, without any other noticeable result than a general rise in prices, accompanied by a natural increase in production. It is easy to speak of a general rise in prices, and of the gradual extension of this rise, but when we descend to details and concrete facts, there is no more difficult problem than to measure such a general rise, and to account for the failure to respond in particular localities, and particular commodities. General prices are made up of particular prices, and the relative prices of particular commodities are influenced by a variety of causes which operate on the demand and supply.

In the sixteenth century we find, at the very time when England was beginning to feel the effects of the new treasure, that all the commodities of Greece,

Syria, Egypt, and India, were obtained much cheaper than formerly—presumably owing to the fact that, by a direct trade through Turkey, the charges of the Venetian carrier were dispensed with.

At the same time, too, if we refer to contemporary writers on the social state of England, and to the statutes passed by paternal Governments to remedy disorders by frantic endeavours to suppress the symptoms, we find, side by side, complaints of the decay of certain places and industries, and dismay at what seems the unnatural and dangerous growth of others.

We find that careful and prudent monarch, Queen Elizabeth, aided by still more careful and prudent counsellors, issuing regulations, on the one hand, to check the growth of London by actually prohibiting new buildings, and, on the other hand, by granting privileges and monopolies to other towns, to restore their former prosperity. As with places and commodities, so it is with classes—some are prosperous beyond measure, others suffer severely. In the famous dialogue of William Stafford, the knight asks of the doctor: "What sorte is that which yee said should have greater losse hereby, than these men had profit?" and the reply shows for the time a singular grasp of economic principles. "It is all noblemen, gentlemen, or others, that live either by a stinted rent or stypend. . . . Therefore gentlemen doe

study so much the increase of their lands and
enhaunsing of their rents, and to take fearmes and
partners to their own use, as yee see they doe; and
all to seeke to maintain their countenances as their
predecessors did, and yet they came shorte therein.
. . . The other sort be even serving men and
men of warre, that having but their olde stinted
wages, cannot finde therewith as they might afore-
time without rauin or spoile."

It was peculiarly difficult for the people of that
time to estimate the force of discoveries of the
precious metals; for, apart from currency causes,
influences were at work which were effecting great
changes in relative prices, and consequently in production. Even before the mines of Potosi were
discovered, English wool had begun to rise in value,
owing to foreign demands; and, as a consequence,
great sheep-walks were taking the place of tillage,
and the outcry against sheep was as loud and bitter
as in the present century in Scotland.

No doubt, however, wool, being very easily carried
compared with other forms of agricultural produce,
felt the influence of the new money most quickly and
most effectively. But apart from these and similar
causes of variations in value, a general rise in nominal
prices had occurred, owing to the debasement of the
coinage by Henry VIII. and his son. The effects of
this debasement were too obvious to be overlooked,

and it was natural for people to expect that, as the abuse was remedied, as it speedily was, by Queen Elizabeth, prices would be restored to their former level.   As it happened, however, the new supplies of silver reached this country in effective amounts just as the coinage was reformed, and consequently prices did not fall.

Before passing from the sixteenth century, let me resume in a few words the general effects of the discoveries.

By a curious coincidence, they were made just at the time when the civilised world was breaking through its mediæval fetters.   The discovery of the New World had given a great stimulus to venturous trading, and the maritime nations were vying with one another in their zeal for appropriating new lands and new treasure ; the Church of Rome, which had weighed down individual freedom, not merely in matters of speculative theology or astronomy, but equally in what we are accustomed to consider matters of practical business, which taught that everything in the form of speculative trade partook of the nature of the deadly sin of usury, and which, with its swarms of dependent paupers, was the most gigantic embodiment of the unproductive consumer the world has ever seen, was compelled to relax its hold.   The old industrial guilds, which had threatened to entail the trade of the nation, as the nobility had entailed the land, in a few families, and had become, in the words of Bacon, fraternities in evil, found, on the one hand, that the craftsmen were fleeing into the country, and to the towns not oppressed with guild regulations, and on the other that the Government, in the interests of the general public, was determined to curtail their privileges, and, in its own interest, to confiscate their wealth. The guilds, like the Church, were discovering that they must yield to industrial freedom and competition; even Queen Elizabeth, in spite of her strong will, had at last to give way in the matter of monopolies. In the country, no less than in the towns, good old customs, which had long since begun to corrupt the world, such as slovenly cultivation in common of old crops and old weeds by old methods, were beginning to yield to individual enterprise, involving, it is true, much hardship and social discomfort, but preparing the way for giving Britain the lead in agriculture; in short, from whatever point it is regarded, the sixteenth century showed signs of the breaking up of an old system which rested on law, custom, and superstition, and the appearance, in its place, of the beginning of our modern world, with its freedom of contracts and freedom of competition. The mediæval edifice was full of cracks and seams, and the new treasure may be compared to villainous saltpetre, which, finding its way into these cracks, regardless of all respect to antiquity, tumbled down huge fragments, and made the whole structure totter. I trust you will not think this metaphor exaggerated; but we are so much accustomed to hear money spoken of as so many counters—so many units of measurement—that it seems desirable sometimes to point out that money governs prices, and that great movements in prices operate in a convulsive, partial, spasmodic manner on the interests of various classes, and the stability of various social institutions; that all the production, distribution, and exchange of wealth, rests on prices —the price of land, the price of capital, the price of labour; that, whether we like it or not, the great mass of the nation is most intensely interested in the acquisition and consumption of wealth; and accordingly, when any great revolution occurs in prices, we are likely to find the most appropriate illustrations of the effects of money, not in children's games of cards, or in the abstractions of the pure mathematician, but in the great forces of nature or art—in earthquakes, tidal waves, or gunpowder. Not that I mean to imply that the effects of the discoveries in the sixteenth century were disastrous. On the contrary, there seems to me no reasonable doubt that if the stock of the precious metals had not been increased, simultaneously with the opening up of new routes to the East and the West, and the growth of individual enterprise, the progress which took place

o

would have been impossible. The metaphors I suggested were intended only to convey an idea of the enormous power of monetary changes; and that in this case the disturbance was beneficial, we have the authority of the 'History of Prices,' by Tooke and Newmarch—the most laborious and judicial work on the historical side of Political Economy ever written. It is there asserted that " we have the fullest warrant for concluding that any partial inconvenience that might arise from the effect of the American supplies of the sixteenth century in raising prices, was compensated and repaid a hundredfold by the activity, the expansion, and vigour which they impressed for more than one generation upon every enterprise, and every act which dignifies human life, or increases human happiness."

Coming now to the discoveries of the present century — in California in 1848, and Australia in 1851—it is interesting to observe that, just as was the case three centuries before, this was a period of great industrial and social changes, and I cannot do better than again quote from the authors of the 'History of Prices' some weighty remarks on the period between 1848-1856 :—

" The rapid increase in railways in every part of the world; the improvements in the navigation and speed of ships; the rapid spread of population into new and fertile regions; the quick succession of important discoveries in practical science; and the ceaseless activity with which they are applied to increase the efficiency of all mechanical appliances; and perhaps, more powerful than all, the setting free of the enterprise, the industry, and the ingenuity of some of the leading commercial states, by the adoption, more or less completely, of principles of Free Trade, are all causes which, singly and conjointly, have assisted to accelerate the rate of progress; [but with all this,] the influence of the *new supplies of gold*, year by year, has probably been that particular cause, or train of causes, which has modified in the most powerful degree the economical and commercial history of the last nine years." The principle of the influence is precisely the same as in the earlier period, but the initial stages are different.

In the sixteenth century silver was obtained by the Spaniards through plundering and slaughtering the unfortunate natives, whose lands they had occupied with the ostensible purpose of spreading the truths of Christianity; it was spread over Europe first of all in payment of further ambitious projects, and it was not till in the course of trade it reached the Dutch, that its full effects on commerce began to be noticed.

In the nineteenth century, on the other hand, from the outset commercial influences alone determined the acquisition and distribution of the precious metals.

The whole of the complicated processes by which the new gold was distributed over the world may be explained by one simple principle. The distribution took place in the precise proportion in which the extended demand for commodities, which originally proceeded from the labourers who picked up the gold, set in motion increased numbers of labourers and increased amounts of capital to supply first the wants of the gold countries, and, secondly, the wants of those who traded with these countries.

Time will not permit me to point out in detail the way in which the great development which had taken place in banking and credit generally, increased both the rapidity and the degree of the influence of the new gold; it is enough to insist on the main result, and that is—*not* that the game of commerce was now played for higher nominal stakes,—for more yellow tokens—but that the whole industry of the civilised world was quickened with new life, and that the production and the consumption of all kinds of real wealth were stimulated. A rise in prices certainly occurred, but the rise was not in many cases in proportion to the increase in the quantity of the precious metals, and it did not merely mean the profit of debtors at the expense of creditors. The new gold was used *not* simply to circulate the same amount of wealth at higher figures, and play the game of trade with more counters, but to circulate more wealth—at higher prices, it is true, but, for all that, a greater quantity of real wealth.

And now I may perhaps introduce, in an appropriate manner, the practical application to our own times of these historical illustrations.

For some years past, since 1874, there has been a diminution in the supply of gold, and an increased demand for it, especially for purposes formerly performed by silver. We have, in fact, the direct converse of what happened thirty years before. Then the supplies of gold were increased, and they were converted at once into standard money; wages of every grade—the incomes of all engaged in production—were increased both nominally and really, and there were all the signs of exuberant prosperity. I would ask those who seek to connect the depression of the last twelve years with improved communication and over-production, to remember the improvements and the enormous expansion of trade in the gold era, and to explain how it is that the same causes can produce such opposite effects. Surely it is simpler to apply what logicians call the method of concomitant variations, and when you find advancing prosperity with increasing gold supplies, and diminished prosperity with diminishing supplies, to argue that there is a causal connection between the two phenomena. And observe, it is not simply as if the gold supplies had fallen off a little—the fact is of equal importance, that the work of gold has been enormously increased.

I must now notice very briefly the *second* subject of inquiry suggested by the title of this address— namely, the effects of great discoveries of the precious metals on their relative values. I have hitherto, with the object of confining the attention to one point at a time, carefully refrained from mentioning the striking fact that, in the sixteenth century, the discoveries were mainly of silver, whilst in the nineteenth they were mainly of gold.

According to the statistics usually quoted,[1] the facts of the case in the sixteenth century are broadly stated as follows :—

At the commencement of the sixteenth century, the relative production of silver compared to gold was about 34·3 silver to 65·7 gold, and the relative values of the two metals were in a ratio of nearly 11 to 1—the highest computation for the value of silver being 10½ to 1 —that is, 10½ to 11 oz. of silver were worth 1 oz. of gold.

In the course of the century the proportion of the production of silver to gold rose to 78·6, as compared with 21·4 of gold, and the ratio of the relative values became only by gradual stages 12 to 1.

It may be interesting to quote the absolute amounts reckoned in pounds sterling.   At the commencement

[1] Compare Soetboer's ' Materialen,' &c.

of the sixteenth century the yearly production of silver was in value about £425,000, and that of gold £800,000; whilst at the end the yearly production of silver was more than £3,750,000, and that of gold only £1,000,000. Surely it is very remarkable that in spite of these great changes in the relative production of the two metals, the ratio of their values should only have moved from 11 to 1 to 12 to 1.

The limits of my subject compel me to pass over the interesting period embraced in the next two centuries, and to come at once to the great gold discoveries of our own century. At the beginning of the century (1801-1810), the relative rates of production of silver and gold were 76·4 silver to 23·6 gold; whilst at the culmination of the gold era in 1856-1860, the proportions of yearly production were 22·1 silver to 77·9 gold—that is to say, just as in the sixteenth century the relative proportions of the production of silver and gold had changed, silver becoming just as much more abundant as gold was before, so in the nineteenth century the converse took place; and whilst at the beginning the proportions were about ¾ of silver to ¼ of gold, they became by 1855 less than ¼ of silver to more than ¾ of gold.

And yet, in spite of these changes, the change in the ratio of the relative values was such that in 1801-1810 the ratio was 15·61 to 1 — that is to say, 15·61 oz. of silver was exchanged for 1 oz. of gold;

whilst in 1856-1860 the ratio was 15.30 to 1—
that is to say, the value of silver, in spite of the
enormous increase in the relative production of gold,
had risen little more than 1d. per oz. And observe
that this steadiness in the price of silver was maintained in spite of the very general belief that its
value, compared with gold, must rise, owing to the
enormous supplies of gold, so that all the speculative
tendencies of a speculative period were in favour of a
general rise.

Now let us look for a moment at the variations
since 1874 in the relative values of gold and silver
inter se.

It is quite true that whilst from 1871-1875 the
relative rates of production were 57·3 gold to 42·7
silver, and that since that time they have gradually
changed to about 43·5 gold to 56·9 silver; but in the
mean time the relative values of the precious metals
have changed from 15½ to 1 to 20 to 1; and not
only has the ratio changed on the whole in this manner, but it has been subject to violent fluctuations.

Thus, while the changes in relative production have
been very moderate compared with the tremendous
changes we have noticed before, the changes in the
ratio of the metals, or their relative values, has been
unprecedented.

The conclusion seems to me then inevitable, putting
all these facts together, that variations in the relative

values of gold and silver are to be attributed almost entirely to changes in the demand; and the changes in demand again are mainly due to the coinage regulations of various Governments.

For the first seventy years of this century, notwithstanding unparalleled changes in the production and distribution of all kinds of wealth, an enormous increase in the population of new countries, gigantic wars and violent political revolutions, a wonderful development of banking and credit with periodical crises, — notwithstanding such vast economical and social movements that the old order of things seems to have completely changed, and in spite of the striking variations in the relative production of gold and silver,—the relative values of the two metals remained practically steady. All kinds of food and clothing, the staple necessaries of life, and the infinite variety of luxuries, fluctuated in their values during the same period; whilst the relative values of gold and silver alone remained undisturbed, until, in an evil moment, Germany, flushed by military and political success, imagined that by adopting one of the accidents of Great Britain's commercial supremacy— namely, the gold standard—she would gain the lead as effectively in commerce as in war and politics. A uniform system of coinage, especially with effective regulations for the prevention of deterioration, is undoubtedly an important factor in commercial prosperity, and it is the recognised duty of every civilised power to provide such a coinage ; but for Germany to imagine that, by imitating the coinage of England, she would achieve her commercial success, is as absurd as for France to suppose she would be a match for Germany in war by clothing her soldiers in German uniforms.

The value of the precious metals compared with commodities—in other words, general movements in prices—and the relative values of gold and silver, which largely determine the course of trade between gold- and silver-using countries, are now more than ever they were beyond the power of any single nation to control.   Monetary independence, in its most essential features, has become less and less possible with the growth of international commerce, and in fact no longer exists.   If, for example, the United States were to repeal the Bland Act, and to throw her silver on the market, the consequences would be a further fall in gold prices, and a further depression in trade, not in that country alone, but in every gold-using country.   Every great commercial nation has, it is true, still enormous power by acting in isolation in monetary policy ; but it is only a power for evil,—any power for good can only be exercised by co-operation.

A moment's reflection will show that this is only one example of the principle which pervades all civilisation. A few fraudulent directors in one great bank may shake the credit system of a whole country; an unprincipled statesman may plunge Europe into war; but the stability of credit and the blessings of peace can only be attained by forbearance. The lines so often quoted in regard to individuals—

> " 'Tis excellent to have a giant's strength,
> But tyrannous to use it like a giant,"—

are as true of nations, and as true of their monetary as of their military policy. I must not, however, detain you with general reflections. In conclusion, let me try to sum up the bearing of these historical illustrations on some of the prominent points in the present controversy on the Currency.

In the *first* place, we have seen how the new supplies in the one case of silver, in the other of gold, gave a real and generous stimulus to the industrial activity of the world. The rise in prices which occurred was not, as we are too often told, merely equivalent to a nominal change of values and a benefit to debtors at the expense of creditors; for as soon as prices began to move in response to the new money, enterprise was quickened, employment extended, and production increased. If in the sixteenth century the trading nations had been afraid of the depreciation of the new silver, and had refused to use it as standard money in unlimited payments, the mediæval system might have retained its immobility for many generations, whilst the only gain to the world would have been a profusion of cheap silver ornaments; and in the nineteenth century, if the nations had listened to the alarmists who urged them to take time by the very tip of the forelock and demonetise. their gold before it became worthless through depreciation, America and California would have been left to sheep and cattle, the enormous expansion of trade which took place over the whole world would have been impossible, and the only gain would have been an addition to the stock of the gold plate of those who held mortgages in one shape or another over the old industries of the world.

But if an increase in the supplies of the precious metals when freely coined has the effect which history reveals, surely it does not require much reason or much imagination to discover that, with diminishing supplies of gold, and a refusal to use silver, the contrary effects — in a word, a dragging depression of trade — might be expected. Surely this explanation is more reasonable than to allege that only wars can raise prices, and that the natural effects of peace are over-production, loss of profit, and depression. It is true that in some cases war may raise prices by. directly diminishing supplies, by increasing the difficulties of communication, and by withdrawing labour and capital from production; and so also may pestilence and famine and earthquake. But political economy would be indeed the most dismal of sciences if it taught that to ensure a period of prosperity we must submit to a period of horror, and that a long continuance of peace is the sure precursor of depression. Political economy, however, teaches no such thing; on the contrary, it shows that, in the long-run, destruction is not good for trade, and that what we call general over-production is, in reality, simply bad organisation.

There are two other lessons to be learned from the history we have examined to-night, which also bear on the present controversy. If is said that for the civilised nations to agree to coin silver freely—to use it as standard money—would no doubt be a good thing for the silver-producing countries, and presumably for no others. Remember, then, that in the sixteenth century it was Spain—the most tyrannical despotism of the day, the home of the Inquisition—which first obtained by plunder and slaughter the new treasure, and tried by every device of monopoly to keep it to herself, and yet in a few years it was diffused over the trading world, and the freest nations, Holland and England, became the greatest gainers. And *finally*, as regards the possible variations in the values of the two metals, history shows that great revolutions have occurred in the relative production of gold and silver with comparatively slight changes in their relative values, and gives us good ground for believing that if the civilised world adopted a conventional ratio, there would be little danger to its stability on the score of supply.

BI-METALLISM BOTH ADVANTAGEOUS
AND PRACTICABLE.

ADDRESS AT THE MANCHESTER ATHENÆUM,
MARCH 31, 1887.

THERE has been a great and rapid change in public opinion on the subject of bi-metallism since the International Conference held in Paris in August 1878. At that time Mr Goschen described the American proposal for a universal double standard as a veritable Utopia, and stated that the English delegates were instructed to say that no change of the gold standard by the United Kingdom would be entertained. But it has never been the habit of the Government of this country to appoint a Royal Commission composed of eminent politicians and practical men simply to inquire into the theoretical advantages of any Utopia; and the appointment of the Royal Commission on Currency last autumn shows clearly enough that bi-

metallism has passed into the sphere of practical
politics. Accordingly the advocates of bi-metallism
at the present time have to show, not that their plan
might be theoretically advantageous, but that the
practical advantages would outweigh the trouble and
expense involved in the actual change of currency;
and to show not simply that the plan is theoretically
possible under certain assumed conditions, but that it
is really practicable under actual conditions.

I do not intend to imply that there is now no
need to appeal to principles, and that we have simply
to collect a mass of facts, for any array of facts and
figures without guiding principles would be as im-
penetrable as a jungle without paths. All I mean is
that the principles must be applied, not to imaginary
examples but to the real facts of the case.

In the *first* place, then, I shall endeavour to balance the principal advantages and disadvantages of
the scheme; and, *secondly*, to examine the practicability of its adoption, and its stability once adopted.

The advantages of international bi-metallism, with
a fixed ratio agreed to by the great commercial countries, are best disclosed by considering the disadvantages of the present system, for bi-metallism is proposed as a remedy for the evils resulting from
mono - metallism. These evils are conveniently
grouped in two great classes, the first embracing the
consequences of a sudden and rapid appreciation of

gold, the second the consequences of a sudden and fluctuating depreciation of silver.

Now although, since Mr Goschen first made the phrase popular, a great deal has been written and spoken about the appreciation of gold and its consequences, it is doubtful whether popular ideas on the subject have yet become very clear and distinct; and perhaps it may be useful, in spite of the able address on this subject recently given to you by Mr Smith, if I say a few words on the general aspects of the question. The price of every particular commodity, from a landed estate or a great ship down to a pound of cotton or a tin tack, depends upon two distinct sets of causes — first, on causes affecting peculiarly the article in question; and, secondly, on causes affecting the general level of prices. The first set of causes is familiar to every one. Every one knows, for example, that a great improvement in any manufacture will lower its price compared with other things.

But the causes affecting the general level of prices are by no means so simple and obvious. In fact, in all the transactions of business and ordinary life, what people practically assume is that the only causes which they need consider are these practical influences: they assume, in fact, that the standard of value remains as invariable as the standard of length or the standard of weight,—that on the average in

P

the long-run general prices will remain the same. But this assumption may in some cases be quite false, and may lead to most unpleasant consequences. If the standard pound weight were defined as the weight of a pennyworth of standard bread, or the standard yard as the length of a pennyworth of standard tape, then the standard yard and the standard pound weight would be on a level as measures of length and weight with the sovereign as a measure of value. The sovereign is simply a certain weight of standard gold; it does not mean a certain value of any one thing or any number of things. If the price of bread and tape were fixed and invariable, a yard or a pound of the imaginary kind described would be invariable, and so also if general prices were quite steady the sovereign would be an invariable standard of value. But as a matter of fact the general level of prices does not remain steady and fixed; and if it becomes lower, that is an appreciation of gold.

No one will deny that the more steady the standard remains, so much the better it is for the whole community. Now for any short period the general level of prices may be considered steady. A prudent and far-sighted trader will discount beforehand any change in relative prices — the successful trader, indeed, is the man who can calculate a day or two, or it may be an hour or two, in advance of his competitors in buying and selling. But in any contract

for any length of time a change in the general level
of prices may become serious, and may upset all calculations. If the change is very slow and gradual,
bargains will be adjusted without any difficulty,
especially when we take into account the fact that
relative prices are always changing; but if the change
is sudden and severe, there will be a great disturbance
of interests. For such changes in the general level of
prices do not operate uniformly and simultaneously,
as is too often supposed. Every farmer will tell you
that the prices of his various outlays have not fallen
in proportion to the fall in his produce, and I imagine
most manufacturers have found since 1874 that prices
have fallen more than expenses.

Now, if the fall in prices is due to special causes
—*e.g.*, over-production of some things—in process of
time a revival may be expected. Production, in the
case supposed, will be checked, and prices will rise.
But the important point to observe is that if the fall
in prices is general, and due to general causes—if the
fall, for instance, in agricultural produce is due not
to the over-supply of commodities but to the contraction of the currency, then there is no such tendency
for a reaction to set in. The years 1872 to 1874
were undoubtedly too fat, and it was quite natural
that they should be followed by lean years; but if
the depression had been due simply to the after-
effects of overtrading, it ought, on the analogy of the

commercial history of a century, to have disappeared
in six or seven years.   Before this time another inflation should have come and gone.

Well, then, the first charge the bi-metallists have
to bring against the demonetisation of silver, or its
general degradation in the West to a token currency,
is that it has caused a sudden and serious appreciation of gold.   As a consequence, agriculturists especially, and all who had made contracts for long periods,
have suffered severely.   Producers of all kinds have
also experienced a loss of profit, because it has been
impossible to readjust money wages, and labour has
suffered through irregularity of employment.   Probably the only class which has gained much has been
that of middlemen, for it is notorious that retail prices
have not fallen to the same degree as wholesale prices.
It is usual to say that those with fixed incomes have
gained ; but I apprehend it would be nearer the truth
to say they ought to have gained, for the middleman
has most effectively broken the fall in prices so far as
the consumer is concerned.

Attempts have been made recently to minimise the
effects of the depression which set in after 1874,
and even in the Report of the recent Royal Commission the general prosperity of the country was considered a subject for congratulation.   But I venture
to think that, under the circumstances, a much greater
amount of prosperity ought to have been experienced

but for some exceptional oppressive influence. Since 1874 there has been a period of profound repose, marked by great progress in the arts of production and the means of communication. There have been neither great wars nor unsound speculations on a large scale. The efficiency of labour and capital has increased, the effects of general education have begun to tell on the habits of the people, crime has been lessened, and thrift has been growing. Now, surely depression of any kind is a very strange result to spring from this general peacefulness and this marked improvement in the *morale* and *physique* and intelligence of the people. Political economy has often been called a dismal science ; but it never gave rise to a belief so dismal as that the causes of a general depression in industry should be looked for in vast improvements in production and better organisation of commerce. Yet that is what we are invited to believe by those who refuse to consider the natural consequences of the great monetary disturbance. They say, in effect, that the causes of the depression have been railways, telegraphs, steamers, and the opening up of new countries. The Suez Canal has done its share in the work of mischief, and the increase in the wealth and population of our neighbours has contributed to the evil. This is, indeed, reading backwards the truths which made the political economy of Adam Smith and his great successors honoured and respected of all who took the trouble to understand it.

Take a rapid survey over the growth of the industrial progress of this country since the end of last century, and you cannot doubt that the principal causes of that marvellous expansion have been precisely those forces which are now said to be the forerunners of depression — the infinite variety of mechanical appliances, both in production and distribution, and the breaking down of international barriers. If I am asked to describe in one phrase, in one word, the real character of this marvellous progress, I should say it is due to constant over-production. Every decade has produced far more than its preceding decade could have produced and consumed. No doubt partial inconvenience may arise from a temporary glut of some commodities; but every increase in productive power, and every extension of the arms of trade, and everything which tends to what may seem like over-production, is, when you look beneath the surface, the mainspring of material wellbeing.

Even then, if the most favourable view possible be taken of the trade and industry during the past twelve years, it is much less favourable than might have been anticipated; but I think the facts of the case do not warrant this complacent survey of the past and this hopeful regard of the future. As regards the past, look at the condition of our colonies, which ought to be advancing by leaps and bounds. In every case their public debts have increased much faster than their population, and it is to be feared that mortgages on land have increased still more rapidly. Consider, again, the condition of the landed interest in this country. It· is well known that arrears are accumulating, that tenants cannot be found for farms even at great reductions, and that the burden of old contracts is becoming intolerable. But agriculture is still by far the most important industry of the country, and no one is bold enough to deny that it has suffered most severely. Sanguine people point to the gross returns made to the income-tax assessments, and say triumphantly that' the gross profits of the country continue to increase. But, in the first place, it is well known that with a declining revenue the fiscal net is thrown farther, and the mesh is made finer; and yet, in spite of all, the rate of increase, allowance being made for population, has dropped from more than 30 per cent in the ten years preceding to less than 3 per cent in the ten years following 1875.

And, again, when we look into the details of these gross profits, we find some surprising official calculations. We see, for example, that from 1875 to 1880 the gross rental of the United Kingdom from lands actually rose, and that down to 1885 the decrease was only about 3 per cent; whilst in Ireland, of all

places in the world, the gross rental in the latter
year exceeds that of the former, and yet Sir James
Caird has made a moderate estimate that the real
rental of the country has lost 30 per cent; and I am
afraid there is reason to suppose that in other cases
the returns have been made on a basis that is no
longer sound. It is significant that the only very
considerable increase has been in houses, the gross
rental having steadily risen 30 per cent since 1875,
whilst population has only increased 11 per cent.
It would be very remarkable if such a rate of increase were to continue, and there are clearly signs
that a depreciation of house property has occurred,
and will continue.

Now, if this depression, or, to put it more mildly,
this absence of prosperity, is to be mainly attributed
to the demonetisation of silver and the consequent
pressure on gold, the natural remedy would appear to
be the restoration of silver to its former level; and,
it must be observed, it is not as if the effects of the
appreciation had been definitely worked out and
everything had been readjusted to the new level of
prices. In that case there would be some excuse for
crying out against another disturbance. We have no
evidence that the readjustment is complete; on the
contrary, we have every reason to believe that a
further appreciation will occur. For with every increase in the volume of trade and the numbers of

people, with every expansion of commerce into new
regions, with every displacement of old customs by
competition and contract, a greater demand is made
on gold for currency. But the amount of gold produced is diminishing, and ·the amount absorbed by
manufacturers and by the East is increasing.

Thus there is every reason to anticipate a diminution in supply, with an increase in demand; and as
the inevitable result, a further fall in prices and a
further increase in the burden of old debts, and a
further dislocation of contracts and agreements. I
wish to discuss the subject in its practical aspects,
and to put the case in a moderate, reasonable form,
and without any exaggeration. Accordingly, I shall
not ask you to believe that even with bi-metallism
you are certain to escape altogether from a gradual
appreciation of the standard when you come to compare a long term of years. But what I do maintain
is, that with the two metals in full use, the general
level of prices will be much more steady, and any
appreciation of the double standard will be much
more gradual than in the opposite case. This appears to me evident, whether we regard supply or
demand.

Under present conditions, there is no doubt that
the abundance of silver would compensate the scarcity
of gold. In this matter our task is very easy, for we
can leave our case to be established simply by allow-

ing our most distinguished opponents to destroy their own case by contradictory arguments. You will find that at one time we are threatened with a perfect flood of silver, which is to drive all the gold from the banks, and the circulation of the West to the secret hoards and goldsmiths' workshops in the East; and at another time we are told that all rich countries naturally prefer gold to silver, that the silver will be boycotted, that gold will rise to a premium, and that there will be no effect on general prices.

The truth is often found between two untenable extremes. The flood of silver is a myth which has no real evidence in its favour: the only scientific evidence worth considering is against it, for the geologist supports in this instance the assertion of Scripture that there is surely a vein for silver, with the addition that veins of silver, embedded in hard and deep rock, are not easily made to pour out in a flood. Again, as regards the opposite extreme, that the silver will make no substantial addition to the world's currency, the argument is a pure conjecture—a piece of guess-work opposed to all experience. In the most advanced communities gold itself is becoming rather the basis of the circulation than a mere medium of exchange. The adoption of bi-metallism will not destroy the banking systems of the civilised world and the payment by cheques of all large sums. Probably one of the first effects, indeed, of bi-metallism would be to extend banking facilities. All civilised nations are familiar with silver for small payments, and the tendency is for all other payments to be effected through the agency of the banks.

But this objection may be met on even more general grounds. For any slight inconvenience (assuming there was any) which might be felt, through the use of silver, would be as nothing compared with the use of inconvertible paper notes issued in variable and excessive quantities. Yet no one will deny that any Government in the world, simply by making its payments and receiving its taxes in that form, and by making such notes legal tender, can force these notes into circulation, and keep them in circulation. This is no mere theory; it has been an accomplished fact at one time or another of all the great countries in the world, and it is only quite recently that America and Italy have reverted to cash payments. Well, then, if highly civilised nations have been induced to accept as their standard money the worst possible form of currency, is there any reason to believe that because silver is raised from the position of a token, a merely limited representative of the sovereign, a cumbrous form of an inconvertible metallic note—for that is the real position of our half-crowns and florins —if silver were raised from this position to that of a standard metal, at a fixed ratio to the other metal, is there any reason to believe that it would cease to circulate, and that new supplies could not be put into circulation ?

The question, put in its simplest form, becomes practically this: If about sixpence worth more silver were put into our florins, and a double florin were made, of about the size of the old silver crown, would the people of the country refuse to circulate these coins ?

The general conclusion on this part of the argument, putting aside the imaginary cases of ingenious theorists, seems to be, that with bi-metallism we should at first have a movement of general prices towards the old level, though in all probability not to the high level of 1872-74, which was under the influence of exceptional causes, and for the future the level of prices would remain much more steady. We should have, as before, credit cycles and periods of comparative inflation and depression, but we should have, on the whole, much greater stability; and it is agreed on all sides that the more stable the general level, so much the better for the public good.

But it is time to observe that bi-metallism is proposed as a remedy not only for the appreciation of gold but for the depreciation of silver. The inconvenience which arises from a fluctuating and uncertain exchange with silver - using countries, must be too obvious to those who export largely to such countries to require any discussion at my hands, and on this simple aspect of the question I shall confine myself to one remark. It is sometimes said that all inconvenience may be avoided by making bargains either on a gold basis or by forward exchange contracts. In precisely the same manner, also, you may avoid the inconvenience of the loss, or partial loss, of your cargoes at sea by the simple device of insurance; but I have never heard it said that you could effect an insurance for nothing. And the fluctuations of exchange due to the uncertainty in the price of silver are on the same footing. It is a matter of risk, and you can either insure against the risk through banks willing to undertake it, or through throwing the burden on native dealers; but neither Indian banks nor native dealers are likely to do insurance business without premiums, and in some form or other the export trade will be made to feel the burden.

This, however, although the most simple and obvious of the effects of the depreciation of silver, is not the only one nor the most important. There are other consequences, more difficult to detect and much more difficult to remedy. For purposes of illustration, the case of India may be taken, and the consequences to which I allude may be described by saying that the depreciation of silver acts like a bounty given on exports from India, and like a protective duty imposed on imports to India. Now, in order to prove this assertion, the first step in the argument is to show how the general level of prices in India is determined. There is a very popular delusion that with every fall in the value of silver compared with gold, the general level of Indian prices, being measured in silver, ought to rise. The case is thought to be the same as that of a country with inconvertible notes — the United States, for example, with greenbacks. It is well known that after a time every addition to the premium on gold marked a further rise—a corresponding rise in the general level of prices measured on paper. If the premium on gold was 150, general prices were 150 per cent above their former level. Now it is imagined that precisely the same thing ought to happen with Indian prices in silver—that is, if silver becomes depreciated, there should be not only the premium on gold which is shown by this depreciation, but a corresponding rise in other commodities. But the two cases are not parallel; theory shows they are not, and experience confirms the theory. In the United States the actual medium of exchange was greenbacks, and the only meaning people attached to these greenbacks was that they represented so much gold. Accordingly merchants really made their bargains on a gold basis, and translated them afterwards into notes—at least, that is what they did if they were wise, and the choice was open to them. And it was only so far as this method was pursued that the fluctuating premium on gold caused corresponding fluctuations in general prices

But at first, as is well known, such was not the case : a premium on gold arose through special demands for it for war or export before general prices were affected, and for some time it continued at a higher level. That is to say, at first the notes became depreciated as regards gold but not as regards commodities, and then not so much as regards commodities.

Now, apply this illustration to India. Silver is there both the actual currency and the standard of value : it is in silver that the people are accustomed to think of values, and they look on gold simply as a commodity, like pearls or tiger-skins. There is from the Indian point of view no more reason why a fall in the value of silver compared with gold, or, what is the same thing, a rise in the price of gold, should raise general prices, than a rise in the price of pearls or tiger-skins, or any other luxury. To the great mass of mild Hindoos the depreciation of silver means simply a rise in the price of gold ; it means that they will have to give more than before for ornaments made of that metal, or for little ingots to put away in their hoards. But the depreciation of silver has in itself no more effect on the general level of prices in India, than a fall in the price of the finer classes of note-paper would have had on the value of greenbacks in America.

This illustration is, no doubt, an extreme one, and that is indeed the principal distinction between an illustration and an argument—the purpose of an illustration is to magnify as with a lens the truth of an argument. And the truth I am trying to enforce is this : unless you throw masses of silver actually into circulation in India (and India is only an example of silver-using countries), you cannot raise general prices. The depreciation of silver compared with gold will, as I said, no more raise general prices than a fall in the price of the paper of which bank-notes are made.

And now I may make use of that part of the American illustration which is really applicable—the failure at first of general prices to rise, in spite of the premium on gold. So long as the notes were used by the mass of the people both as currency and as the standard, prices could only rise by an enormous increase of issues ; and in precisely the same way, general prices in India will rise only through enormous importations of silver. This, then, is the first position, and it is borne out by the well-known fact that general prices in India have not moved, or if they have moved at all, it has been downwards.

The next step in the argument is that the gold price of silver is practically determined by the· demand and supply of the metal in the London market. And here we get precisely the reverse of what happens in India. A large quantity of silver might be added to the currency of that country, and dispersed through its vast population, without having any appreciable effect on general prices ; but a comparatively slight increase in the supply in London, or a falling off in the demand, at once operates on the price. Thus silver has fallen 30 per cent in London without any response being made by general prices in India. These, then, are the two steps by which we attain to the position that the depreciation of silver is a bounty on exports from India and a protective duty on imports into India.   For since general prices have not moved upwards, the same amount of silver as before will give the Indian producer his usual or expected profit ; but this is the same thing as saying that Indian produce can be sold for less gold than before in Western markets, and the effect is similar to a bounty on Indian exports.

We know from other cases how a bounty operates : it increases the quantities exported, lessens their price in the foreign country, and cripples foreign competitors.

In exactly the same manner it may be shown that prices in India remaining about the same, depreciation of silver acts like a protective duty on imports ; and I was not surprised to read in Mr Ellison's valuable and interesting work on the cotton trade, that Lancashire has more to fear from India than from Europe and America in competition.

The fall in Eastern produce may have a depressing effect on other markets and other produce, and the

Q

general fall in Western prices is probably due partly to the indirect effects of the depreciation of silver as well as to the direct effect of the pressure on gold. If, for example, the fall in the price of silver has encouraged the export of wheat from India, and has caused a fall in its price, it is easy to see that a sympathetic fall will take place in other grain- and food-stuffs; and then if all the gold-using countries try to improve their position by raising sheep and cattle, the increase in quantity will tend to lower the price of beef and mutton, and of wool and hides, and thus the depreciation of silver, though it strikes most severely at the producers of wheat, indirectly affects the whole farming class.[1]

[1] It is not maintained that *in all respects* the depreciation of silver acts precisely like a bounty in one case and a protective duty in the other. It is sometimes said that there is no bounty on Eastern exports, *because* their gold price has fallen. But it was shown by Adam Smith, and the recent experience of the sugar bounties furnishes a good illustration, that the principal effect of a bounty is a reduction in price to the foreign consumer. A bounty cannot, except at first, give *exceptional* profits. But growers and exporters of Indian wheat will do a profitable business so long as they obtain the same silver as before, and thus the production can be extended, whilst English farmers cannot grow the wheat profitably for the same silver (because it means less gold) until all other prices have been adjusted. Thus the general effect of the depreciation is so far analogous to a bounty.

In the same way, a protective duty is a convenient analogy for showing that, if silver prices remain the same, and the price of silver falls, exports to India are only possible if a lower gold price is accepted—just as in exports to protective countries in general, the prices actually obtained are less than they otherwise would be. For the full theory, see p. 351 *et seq.*

Let me resume in a sentence the principal points
in the argument.   I have been labouring to prove
that bi-metallism would be a remedy for certain evils
which have arisen from the demonetisation of silver,
and the consequent depreciation of that metal and
the appreciation of gold.   Now it may seem that the
last disadvantages which I have just mentioned must
be an unmitigated blessing, and that every member
of the general public ought to pray for a still further
depreciation of silver.   And if all the consumers of
this country were in receipt of fixed money incomes,
and the middlemen were simply brokers with a fixed
and modest charge per cent, undoubtedly every fall
in prices would mean an increased power of consumption; but just as this point requires neither
introduction nor illustration, neither also does the
position that the mass of the community are not
in receipt of fixed money incomes, even if we grant
for the sake of argument that the middleman never
receives more than the minimum rate of profits.

The three great classes of income in every great
country — wages, profits, and rent — all depend on
prices, and the remaining class of those who receive
fixed interest on former investments is comparatively
small.   Any disturbance of the general level of prices
must in time affect the nominal amount of incomes.
Profits and rents have already felt the reduction, and
if regard were paid to the regularity of employment,

wages have already suffered, and will probably suffer still more. The question is one of comparison—we must compare actual receipts with actual expenditure, and not possible nominal receipts at high figures with actual expenses at very low figures. It is possible that hitherto wages, or the real consuming power of labour, has suffered least—that nominal wages have not fallen so much as real expenses. But it is contrary to all principles and to all experience to suppose that the labouring classes can derive more than temporary benefit by a disturbance of the currency, even if that disturbance leads to lower prices. The price of labour cannot be an exception to the general fall in prices. If profits fall, enterprise is contracted; and if enterprise is contracted, wages must fall, and employment become irregular.

It is sometimes said that the fall in the price of agricultural produce has simply had the effect of diverting the rents of great landowners—who have long loved to reap where they have not sown—into the pockets of the people. But I think you will find with a very little examination that no such simple redistribution has happened or was possible. The blow could only reach the landowner through the tenant-farmer, and it is that class which has suffered most severely. Again, it must be remembered that a large part of the rental of this country is simply profits, and very low profits, on capital sunk in the soil, and that this capital can only be received from year to year through agricultural profits, and so far it would be just as reasonable to look at the failure of the railways to pay dividends as a cause for congratulation. During the agitation for the repeal of the Corn Laws, nine out of ten educated people had mastered that elementary proposition in political economy which shows that the rent paid for natural superiority of fertility or situation cannot enter into the price of the produce; and since that time the truth may have been forgotten, but it certainly has not been disproved.

I must not, however, make any further digression on this interesting topic, and I will only add that the cheapness which springs from improvements in the efficiency of labour and capital, and from the extension of foreign commerce on the basis of a world-wide division of labour, is in its causes and in its consequences altogether different from the cheapness which springs from a disturbance of the currency. In the former case there is a common gain by all parties concerned; in the latter the gain of one class is only possible through the still more serious loss of another.

There could be no greater delusion than to suppose that cheapness which is caused by the scarcity of gold, and which must in a short time make labour also cheap, is a benefit in the same sense as cheapness caused by the bounty of nature or by the ingenuity of men. If it were so—if artificial cheapness of this kind were desirable—you have only to make your sovereign of greater and greater weight, whilst retaining the same nominal value, and the consumers will be filled with plenty. Make your pound sterling into a pound-weight of gold, and you will find by an easy calculation how wonderfully cheap the quartern-loaf will become. At present an ounce of gold makes nearly four sovereigns, and twelve ounces, as we know, make a troy pound. So that the new sovereign would contain as much gold as forty-eight of the old sovereigns, and everything would fall to one-forty-eighth of its former price, and the quartern loaf, instead of being 5d. or 6d., would become less than half a farthing. The mono-metallists accuse us of wishing to give a semblance of prosperity to commerce by raising prices; we may fairly retort that they wish to give a semblance of cheapness to consumers by lowering prices. The truth, however, is that what bi-metallists contend for is steadiness of prices and a cessation of the irregular, spasmodic actions of independent Governments. They wish to restore on a rational basis the monetary equilibrium which was upset by the ill - considered action of Germany when glutted with the ransom of France.

I have addressed myself mainly to the advantages of bi-metallism, because that is the best mode of

showing the practicability of the proposed reform.
As matters stand at present, there can be no reasonable doubt that if this country were to make a proposal for a fixed-ratio bi-metallism to the other great
commercial nations, such a proposal would be readily
and gratefully adopted.   It would have been adopted
in 1878, and every year since then the reasons for
its adoption have gained strength.   The only obstacle
to general bi-metallism is the public opinion of this
country, and public opinion is rapidly turning in its
favour, simply because the merits of the proposal are
every day becoming more widely known and appreciated.   The traders with silver-using countries have
begun to see the evils of the depreciation of silver
and the unaccountable fluctuations in its value.   The
agricultural interests here, as in Germany, are beginning to open their eyes to the evils of the appreciation of gold; and the greatest class of all, the
taxpayers, are becoming aware of a want of elasticity
in the revenue, and the increase in the real weight of
public burdens.   It seems, then, that we have only
to give our proposals plenty of light and air, to put
them before the public in the plainest manner possible, and the details of the method of action will
soon be decided.   In the world of practical politics
it is the advantageous which is the practicable.
Every important reform has been branded as impracticable until its advantages have been shown to

be unquestionable, and then party has vied with party and leader with leader for the honour of practical achievement.

At the same time, it may perhaps be desirable to make a few specific observations on the practicability of international bi-metallism, and to answer some objections commonly urged on that ground. We may, I think, take it for granted that if the great commercial nations agreed to a fixed ratio and kept to their agreement, the ratio adopted would remain steady. I assume this not simply because it has been demonstrated over and over again by bi-metallists, but because a strong advocate of mono-metallism, Mr Giffen, has taken pains to show that even without any convention, if only the countries of the world would avoid changing their standards, the ratio would remain practically steady. His object was to show, not that a convention could not preserve the stability of the ratio, but that there was no need for a convention, as natural causes were sufficient. Bi-metallists do not think Mr Giffen is right in this belief; but they have no need to fight for a position which is already more than granted.

But if the stability of the ratio is admitted, provided the great nations make an agreement and keep to it, the only practical difficulties to overcome are— first, to show that such a convention is possible; and, secondly, that if entered into it would be observed. As regards the possibility of the convention, it might be sufficient to repeat the opinion that England alone bars the way; but with many people the mere mention of a general international agreement makes them quite deaf with their own volubility. In the first place, they say, we can never get all the nations of the world to agree. The answer is, that the four great commercial nations would be more than enough. Countries such as Turkey or Greece or Portugal, or even Russia, might join the convention or not join it, and it would make no more difference than two or three old ladies moving to the side of a great steamer would capsize it : such countries, if they happened to have any metal to coin, would probably find it convenient to keep within the rules of the convention, just as the old ladies would find it convenient to keep within the steamer, though it would make no difference to the steamer if they fell overboard. Then, when the word general or universal is seen to be intended in a practical and not a metaphysical sense, an attempt is made to magnify the initial difficulties — to show that any agreement on such a mysterious subject as coinage is impossible. The way to make a molehill appear like a mountain is to cover it with a thick fog, and the way to make a moderate difficulty appear insuperable is to clothe it with vague and mysterious language.

Now, what is in reality the essence of this agreement which appears to be so formidable ?   It is simply this—that on and after a certain date the countries which are parties to the convention will coin all the silver and gold brought to them at a fixed ratio. Each country will please itself as to the names and weights of its coins.   One thing is enough at a time, and for the present nothing need be said of the ultimate possibility of an international coinage.   The essence of international bi-metallism is simply that both gold and silver shall be freely coined and shall be unlimited legal tender on a fixed ratio, and all that this country need do would be to make the florin or half-crown of full weight at the ratio agreed to.   As before, small coins might, if it were thought desirable, remain token-money.   So long as both gold and silver are coined freely at the fixed ratio, it makes no difference how many or how few different sorts of coins are used.   One of each metal is quite enough.   Now, as regards this country, the half-sovereign seems to be slowly dying of consumption, and our currency would certainly be brought to a much better state if this emaciated half-sovereign were replaced by five robust and full-weighted florins. Surely such a revolution in England is not beyond the genius of the present Chancellor of the Exchequer, and in France, America, and Germany the actual disturbance would be still less.

Then the difficulty is raised, What is the ratio to be ? Between the old ratio of 15½ to 1 and the market ratio, which occasionally happens to prevail, of 20 to 1, there are, as every mathematician knows, actually an infinite number of possible ratios to choose from ; and to choose precisely that ratio which, having regard to all past and present and future interests, would cause the very least possible disturbance —that, I admit at once, is impossible. But it is only impossible in the same way as 'every other realisation of perfect justice is impossible. And in all probability the difficulty would be solved in reality before the commissioners appointed to decide it had elected their president. For there can be no doubt that what most people would expect to be adopted is the old ratio of 15½ to 1, and any general belief of this kind would gradually cause the market price to move up towards that ratio, and on the day the decision was announced in all probability the market ratio would have reached the old ratio. No one would sell silver to-day at 59d. per ounce if to-morrow he expected the price would be 60d.

And now only one other practical difficulty remains. It is often said, How can you expect the nations to keep to their agreement ? and again the language of mystery and foreboding is employed to obscure a very simple set of facts. Suppose that the great commercial nations have respectively adjusted their coinage on the basis of bi-metallism at a fixed ratio, the question is asked, How can you be sure that each nation will observe the compact,—that none will break away, regardless of the others, simply for its own convenience? The answer to this question reminds me forcibly of the answers to the most foolish and irritating of all riddles—those answers which are overlooked because of their extreme and obvious simplicity. The question is, Why will any nation not recede from its engagement? And the answer is, that by doing so it will cause more injury to its own subjects than to any one else. We cannot allow the mono-metallists to oppose us with contradictory arguments. They must make their choice. Well, then, if they say — and certainly they very often do say—that it is next to impossible to get any nation to change its currency, then they must admit that if once any country adopted bi-metallism at a fixed ratio, it would be next to impossible to induce it to change.

But I do not wish to rely on the inconsistencies of opponents, for of course one opponent may say one thing and another a different thing. Let us assume, then, that the great commercial nations have adopted bi-metallism at the fixed ratio, which, so long as the compact is observed, will remain perfectly stable, and try to imagine the circumstances under which one or more of these nations might recede from the agreement, and the consequence of doing so. The case which is apparently most dreaded is that silver will come to the mints in excessive quantities and choke the channels of circulation, and that a desire for a single gold standard will arise. Let us suppose that in England the robust florin of which I spoke has largely replaced the sovereign, and that in an unreasoning panic a weak Government wishes to restore the gold. How is this to be done? Now there is only one answer, and I recommend it to the careful attention of our opponents, who are never tired of quoting Gresham's law—that the worse metal always drives the better from circulation. The only way to get rid of this silver, unless the Government buys it up at a loss, would be to debase the gold standard—to make the gold in a sovereign equal to nine florins and still call it equal to ten. Recall the conditions of the case. The country is full of silver, and the reserves of the banks are in silver, and this silver is supposed to be either actually depreciated or in danger of depreciation—that is, the gold in the sovereign is considered to be worth more than ten florins. Well, then, to drive this silver from the country and bring back gold, you must not only declare that the legal-tender sovereign is worth less than ten florins, but you must actually make it worth less than ten florins — you must diminish its weight. But this really amounts to saying that you begin your reform

by compelling the banks to sell their stores of silver
under the market value, and you debase the standard
you wish to adopt.

I will not weary you with further imaginary cases
—we are not bound to provide our opponents with
objections; it is enough to answer the objections
they raise themselves, and no one yet has shown even
an imaginary case in which a nation might gain by
breaking its engagement.   In the mean time we may
rest assured that if the great nations agreed to remodel their coinage on the same plan, and enter into
an agreement for the purpose, there would be very
obvious and forcible reasons why they should keep
that engagement.   There is the importance of public
credit, there is the probability that the country which
broke faith would cause more inconvenience to its
own subjects than to any one else, and there is the
danger of provoking retaliation.

We must remember that in the convention proposed, every nation in reality enters into an engagement with its own subjects in the first place: it declares that it is about to remodel its currency on a
bi-metallic basis, one reason being that other nations
have agreed to do the same.   Every nation enters
into the agreement for its own interest and keeps it
for its own interest, and surely that is such a simple
kind of international convention that even Russia
might see the advantages of observing it.   It is just

as if the nations agreed to adopt the same weights and measures—the only difficulty is in making the change. Once the change was effected, no nation would give itself the trouble of making another change.

This, then, is the only real practical difficulty, and that difficulty would be solved if the great English statesman who is now Chancellor of the Exchequer were to set himself to the task. Fortune has thrown in his way a splendid opportunity of doing a great service to his country and to the world, and at the same time of converting a reputation founded largely on criticism into a reputation founded on a great practical reform. Something more is expected of Mr Goschen than the recitation of a humdrum Budget and an ingenious display of the anomalies of taxation and the difficulty of making any change. Mr Goschen ought to abandon the microscope for the field-glass. He stated the other day that too roseate a view had been taken of the elasticity of the revenue, and of the revival in trade; and the man who first directed the attention of the general public to the appreciation of gold knows very well that neither the revenue nor trade can expand when fettered by a contracting currency. He is perfectly familiar with all the arguments and all the facts of the case, and he has had ample time to strike a balance, and he ought in this matter to lead and not follow public opinion.   If to one who is always swayed by the nicest ideas of justice an appeal may be made through personal ambition, I would venture to say that if, in attempting to make this practical reform, by any accident of fortune he made a mistake—and there was never a practical proposal in which the chance of a mistake was less—such a mistake would gain for him the regard and sympathy of the public.   It is only the critic who never runs the risk of making mistakes.   In ancient Greece there was a celebrated conservative statesman named Aristides, and surnamed " The Just."   He was ostracised and driven into honourable banishment for ten years, and the reason given by one of the voters has become historical. " I was tired," said he, " of hearing him called The Just."   Let Mr Goschen beware of the fate of Aristides.   He could wish for no better opportunity of passing from criticism to performance than by taking the lead in a great reform which would restore prosperity to industry and commerce, and remove one more barrier from the friendly intercourse of nations.

THE MORALITY OF BI-METALLISM.

ADDRESS TO THE GLASGOW PHILOSOPHICAL SOCIETY,
ECONOMIC SECTION, MAY 16, 1887.

THE advocates of bi-metallism have to defend a position which is open to attack on many sides. In the first place, they are told that the system is theoretically impossible and contradictory, and the heavy artillery of distinguished authority is dragged out from ancient arsenals. But it often happens in currency as in war, and many other interesting matters, that a position which is proved to be untenable according to all the recognised rules, is, as a matter of fact, impregnable.

Then when it is reluctantly admitted that the bi-metallic theory is possible, the practical man delivers an assault, and the artillery has to stop fire for fear of injuring its own side. The practical man rushes to close quarters and lays about him with hard facts

R

drawn from his own particular calling; but owing to the divergence of interests in this world, there are in most controversies practical men on both sides. Thus the debtor hammers the creditor, and the exporter the importer; the consumer raises his battle-cry of cheapness, the producer answers him with profit, and the working man drowns both with a cry for regularity of employment.

When the battle of the standards has thus reached a condition of most admired disorder, and both sides think they are getting the victory, a peacemaker in the garb of a moralist appears on the scene. He shows in the usual way that there is much to be said on both sides, that mono-metallism inflicts some hardships, and that bi-metallism might confer some benefits. But a peace-maker is generally a person of strong opinions, and the conclusion of the sermon is the sanctity of contracts and the horrors of disturbance. Thus, in the end, bi-metallism is declared to be not only theoretically absurd and practically impossible, but morally most wicked in general and dishonest in particular,

It is to this last aspect of the question alone that I wish to direct your attention, and, accordingly, I must ask you to grant, for the sake of argument, some large admissions. I shall assume that bi-metallism at a fixed ratio would be quite possible if the great commercial nations entered into an agreement, and not only that it is theoretically possible, but that it is actually practicable, and that after the necessary stages of agitation, Royal Commission, Parliament, diplomacy, conference, convention, and ratification, it becomes an accomplished fact. Having thus cleared the ground, I invite you to take up the position of the future historian of British civilisation, and to declare whether this monetary revolution was or was not justified.

The first charge brought by the moralist against bi-metallism is, that it is an interference with contracts; and it is gratifying to find, in spite of the large inroads made by Governments on the field of contract, that this objection is still considered perfectly valid if it can be established. The contention is, at any rate so far as this country is concerned, that there is an almost infinite number of contracts which have been expressed in terms of the pound sterling, and that the pound sterling means a certain weight of standard gold.

If bi-metallism is adopted, it is urged that all debtors will have the option of paying in silver instead of gold, and that in consequence creditors will be defrauded. Now it must be admitted at once that this difficulty cannot be evaded by providing that the option of paying silver shall be confined to contracts made after the change in the standard has been adopted. For, to take only one example, it would follow from such a provision, that whilst the Government received its taxes in silver, it might have to pay the interest on its debt and all fixed charges in gold, and the confusion introduced into banking would be extreme. Apart from this, the mere insertion of such a clause in the new Coinage Act would of itself tend to discredit silver, and to render it liable to depreciation, and thus defeat the primary object of the change.

Accordingly, in dealing with this objection, I shall suppose that the new interpretation of the pound sterling is made to apply to all contracts drawn up in terms of money, and that the pound sterling will mean in the option of every debtor either a golden sovereign or five double florins, if we may assume the double florin to be the standard silver coin. Well, then, the charge made is essentially that a vast multitude of persons who had covenanted to pay so much standard gold, are to be allowed to pay instead fifteen times and a half as much silver —supposing that is the ratio adopted.

Now at first sight this appears a terrible interference with contracts, and I will try to make it appear as heinous as possible by illustrations. Suppose that a man had ordered a golden spoon or a golden candlestick, and, owing to the interference of Government, the goldsmith sent him instead fifteen or sixteen silver spoons or silver candlesticks, he would certainly have serious cause for complaint; and similarly a manufacturer of teeth, who absolutely needed gold in his trade, would do well to be angry if he received some fine morning a mass of silver instead of the more precious metal. And even if we come a little nearer to the essence of the proposed change, it may be admitted that an ounce of gold is much more easy to carry about than a pound-weight of silver, and that two pockets full of silver would be much more inconvenient than a little purse of sovereigns.

But this objection, formidable as it may seem when thus stated, only gains the appearance of strength by neglecting the principal elements in the case. A pound sterling may be defined as consisting of so much gold at present, just as in early times it meant really a pound-weight of standard silver, and to dealers in bullion and to exchange-brokers the metallic meaning of the pound sterling is of real importance; but to say that contracts expressed in terms of pounds sterling are to be fulfilled by the actual transfer of gold, is to overlook the most striking distinction between the trade of civilised nations and the rudimentary barter of savages. At a low computation 97 per cent of wholesale transactions are settled without the use of gold, and so long as the ratio of gold to silver remains constant, silver would answer equally well the purpose of reserve in the vaults of the Bank of England, which is the ultimate reserve of the United Kingdom. With the ratio fixed and stable, the bank would adjust the proportions of the two metals held as reserve, so as to meet the convenience of its customers, and it would not make the smallest difference to the trading community whether the £18,000,000 or £20,000,000 of bullion usually held against the issue of notes, and lying dead in the issue department, consisted of gold or silver. And it is worth while pointing out that according to the Bank Charter Act of 1844, the Bank of England is actually entitled at this moment to hold against its issues an amount of silver equal to one-fourth of its gold reserve.

Thus, so far as large payments are concerned, the adoption of bi-metallism would possibly affect the nature of the reserve held against notes. We may test the truth of this argument in a very simple manner. I am contending that contracts expressed in terms of pounds sterling do not mean in the minds of the parties concerned certain weights of gold of a certain fineness; and in support of the contention, I venture to say that not one merchant in a thousand could tell you the weight of a sovereign, or the proportion of alloy to fine gold of which it is made. All that the ordinary merchant knows or cares about the pound sterling is, that it is the unit in which his banking account is kept, and he need have no more fear of being invited to carry on his back a ton of silver than a sack of coal or a bale of cotton. A dealer in cotton goods examines his samples with a lens, to such a pitch of carefulness has competition pushed him, and a wool-broker will divide wool into dozens of different qualities, but the money with which they are paid is practically "bank" money, and if the banks were called on to furnish immediately the gold which this money represents, they could not pay sixpence in the pound. The argument may be summed up in a sentence by saying that the great mass of wholesale transactions are settled not in bullion but in money, and that any large use of metallic money is, like bi-metallism according to its opponents, inconceivable in theory, and quite impossible in practice; and if a large use of metallic money in wholesale transactions were conceivable and possible, it would, at any rate, be a most intolerable nuisance. I will conclude these remarks on the hardship inflicted on the creditor by taking from him the right to receive gold, with the observation that at present he may be compelled to take Bank of England notes, and that a cheque duly honoured by a bank by a transfer in its books is the usual form of giving the creditor his gold.

Turning for a moment to the question of small

payments and retail transactions — to the expenditure of the creditor on consumable commodities in which metallic money is more generally used—it is only necessary to remark that to a great extent silver is already used, and silver which is by law merely token-money, and that even in retail transactions bank money plays an important part, especially in Scotland, where most people have the sense to prefer £1 notes to sovereigns.

The argument which I am advancing may be supported by an interesting reference to the champion of gold mono-metallism, Lord Liverpool. In his celebrated letter to the king on the coinage, he has to meet the objection that hitherto contracts had been based on silver as much as gold, and he rejoins that, as a matter of fact, owing to well-known causes, gold had become the principal medium of exchange. Well, we may say at present that "bank" money has replaced gold. And even when Lord Liverpool wrote, in comparing the relative market values of gold and silver, for that was before the price to be paid by the Bank of England was fixed by law, he found it most convenient to express the values in terms of Bank of England notes. Thus, even at the beginning of the century, when England was on the point of adopting gold mono-metallism in place of the historical bi-metallism, we find as a matter of fact that the principal medium of exchange was bank money resting on both gold and silver.

Thus an examination of the facts of the modern industrial world shows that the adoption of bi-metallism would directly, and in the strictest sense, imply no real interference with the vast majority of contracts; but the real difficulty lies in the indirect effects attributed to the system.

From this point of view, two accusations may be brought—first, the alleged injury to trade with, and in, silver-using countries; and, secondly, the alleged inflation of prices in gold, and the consequences of such an inflation in the relative distribution of wealth. The first of these accusations need not detain us long, so far as trade proper is concerned, for there can be no doubt that fluctuations in the relative values of gold and silver, in the sovereign and rupee for example, introduce an element of uncertainty, which, like all other risks, must on the whole operate injuriously. It is of course possible that, just as insurance companies make a profit on shipwrecks and fires, accidents and diseases, and all kinds of evils by land and sea, certain banks and brokers may make a profit out of the fluctuations in the gold price of the rupee. But, as regards the great mass of commercial transactions, the flow of capital to the places in which it is required, the fulfilment of prior obligations, and the provision for enterprise in the future, these fluctuations in the ratio of gold to silver must be the reverse of beneficial. The advantages of a stable ratio, provided the difficulty of adjustment has been surmounted, will not, I think, be seriously disputed by any one. It is, however, on the ground of the immediate consequence of the actual readjustment that the moral accusation is based.

It is said in the first place, that if the price of silver were suddenly raised by 20 to 30 per cent, a great dislocation of trade must ensue. But in the matter of reform, Royal Commissions are slow, diplomacy is more slow, and the Parliament of Great Britain and Ireland is most slow, and we may be tolerably certain that the rise in the price of silver towards the conventional ratio would not be characterised by a few leaps and bounds. It is of course very gratifying to bi-metallists to find the power of international legislation so fully recognised; but in this case, at any rate, they are content to have the pure theory tempered with facts. They argue that an international convention could fix the ratio and keep it stable; but if there appeared to be any danger of excessive haste, they would be quite willing in the interests of morality to press for a little delay. For my own part, however, I think the danger is all the other way, and that the moralist should set himself to hasten the readjustment. For, in the mean time, a great disturbance of industrial relations is in progress. India, for example, is receiving in some departments of production a purely artificial stimulus compared with Western nations.

In the natural course of things, after a painful and tardy process, we may expect the reaction to occur.

It is generally agreed that every fall in the value of silver acts at the time as a stimulus on Indian exports, and as a check on imports into India. Taking into account merely the fall in exchange, that must be the effect, and the actual statistics of large imports into India only show that in some way this check has been neutralised.

I will take the effect on the imports into India first.

The Lancashire manufacturer, in order to cope with the fall in exchange, has had to reduce profits to a minimum, and to strive to the utmost in every way to economise production. To some extent he has been able to throw the loss on the raw material; but the general result is that, owing to the difficulty of forcing up prices in India, some kinds of manufacture cannot be sent at all now, and other kinds are subject to most severe competition. And when you look beneath the surface of things, that means that, purely owing to monetary changes, the Indian manufacturer is for the time being protected.

Well now, suppose silver begins to rise again, or

that prices in the East begin to move upwards, then suddenly this protective duty is repealed by the high court of nature which we are invited to treat with such respect, and the Indian manufacturer has to compete with Lancashire, educated to a high pitch by years of constant effort.

India would then feel the burden which Lancashire feels now.

Now consider the export trade of India, with wheat for the example. Every fall in silver acts like a bounty on the production of wheat in India, and the area under cultivation is rapidly extending.

But again, suppose that silver ceases to fall, and that silver prices begin to move upwards.

The Indian producer, in this case, will require more gold than the Western producer : he wants not only the same number of rupees, but more, and then he can only afford to sell for more gold. But if gold prices rise, the west of America and the Lothians of Scotland may again find it profitable to grow wheat, and the Indian producer may suffer.[1]

It is only with the morality of bi-metallism that I am concerned at present, and the objection I am trying to meet is, that the present condition of things gives a benefit to India, and that it would be unjust to India to return to the fixed ratio. Unjust it would be, certainly, if we were, simply in the inter-

[1] On this subject compare p. 242.

ests of England, to propose a monetary change to the detriment of India.

But nothing of the kind is contemplated.

The proposal is simply to neutralise a stimulus which cannot be permanent, and to put Indian trade on the firm basis of natural advantages; to balance the interests of the future against the gain of the moment—for in the life of a nation a few years is but as a moment; and, in a word, to reduce money as far as possible to its proper position as the medium of exchange, and not to allow it to assume the guidance of production.

For the moment, India might lose, but even the momentary loss would be subject to compensation. The capital of the West would again be advanced for the development of her resources, and the reduction of usury by her money-lenders, and the burden of taxation and the interest on debt, would be proportionately lessened.

I pass on to consider an objection which rests on a wider basis, and which concerns this country more directly.[1]

It is said that bi-metallism would lead to a great inflation of prices, that all creditors would be prejudiced at any rate, and that probably a wild out-

[1] For a full discussion of the nature of the stimulus in different cases, see p. 351 et seq.

burst of speculation would ensue.   It is mainly on
the ground of this prospective inflation that the
argument as to the interference with contracts rests,
for, as we have seen, the feature of money which is
of importance is not the material of which coins are
made, but the command of money, in whatever shape,
over things in general.

Now it seems to me it is impossible to deal with
this objection unless we can roughly estimate the
degree in which prices will be affected.   Over and
over again various nations have suffered from excessive issues of inconvertible paper, and from a debasement of the coinage.   It is thus quite possible, theoretically, that an inflation of prices may be injurious,
and it is quite conceivable that if silver were made
into standard money such an inflation might ensue.
It is quite conceivable, and the morality of the operation will depend on the way in which it works.   But
it must also be observed, on the other hand, that the
world as a whole, and also particular countries, have
also suffered at times severely from an *insufficiency*
of currency and a consequent fall in prices.   There
can be little doubt that throughout the middle ages
commerce was hampered and restrained by the deficiency of the precious metals, and the large discoveries of silver in the sixteenth century gave a generous
and perfectly healthy stimulus to trade.   In the
modern world an elaborate system of credit has

economised the use of the precious metals in a wonderful degree, and we have an abundance of what is
practically representative money.   The evils which
spring from any contraction of credit, which is, so to
speak, the raw material of this representative money,
have been made familiar in every commercial crisis.
A commercial crisis does not merely burst the bub-
bles of speculation, but it puts a drag on the course
of legitimate trade, and it does so mainly by causing
a fall in prices.   The suspension on these occasions
of the Bank Charter Act of 1844, with the express
object of increasing if necessary the note circulation
and of rendering advances possible, has been the
recognition on the part of the Government of this
country, that it may be its duty to endeavour to check
the fall in prices, or the consequences of such a fall.

For the sake of argument, and in order to put the
objection in its strongest form, let us assume that
the ratio to be adopted is the well-known ratio of
$15\frac{1}{2}:1$, which would involve a rise in the gold price
of silver of from 25 to 30 per cent.   The question
then is—What would be the effect on general prices ?

Well, in the first place, the advocates of bi-metallism would argue that the adoption of this ratio
would be simply a return to the monetary position
which was upset by the action of Germany.   For
seventy years this ratio had been practically maintained, and its stability was really taken for granted.

For example, in Tooke's 'History of Prices' (vol. iii.
p. 213), issued in 1840, I find it stated in an argument against the adoption of bi-metallism by this
country : " There is always a market for silver in this
country for any quantity, and the utmost variation in
the market price is very trifling, rarely so much as 1
per cent ; but for this variation, trifling as it is, the
merchant shipping it obtains an abatement in the
price."

The ratio remained practically steady for seventy
years, and was disturbed, not through the super-
abundance of silver, as was demonstrated in the
report of Mr Goschen's Committee, but simply by
the legislative action of Germany and other nations.
Accordingly, it may be fairly argued that, so far as
the general level of prices was affected, if bi-metallism
were adopted on what is essentially the old basis, it
could not be raised higher than it would have been
in the natural course of things, but for this ill-con-
sidered action of foreign States.

But we may go much further than this in answer
to this supposed inflation of prices. For there can
be little doubt that even under the old conditions,
when silver did part of the work which is now done
by gold, even then there was really a tendency towards a general fall in prices. Many people at the
time believed that the great gold discoveries about
1850 would cause such an inflation of prices as to

produce a commercial catastrophe; but, as a matter of fact, this enormous increase in the supply of gold was no more than sufficient to meet the growing demands of the commercial world, and before the speculative inflation of 1872 to 1874, the old level had again been reached. It is of course difficult to estimate the general level of prices, but that is the result taking the one hundred important articles of the Hamburg list; and by other methods of calculation, the level seems to have become really lower in less than twenty years after the great discoveries. An elaborate essay would be required for the full investigation of this intricate problem; but I have no hesitation in saying, as the result of a careful inquiry, that quite apart from the monetary disturbance about 1874, general prices could not be maintained by the existing supplies of the precious metals. But since that time a very great increase has taken place in the trade and commerce of the world, so that if the old monetary position were restored, we should expect, so far as the metallic supplies are concerned, that we should still fall short of the old level of prices. In fact, instead of any great inflation from the adoption of bi-metallism, we ought, perhaps, only to anticipate a check to the downward movement, and thus bi-metallism would be rather a preventive of further disorder than a simple restoration of the old order.

S

There is, it seems to me, only one possible answer to this argument, and that is the assumption of a tremendous increase in the supplies of silver. Recently calculations have been placed before the public tending to show that silver can be produced in abundance at 1s. 6d. an ounce, or even lower figures. I think it is only necessary to say in reference to these calculations, that with the present low price of silver this would be a minimum profit of 150 per cent, and if that is not enough to bring out a flow of silver, the owners of the mines must be hard to please, and the promoters of mining companies must be in a lethargic condition ; or else the investing public must, for this time only in the annals of speculation, be more distrustful of mining than it ought to be, for a profit of 150 per cent translated into the language of the money prospectus would be, on all analogy, about 3000 per cent. I will only add, that if under present conditions silver is likely to fall rapidly to 1s. 6d. an ounce, the world will be compelled to choose between international bi-metallism and a practical silver currency, or mono-metallism on a gold basis, involving, so far as prices are concerned, a choice between a tropical sun of inflation and a polar night of depression.

But when we are discussing a question of morality, it seems proper to consider rather the facts of to-day than the chances of to-morrow ; and taking the facts as we find them, there is no reason to expect that gold and silver together would more than suffice to check the natural tendency of prices to fall with the enormous expansion of population and trade.

Well, then, if this position is granted, it follows that under bi-metallism the standard of value would be much more steady, and thus the real meaning of contracts expressed in terms of money would be less variable under the proposed than under the present system. Thus the charge of inflation falls to the ground, and those who wish to reap where they have not sown are not the advocates of bi-metallism and debtors of all kinds, but the approvers of the recent revolution, and the creditors who want their pound of gold to grow year by year more valuable.

An illustration on a large scale may be drawn from this year's Budget. The foundation of Mr Goschen's financial proposals rests on the fact that, in spite of a great growth in the consuming power of the people, the revenue has lost its elasticity; that the income-tax in particular, in spite of the greater strictness of collection, is not expanding—in a word, that the value of the national wealth is not increasing in proportion to its volume, and accordingly, that the burden of the old debt must be lightened. The point is, that every million of taxes is heavier than it was, and the national debt is only a large example of similar burdens carried by municipalities and corporations, by companies and by individuals. Thus if, in the matter of contracts expressed in terms of money, the moralist says we must beware of lightening the burden of just debts, the obvious retort is, we must beware also of increasing their burden.

There is another charge brought against bi-metallism closely allied to that just noticed, and depending in the same way on the supposed results of this supposed inflation. It has been observed in the recent depression of trade that rent and profits have suffered more than wages, and some people go so far as to maintain that wages have not fallen so much as the prices of commodities consumed by labour, and therefore . that the so-called depression has actually benefited labour, and that any check to the fall in prices, and still more, any reversal of the fall, would really be injurious to the masses of the community. Now this is a very plausible argument, because it is founded on a principle which, under certain conditions, is quite true, and which has been illustrated in the practical experience of nations. It is generally admitted, for example, that a rise in prices due to excessive issues of inconvertible paper has given profits a relative advantage over wages, because wages do not rise so quickly as the prices of wholesale commodities ; and when, owing to particular influences, a great rise has taken place in some commodity, *e.g.*, coal, it is generally allowed that, in the first place at any rate, capital has gained more than labour.   In the converse case of a fall in prices, it is quite possible that profits may vanish before any attempt is made to reduce wages; and if the prices of food and other necessaries fall, and employment remains regular, it is clear on arithmetical grounds that the wage-earners must gain.   The truth of this general theory, and the validity of these particular illustrations, I am quite prepared to admit; but that a continuous fall in prices, with a conse-quent shrinkage of profits, is, on the whole, a good thing for labour, I strenuously deny.

The whole position rests on the exploded doctrine, which used to make political economy .seem so dismal and immoral, that profits can only rise at the expense of wages, and wages at the expense of profits,—a doctrine which contains just enough super-ficial truth to make it plausible.   For if we take the industrial world as it is actually constituted at the present time, we find that the whole of industry depends for its stimulus upon profit, and if profits fall to a minimum or vanish, enterprise is at once contracted, and there is less scope for employment. If an employer cannot reduce wages, he will at any rate try to economise labour; and if he cannot trans-fer his loss through a fall in prices to other capitalists in the chain of producers, in the end that loss must fall on labour. Capital may for a certain time be employed without profit, and machinery and plant may be kept up out of previous accumulations, but that is only possible for a limited time, and when the limit is reached, wages must suffer. I have been told on excellent authority that in some parts of England agricultural wages have recently fallen 30 per cent, and every one knows how much the wages of miners have fallen with the fall in the price of coal. In fact, the modern doctrine of the relation of wages and profits rests on the basis that both wages and profits are paid out of the price of the product, though wages may in some cases be advanced out of capital. Accordingly, what we ought to expect in the natural course of things is that wages and profits will rise together and fall together. It is of course quite true, if the proceeds of a sale are divided into two shares—the share of labour and the share of capital—that the larger the one the smaller the other : every one pays sufficient respect to arithmetic to admit that, and if prices were fixed and unalterable, wages could only rise at the expense of profits. But with falling prices both wages and profits will fall; and though profits may fall first, we may be sure that wages will follow.

If we look beneath the surface, what are the real changes produced in the distribution of wealth by a rapid appreciation in the standard or a general fall in prices ?   In the first place, incomes of all kinds which depend on prices—and they are by far the greater number—are paid at the lower level, whilst all prior obligations must be honoured in terms of the letter of the bond.   Consider, for example, the case of agriculture.   The farmer's surplus will depend over a term of years on the run of prices.   Well, suppose prices fall, and for the time being he cannot or does not reduce wages.   Not only may he have to pay his rent out of capital except for the indulgence of his landlord, but he may have to trench on his funds to pay these high wages, and to keep up his stock and implements.   Well, the farmer may suffer first, and the landlord may suffer next, but in the third place the labourer will suffer.   And the labourer will suffer not merely by having his wages reduced to the level of the articles of his usual consumption, but he will probably find that after a time less capital will be available for agriculture, land will be idle, and the hands of labour will be idle too.

These are elementary truths, and I should apologise for bringing them under your notice, were it not for the fact that many who profess to be the friends of labour are endeavouring to show that what is to the capitalist dulness and depression must, by a kind of see-saw, be for the labourer a time of joyful-

ness' and elation. Bi-metallists are charged with a
desire to rob labour of the gifts of fortune, and to
check the beneficial and natural tendency of profits
to a minimum. In truth, all that they propose is to
minimise, as far as possible, fluctuations in the
standard of prices, and their moral position is that
all fluctuations are of themselves injurious, and that
fluctuations with a downward tendency are far more
injurious than in the converse case. To tell the
working classes that an appreciation of the standard
is a good thing for them though a bad thing for their
masters, is not only misleading in fact, but rests on
the most immoral and degrading of all economic
sophisms—namely, that any gain by one class is
only possible through the loss of another; that the
only way to elevate labour is to depress capital; and
that industry is not becoming more and more a
highly organised system, the life-blood of which is
good faith, confidence, and fidelity to the real meaning of contracts, but that it is a state of war and
hatred, of deceit and mistrust, of tyranny and slavery.

I must pass on, however, to another species of
immorality of which bi-metallists are accused, and
for which it is difficult to find a name, but which
may be described negatively as a culpable want of
common-sense, of patriotism, and of foresight. This
charge arises from the fact that bi-metallists advocate
the adoption of an international convention as regards

the coinage of gold and silver. It is argued that this country already possesses an excellent monetary standard, known all over the world, and that we have no right to sacrifice our interests to the interests of other nations; that the silver-using countries may be left to take care of themselves, and that in any case a convention would be probably impossible, and if possible, would not last. To be possessed of too little prudence and too much credulity and enthusiasm, is not perhaps on a level in respect of immorality with the deadly sin of depriving the poor of their wages; but so perverse is human nature that many people would rather be accounted positively wicked than simply foolish, especially in money matters.

In the first place, as regards the supposed monetary independence of this country, and the assertion that we may well leave silver to the silver-using countries, I should rejoin that in all essentials monetary independence would be only possible with commercial isolation. The most important characteristic of a good monetary standard is, that it should preserve comparative stability of value. The principal reason why, of the multitude of commodities that have been used for the material of money at different times, gold and silver have survived as the fittest, is because their great durability renders the total stock always extremely large compared with the annual supply, and thus eliminates one element of instability of

value. But when we speak of stability of value, we
can only refer to prices; for, as every schoolboy
ought to know, if political economy had its proper
place in education, the value of money is the same
thing as the level of prices. Now the fact which has
been forced upon the attention of the least observant
with increasing emphasis is, that foreign competition
and foreign influences determine to a very great extent the level of prices in this country—that, in a
word, prices are more and more determined by international and not by purely national causes. The
very land on which a nation is located, and all the
necessaries and luxuries which it consumes, may rise
or fall in value by influences which spread from India
or America, and it would hardly be possible to name
an article the value of which does not directly or
indirectly depend upon foreign competition. But if
every item in the endless series of purchasable commodities is thus influenced, how is it possible for the
series as a whole to escape ? If every particular price
is affected, the sum-total of prices must be affected,
and the sum-total of prices is the real meaning in
this country of the value of gold. This seems to me
one of those facts which, like the standing up of the
egg by Columbus, requires only to be mentioned to
be understood. Every nation can of course make its
coins exactly as it chooses, but as regards the real
value of its coins, it has no such power.

Under present conditions, some nations use gold and some silver as their standard, and, owing to the monetary disturbance, the relative values of these standards are constantly changing. Again, all the Western nations have practically adopted a gold standard; for although several of them hold large masses of silver which is still legal tender, they do not coin it freely. As a natural consequence, there is a pressure on gold which must make prices fall. All that the bi-metallists do is to invite the nations to recognise the very palpable fact that they are mutually dependent, and once for all to destroy these purely artificial causes of instability of value.

Now, if it be granted that an international convention on the lines proposed would benefit every party to the convention, and if it be further granted that, whether they like it or not, the value of money depends actually on the resultant action of many nations, surely it does not savour of very extreme enthusiasm or credulity, or of a want of patriotic independence, to urge that this cosmopolitan character of money should, in the interests of each, receive the recognition of all. When, for example, every one knows that, for the Government of India, the most important financial fact is whether the Bland Act will or will not be repealed by the United States, and that Germany, by forcing sales of silver, can dislocate our trade with the East; when the mutual dependence of nations in their monetary policy is forced on the attention every day,—surely the immorality of imprudence must be charged, not against bi-metallists, but against those who wilfully blind themselves to obvious facts. The choice lies between joint action on a reasoned and settled basis, and a conflict of interests in which all must suffer—between the benefits of a real and recognised combination, and the dangers of actual and unrecognised dependence.

Now, in conclusion, I should like to touch for a moment on a very general aspect of the question. It is said that the adoption of a fixed ratio would be an interference with nature, artificial protection to silver, and a contravention of the principles of free trade. I suppose I shall be told that in this city opposition to free trade is at present rather a merit than otherwise. I cannot enter into any general discussion of the question, but from a moral point of view I do not suppose there is one person in a thousand of those who advocate protection who does not profess to desire universal free trade. The strength of the opposition to free trade lies in the idea that other nations are doing their best to injure us, whilst we do nothing but heap coals of fire upon their heads without burning them; and the weakness of free trade lies in the exaggerated dogmatism of its supporters.

I shall try to say one word to lessen the opposition to free trade, and one word to strengthen the defence.

It seems to me that every impartial reader of the recent report of the Royal Commission who takes the trouble to weigh the evidence as a whole, must allow that the principal feature in the depression is the continuous fall in prices and the consequent loss of profit. Now, if this fall in prices is mainly due to currency causes, the natural remedy to apply is not protection but bi-metallism; and there can be no comparison, on moral, political, and economic grounds alike, of the superiority of the latter remedy. The essence of protection is selfishness; at the best it is retaliation,—the hopeless attempt to secure love and peace by a preliminary trial of hatred and war.

The old objection urged by Adam Smith, when he laid the foundations of the 'Wealth of Nations' in lectures in the University of Glasgow, is as true now as it was then. The adjustment of interests under a system of protection is a task which is too difficult for any council or senate whatever, and certainly for any Parliament with three mountains on its back.

On the other hand, international bi-metallism is one more step towards the federation of nations, one more advance in the path by which civilisation has progressed. Let protectionists remember that we were free-traders during the leaps and bounds of trade fourteen years ago, and let us see what the restoration of the old monetary position will do before we turn our backs on the teaching of Adam Smith and the work of Cobden and Peel, and try to re-establish the fiscal position which they destroyed.

And let our fervid friends, the dogmatic free-traders, who have in some cases converted free trade from a generous belief into a narrow superstition, refer for edification to the Authorised Version. They will find that freedom and liberty are not identical with anarchy and lawlessness; but that everything that increases the mutual dependence of nations is a guarantee for peace and an extension of the sphere of freedom of contract. A monetary convention of the simple character proposed would, under present conditions, do more to further real freedom of trade than the most adroit and unpleasant retaliation on foreign nations, or the closest practicable union of our colonies and dependencies in a nominal federation. Do not let us, through fear of protecting silver, encourage the gold-using nations to protect themselves against every export from silver-using countries, and, through a narrow observance of the letter, break the spirit of our orthodoxy.[1]

[1] It ought to be remembered that bi-metallism did not become a question of practical politics in this country until long after the battle of free trade had been fought. So far as I know, Cobden has given no opinion on the question, and even if he has done so it must have been under widely different conditions, since his death occurred in 1865. There is, however, ample evidence in his speeches and

writings that he did not regard international conventions as an infringement of the true liberty of nations, or as useless and unstable in their nature. When, for example, he was arguing in favour of reforms in maritime law, in the interest of neutrals in time of war, he said (Speeches, p. 459): "With the general spread of free-trade principles—by which I mean nothing but the principle of the division of labour carried over the whole world—one part of the earth must become more and more dependent upon another for the supply of its material and its food. Instead of, as formerly, one country sending its produce to another country, or one nation sending its raw material to another nation, we shall be in the way of having whole continents engaged in raising the raw material required for the manufacturing communities of another hemisphere. It is our interest to prevent, as far as possible, the sudden interruption of such a state of dependence." . . . The argument is, as stated above, in favour of certain international agreements as to contraband, but it applies equally well *mutatis mutandis* to an international monetary convention, and so also does the reply to objections with which he proceeds : "To what I am urging, it may be said, 'But you won't get people to observe their international obligations even if they are entered into.' That remark was made in the House of Commons by a Minister who, I think, ought not to have uttered such a prediction. Why are any international obligations undertaken unless they are to be observed ? We have this guarantee that the international rules I am now advocating will be respected, that they are not contemplated to be merely an article in a treaty between any two Powers, but to be fundamental laws regulating the intercourse of nations, and having the assent of the majority of, if not all, the maritime Powers in the world. Let us suppose two countries to be at war, and that one of them has entered into an engagement not to stop the exportation of grain. Well, we will assume the temptation to be so great that, thinking it can starve its opponent, it would wish to stop this exportation in spite of the treaty. Why, that would bring down on them instantly the animosity, indeed the hostility, of all the other Powers who were parties to the system. The nation which has been a party to a general system of international law, becomes an outlaw to all nations if it breaks its engagement towards any one." To this argument, as applied to a monetary convention, it need only be added that every nation has learned the value of keeping its word in financial more than in any other obligations.

STABILITY OF THE
FIXED RATIO BETWEEN GOLD AND SILVER
UNDER INTERNATIONAL BI-METALLISM.

SCOTSMAN, DECEMBER 7, 1886.

IT has often been asserted by bi-metallists that if a fixed ratio between gold and silver were adopted by an International Convention, it would be theoretically impossible, except under very exceptional circumstances, that the market rate should vary from the conventional rate, or that gold should to any large extent be demonetised. But, so far as I am aware, no attempt has been made to show in detail the practical application of the general argument to present circumstances. There is no doubt, however, that practical men to a great extent distrust theoretical reasonings, even when they appear of the most convincing kind: they have too lively a recollection of the failure of theories in their practical application

in many economic questions, to believe that on such
a mysterious subject as currency the theory is sure
to be right because it is expressed with emphasis and
a great appearance of wisdom.   What they know for
an undoubted fact is, that since 1874 silver has fluctuated in value, compared with gold, more than 30
per cent; and, besides this, they have a general distrust in the power of Governments to interfere with
market price of any kind.   Accordingly, they will
not believe that any Government can do any good
in the matter, and they refuse to admit that a union
of many Governments would be better than one—
probably, indeed, they think it would be worse—and
it is impossible to convince them by any theory of
compensatory action, and still less by any simile,
such as that a stool may stand on three or more legs,
though not on one.

The working out of the theory in actual figures is,
however, so startling in its results that it seems to me
opposition to bi-metallism on this ground must be
abandoned by all who take the trouble to follow out
the investigation.   The statistics in this paper, when
no special reference is made, are taken from Mr Palgrave's Appendix (B) to the Third Report of the
Royal Commission on Trade, and refer to 1884, the
last year given.[1]

The   estimated   stock   of   gold   in   money   and

---

[1] Mr Palgrave relies mainly on Soetboer.

hoarded in the civilised nations was, in 1884, about £654,000,000, and of silver, £437,000,000. The total production of gold for 1884 is estimated at about £19,500,000, and that of silver at less than £26,000,000.

The net consumption of gold in the arts and manufactures is 90,000 kilogrammes, equal (at £139, 10s. per kilogramme) in value to about £12,500,000 ; and the flow to the East (deducting imports thence) is, for the four years 1881-84, 120,000 kilogrammes —say, for 1884, 30,000 kilogrammes of the value of £4,000,000. Thus the total consumption of gold for other purposes than monetary is £16,500,000, which leaves £3,000,000 of new gold available for maintaining or increasing the coinage, or hoarding.

The net consumption of silver for the arts and manufactures is 515,000 kilogrammes, equivalent to (at £9 per kilogramme) about £4,500,000 ; whilst the net flow to the East is 1,603,000 kilogrammes, equivalent to about £14,500,000. Thus the total consumption of silver for non-monetary purposes is about £19,000,000, leaving a balance of about £7,000,000 for coinage purposes and hoarding.

These being the facts of the case, suppose that the civilised nations adopt bi-metallism at a ratio of 15½ to 1, which is the ratio on which in these figures the value of silver has been reckoned. The adoption of bi-metallism will involve free mintage of both metals to any extent, and un-limited legal tender of either metal at the option of the payer.

Assume, if it is possible, that the market ratio of gold and silver diverges from the conventional ratio, and observe what will happen. It must be premised, in the first place, that operations in bullion are con-ducted by special dealers at a small rate of profit per transaction, and that there is very keen competition. Under the assumption made of a possible divergence in the market rate, gold as bullion will exchange for more silver than gold coins will obtain of silver coins at the legal ratio. Accordingly, so long as the divergence exists, no gold will be taken to the mints, either new or old, and gold coins will be melted. It is, however, clear that these gold coins which are to be melted must be obtained by a substi-tution of silver coins for them, either in the banks or in the circulation. Where, then, are these silver coins to come from ? Plate is protected by being in a manufactured form, and it is quite opposed to the law of demand that, because silver is comparatively cheap, people should demand less of it for general purposes. Besides, how are the dealers in bullion to buy the plate ? There can, then, be no doubt that the silver which is to take the place of the gold coins must come from the new silver available for coinage. It may, perhaps, be thought it would come from

hoards.   But, apart from the fact that in the civilised
world hoarding is becoming less common, it is
quite clear that any one who hoarded would only
exchange his hoard of silver for a hoard of gold;
so that the deficiency in the gold coinage caused
by melting coins must be met by the new silver.
But, according to the present rates of consumption of silver in the civilised countries for non-
monetary purposes and for transmission to the East,
there are, at the present rate of production of silver,
only £7,000,000 available for monetary purposes.

Since, however, no new gold is sent to the mints,
owing to the assumed disturbance of the ratio, the
£3,000,000 of new gold formerly available for coinage must be replaced by silver, and this will reduce
the amount of new silver available for driving the
£654,000,000 of gold from circulation to the sum of
£4,000,000.

The question must also be regarded from the point
of view of gold.   The amount of gold available for
non-monetary purposes will now be increased by the
£3,000,000 of new gold formerly minted, and by the
£4,000,000 of coins driven out by the silver—that
is, by £7,000,000.   Thus there will be available for
the non-monetary purposes of the civilised nations
£23,500,000 of gold per annum in place of
£16,500,000; but such a sudden increase in the
demand for gold for non-monetary purposes is pal-

pably incredible, especially when we assume that a similar demand for silver is stationary.

Another step in the argument may now be taken. Suppose that, owing to the rise in its value (though, be it observed, we are assuming it is still to some extent depreciated), the use of silver for the arts is diminished, and also its use for exportation to the East; and suppose that in this way £20,000,000 is available for driving out gold. Then £20,000,000 of "driven-out" gold and £3,000,000 formerly used for coinage must be added to the £16,500,000 at present used for non-monetary purposes. But where in the world—in the East or the West—are the consumers of this amount of gold to be found ? Is it conceivable that, the range of prices remaining the same (for no absolute addition to the currency has been assumed), and the general distribution of wealth being unaffected—is it conceivable that 140 per cent more gold could be consumed ? Now, suppose that the amount of silver produced is largely increased owing to the nominal rise in its value; suppose it is more than doubled, and that £50,000,000 is available yearly for "driving out" gold, so much the more difficult will it be to find a non-monetary consumption for the gold. For so long as gold continues to be driven out, the silver will simply take its place in the currencies of the world, so that there will be no general rise in prices and no fall in the value of gold. Thus the supposition of any deviation from the fixed ratio on an international basis leads to glaring absurdities, and those who speak of international bi-metallism ending in silver mono-metallism cannot have realised the amount of the present stock of gold, and the limited extent of the demand for other than coinage purposes. They make absolutely contradictory suppositions, without any discoverable reason, concerning the production and concerning the demand for the two metals. They assume that, as regards production, gold will steadily diminish, and silver enormously increase; whilst, as regards consumption for non-monetary purposes, they assume that the use of gold will be enormously increased, whilst that of silver will remain stationary or decline. It is, of course, impossible to foretell the relative rates of production of the two metals, but it is quite certain that if, owing to excessive production, silver became of less than the ratio value, it would drive out gold, and this gold must be added to the stock available for non-monetary purposes. Accordingly, the more silver there is produced, the more gold (if the ratio is disturbed) will be turned from monetary to non-monetary purposes. But if the world suddenly becomes so rich, or distributes its wealth in such a manner that the demand for gold plate is doubled, trebled, or multiplied in proportion to the increased production of silver, can we suppose, with any show of consistency, that the demand for silver plate, in spite of silver being assumed to be relatively cheaper, will not increase equally? Can we suppose that the world and his wife will be in a position to demand an indefinitely larger quantity of gold ornaments, and yet that there will be no corresponding demand for silver? But the silver cannot be used both for the arts and for driving out gold.

It follows, if the foregoing reasoning is sound, that the stability of the fixed ratio, if generally adopted, could only be disturbed and lead· to silver mono-metallism under hypotheses which are opposed to all experience—namely, coincidently with an enormous increase in the production of silver there must be an effective demand to the same amount for the gold which is to be displaced for non-monetary purposes, and yet at the same time there must be no corresponding increase in the demand for silver for such purposes. Increased production of silver alone will not disturb the ratio; there must be an equally increased demand for gold, and no corresponding demand for silver, for non-monetary purposes.

What we ought reasonably to expect, if the rate of $15\frac{1}{2}$ to 1 were adopted, is something very commonplace and unromantic in comparison with these wild hypotheses. (1) The production of silver would be to some extent increased. But since silver is at present produced at very different rates of cost, the increase would only be effected by opening or re-opening less fertile mines or working more difficult veins. (2) Any silver not required for the arts or for the East would be added to the coinage of the civilised nations. (3) There would be just as much gold used as before, unless the demand for the arts and the East increased so much as to absorb more than the annual production. In this case, the deficiency must be made up from the existing coinages ; but if any such increase in the non-monetary demand for gold is probable, the sooner gold-using countries make use of silver as standard money, the better for their commerce. The mere adoption of universal bi-metallism would not cause such an increase in the demand for gold for the arts, which can only arise from the growth of wealth and population, or some change in the distribution of wealth that would increase the relative power of gold consumers. It is, however, possible that the more equal diffusion of wealth will cause a greater relative demand for silver, and at any rate there must be an increased demand for silver to some extent. There is, again, no reason why the adoption of bi-metallism should increase the flow of gold to the East, or diminish the flow of silver. The East requires silver for coinage, and imports gold as a luxury ; and so long as this is the case, the value of the former is likely to exceed greatly that of the latter. At any rate, taking the facts of the case as they are at present, any disturbance of the ratio once generally adopted, and any extensive substitution of silver for gold as coinage, are plainly impossible. In former times it was simply the want of agreement between the nations which rendered it possible for dealers in bullion to make a profit by altering the local distribution of the metals ; and it should never be forgotten that, whilst in the sixteenth century the production of the precious metals was at the commencement about 2 of gold to 1 of silver, and became at the end more than 3 of silver to 1 of gold, the ratio only moved from 11 to 1 to 12 to 1 ; and in the nineteenth century, whilst the production of silver to gold was at the beginning about 3 to 1, and in 1860 about 1 to 3, the ratio was practically stable, and continued stable until the *de facto* agreement of the Governments was broken.

THE MEASUREMENT OF VARIATIONS IN THE VALUE OF THE MONETARY STANDARD.

READ BEFORE THE ROYAL SOCIETY OF EDINBURGH, MARCH 21, 1887.[1]

IT may seem at first sight almost contradictory to speak of variations in the value of the monetary standard. How, it may be asked, can the standard, which is the measure of values, itself vary in value? At present in this country the sovereign is apparently the standard measure of value, just as the yard is the standard measure of length, and it would certainly seem odd to most people to speak even hypothetically of variations in the measuring power of the standard yard. It may be useful for purposes of comparison and contrast to quote the definitions of the standard yard and of the sovereign or pound sterling. By Act of Parliament, 30th July 1855, it was enacted, "That

[1] Published in the Journal of the London Statistical Society, March 1887.

the straight line or distance between the centres of
the transverse lines in the two gold plugs in the
bronze bar deposited in the office of the Exchequer
shall be the genuine standard yard at 62° F., and if
lost shall be replaced by means of its copies." According to the Coinage Act, renewed in 1870, "the
sovereign is defined as consisting of 123·27447 grains
of English standard gold, composed of eleven parts of
fine gold and one part of alloy, chiefly copper."

When we compare the two definitions, we see that
whilst the former refers definitely to the distance between two points or to length, the latter refers only
to the weight of a particular substance, and says
nothing of value.

In the definition of a standard yard, a definite place
and a definite temperature are mentioned (and other
precautions are implied), which render the standard
for practical purposes invariable. In the definition
of the sovereign, also, similarly precise elements are
found, but they refer only to weight and chemical
composition, not to value. Strictly speaking, then, it
is only by accident that the sovereign can ever be a
standard of value at different times and places in the
same way as the yard is the standard of length. "At
the same time and place," says Adam Smith, "money
is the exact measure of the real exchangeable value
of all commodities. It is so, however, at the same
time and place only."

I will try to show how a standard yard might be constructed which would correspond logically to the sovereign as the standard unit of value, and under what conditions the sovereign would really correspond to the standard yard actually adopted. There are, of course, an infinite number of ways in which a thoroughly bad standard may be chosen. The one I have chosen is this: a standard yard might be defined as the length of a shilling's worth of standard mercury enclosed in a standard tube placed on a standard sun-dial in every market-place at noon-day by Greenwich time. Now in the standard yard as thus defined, there would be no dispute as to the meaning of the term at any given time and place, at least in any market at noon-day. Any merchant who had agreed to sell a yard of cloth need only repair to the market-place at noon-day to find out how much or how little he must cut off the roll. The contract would be capable of a certain interpretation. If standard mercury were cheap, and the sun hot, the buyer would gain and the seller would lose, if the contract had been made beforehand. At the same moment, and in the same market, however, all traders in all kinds of goods sold by the yard would be able to conduct their business in a perfectly accurate manner.

This will perhaps seem an extreme illustration of the nature of the standard unit of value, and I admit that in degree the sovereign is not quite so bad as

the standard yard I have just described, if the standard tube were a very sensitive thermometer and the
price of mercury were very variable.   But in one
celebrated case in history this illustration, even in its
most exaggerated form, would have been really in-
adequate.   The *assignats* issued by the Government
in the great French Revolution in about four years
sunk to $\frac{1}{30,000}$th part of their nominal value.   The
assignat was, it is true, an inconvertible note, but it
was for a time the standard unit of value, and in
different times and places the value was much more
uncertain than the length of a standard yard of the
kind just described.   We could, however, easily
imagine a standard yard of this kind being quite
stable under certain conditions.   Suppose, for example, that the price of mercury were fixed by law,
the climate of the country uniform, and the tube of
a particular kind, it would be possible for the new
standard yard to be as accurate as the old.

Under certain conditions, also, the sovereign might
be as good a measure of value as at present our
standard yard is of length.   Such, for example, would
be the case if prices, whether by law, or custom, or
accident, were always the same.   If the price of
everything bought and sold were fixed, the sovereign,
as defined by the Coinage Act, would be a perfect
measure of value, but with every movement in prices
the purchasing power of the sovereign varies—that is

to say, so far the sovereign fails in its primary function as a standard measure of value. It is not a standard in the same sense as the other standards of the country. The use of a standard of value, as distinct from a mere medium of exchange, is to measure values at different times and places, and it is only so far as the sovereign of specified weight and fineness happens to preserve the same purchasing power that it can be considered even sufficiently accurate for practical purposes. The difference between the standard of value and other standards is shown in the case of an agricultural lease. Acres, bushels, tons, have a precise meaning as regards extension, capacity, and weight, but the pound sterling has no precise meaning as regards value. So many pounds' weight of ten thousand different articles of a certain quality would, so long as the Act defining the pound weight remains in force, mean precisely the same thing, a definite amount of commodities; but so many pounds' worth of ten thousand articles would, in all probability, vary in meaning every day, although the Act defining the pound sterling were observed most religiously.

Against some kinds of uncertainty in the interpretation of contracts, the legal definition of the sovereign is ample guarantee. Illogical as it may seem, as now defined, the sovereign as a standard of value would be much worse if, according to the needs of a tyrannical

Government, its weight and fineness were constantly changing.

A contract for a certain amount of standard gold is certainly to be preferred to a contract for an uncertain amount, and after repeated warnings from history, civilised nations have recognised the foolishness of making petty gains by debasing their standard.

Still, a certain weight of standard gold is a very different thing from a certain amount of purchasing power ; and the inquiry into the variations in the value of the monetary standard is probably by far the most important problem or group of problems in the wide field of economic science. For, in other words, such an inquiry is an attempt to give precision to the vague expression, general movements in prices. A general movement in prices is, however, the resultant of a number of particular movements ; and in these particular movements, again, we find the proximate causes of the distribution of the industrial forces of the world, and of the wealth which these forces create. " Every science," [1] says Clerk - Maxwell, " has some instrument of precision which may be taken as the material type of that science which it has advanced, by enabling observers to express their results as measured quantities. In astronomy we have the divided circle, in chemistry the balance, in heat the thermometer ; while the whole system of

[1] 'Theory of Heat,' p. 75.

civilised life may be fitly symbolised by a foot-rule, a set of weights, and clock." To these symbols of civilised life I would add a piece of standard money ; and in illustration of the general observation, I would point out that the principal quantities with which the economist has to deal are prices.

In discussing variations in the value of the monetary standard, two kinds of inquiries of a very different nature are usually blended together, which it would be much better to keep distinct. In the *first* place, we have a purely statistical problem—namely, the observation and classification of prices, and the measurement of the rise or fall observed in particular groups, in combinations of these groups, and, finally, in the whole mass of exchangeable commodities. Further, the record of prices may refer to different places at the same time—a comparison may be made between different industrial areas in the same nation, or between different nations.

But there is a *second* kind of inquiry implied in the general expression, which is still more difficult and complex. The primary object of all scientific classification is the discovery of causes ; and, even for practical purposes, the mere observation of variations, without any further inquiry into the causes, would be incomplete. It is only when the causes have been estimated that any idea can be formed as to whether the variations are likely to be temporary or prolonged, or whether, by any action of Government or individuals, they may be reversed or modified.

There ought to be no difficulty in seeing that these two inquiries are quite distinct, and that it is one thing to measure variations in the purchasing power of the sovereign, and quite another to give a scientific explanation of the variations.

I propose, then, for the present to postpone altogether the second inquiry as to the causes of variations in the value of the monetary standard, and to discuss in the first place the methods by which such variations may be measured. The principal difficulty arises from the fact that relative prices vary, whether we consider times or places. Between two dates, for example, bread may fall, and meat may rise—or, taking a wider illustration, all kinds of manufactures may fall, whilst all kinds of agricultural produce rise in price; and similar differences may be observed when comparing different industrial areas. Even if there is a rise or a fall in every particular commodity, or a variation in the same direction, still there is almost certain to be a difference in the degree of the rise or fall in different articles. Take, for example, the comparatively simple case of the purchasing power of the nominal or money wages of unskilled labour. Suppose that, in comparing two points of time, it is found that every other article of the labourer's usual consumption has fallen in price, but that bread has

U

risen. If the rule of one commodity one vote is adopted, the result would be that the purchasing power of wages had risen, whilst in reality the labourer was compelled greatly to curtail his consumption. A similar difficulty arises when comparing the purchasing power of wages at different places.

It would be easy to give a number of particular examples of temporary and local variations in the value of the standard. The same nominal rent for land may mean at different times very different things, both to the landlord who receives and to the farmer who pays, and the purchasing power of the sovereign compared with various groups of articles in London and in the rural districts would vary very much. It would be easy both as regards rent and wages to construct a better standard than is given by the pound sterling, and practically such standards have been resorted to in produce rents and sliding-scale wages.

But it is important to observe that in every one of these cases we should assume that the particular movements in prices between different times are caused partly by special causes—*e.g.*, improved processes of production, &c.—and partly by causes of a general and wide-reaching character. In other words, every particular price depends partly on the relative value of the commodity compared with others, and partly on the relative value of money compared with things in

general. In some cases this distinction is quite obvious, as for instance when there is a sudden and
general rise in prices owing to large issues of inconvertible paper. But usually the cause of any general
change may for a long time remain unobserved.
Often the change is gradual, and can only be detected
after a long interval, and in any case it does not
affect all commodities simultaneously in the same degree—that is to say, a disturbance of relative values
is caused by the process of a readjustment. The
object of the present paper is to show how any
general change between two points may be measured,
it being assumed that such general changes are possible. I say nothing for the present either of the
causes or the consequences of such variations. The
present inquiry is simply a problem in the method of
statistics, with a few examples which must be considered rather as illustrations than deductions.

In the first place, what are we to understand by
the purchasing power of the standard over things in
general ?

At any date taken as the basis of comparison, the
aggregate of purchasable commodities in the widest
sense in any country may be expressed thus:—
$£_1 w_1 = (q_1 \cdot p_1 + q_2 \cdot p_2 \ldots + q_n \cdot p_n)$, where q represents the total quantity of any item in the national
inventory and p the price per unit. Strictly speaking, every item should be stated separately which,

through quality or locality, has a special price, and
the series would be practically infinite. Suppose, for
example, that in 1870 the total mass of purchasable
"things" was £8,000,000,000, then the purchasing
pound of the pound sterling would be strictly
$\frac{1}{8,000,000,000}$ part of each item (q_1, q_2, &c.) in the series.

Such a conception of purchasing power, or of the
value of money, would be of no practical use except
for clearing up the obscure phrase, "the value of
money in terms of things in general." The series,
however, might be simplified (1) by various devices
of grouping. Thus, instead of various prices of land
of all qualities, and in all situations, we may take
only a few classes, and finally only two—agricultural
and building. So again of houses, we may take a few
classes, or even group all together. By proceeding in
this process, we might reduce the series to a limited
number of terms. (2) This number might be further
diminished by neglecting all below a certain value, and
the idea formed of the purchasing power of the standard would be adequate, according to the proportion
of the total rejected to the aggregate. In proportion,
however, as the series was simplified and abbreviated,
the conception of purchasing power would become
illusory, for it would lead to something of this kind :
the purchasing power of the sovereign would be represented as $\frac{1}{8,000,000,000}$ part of the land of the country,
of the houses, of the furniture, of the railways, and of

the services of labour; or dividing out the quantities, we should say that a sovereign would purchase $\frac{1}{100}$th part of an acre of cultivated ground, plus $\frac{1}{1000}$th part of a house, plus $\frac{1}{1000}$th part of the furniture of a house and the labour of a British working man for a quarter of an hour. Thus the whole meaning of the expression has been squeezed out in the process of condensation.

But although the unit of purchasing power has been thus reduced to an imaginary or impossible quantity, it is quite possible, as in many mathematical problems, that it may for some purposes be used and not appear in the final result. Such might be the case if we measure the appreciation or depreciation of the standard or the change in its purchasing power between two points of time.

The national inventory at the second date would consist of the old inventory, plus or minus any difference in the old items and plus the new items. This might be expressed symbolically by saying that $£_2w_2 = £_2w_1 + d\ (£_2w_1) + £_2N$. Now if there has been only a relatively small addition to the national wealth, either by an increase in the old or an addition of new elements—if, for example, the population has remained nearly stationary, no great changes in the production of wealth have occurred, or in its distribution, or in the material wants of the community—then the two last terms may be neglected, and the change in the purchasing power of the £ is equal to the fraction $\dfrac{w_1}{w_2}$.

I propose to call this fraction the coefficient of appreciation.

Thus, if the total value of the old inventory at the new prices be doubled, that means that the purchasing power of the £ is one-half of what it was.

The simplest case would occur when the two last terms vanish, and the movement in prices has been perfectly uniform, for then $\dfrac{w_1}{w_2}$ would measure exactly the change in purchasing power.   Such a case would occur theoretically on excessive issues of inconvertible paper as soon as equilibrium is restored.

In the series given, in every case p has become $n\,p$.

Again, if the increase in the quantities of the national wealth has been uniform, and relative prices have remained the same, q in every case becoming $m\,q$, and p in every case $n\,p$, then, $£_2 w_2 = £_2 \,.\, w_1 \,.\, m\ n$, and $n = \dfrac{w_2}{w_1 \,.\, m}$, and the new purchasing power of the standard is $\dfrac{w_1}{w_2} \,.\, m$ of the old; that is, $\dfrac{w_1}{w_2} \,.\, m$ is the coefficient of appreciation.

The case might, however, be reduced to the former under the conditions assumed, for the purchasing power of the standard will obviously be the same for

the old inventory, and for every uniform addition to
it.   Thus the change in the standard may be measured by the old inventory at the old prices, divided
by the old inventory at the new prices.

Suppose in any interval the nominal wealth of the
country has increased : this may be due either to an
increase in quantities or to a rise in nominal prices
(or depreciation of the standard), or to both causes.
Now if the increase in both q's and p's has been uniform, the change due to the standard may be found,
and the change in quantity deduced.   We first find
n and then m.

It may be objected that if we assume relative
prices remain the same, we might calculate the
change in the standard by the change in the price of
any single article.   The objection is quite valid, but
it does not destroy the value of the method proposed.
For the use of the method is as the basis of an
approximate calculation.   As a matter of fact, relative
prices are constantly changing, by peculiar changes
affecting the demand and supply of particular commodities.   No one would dream of saying : the price of
potatoes has fallen one-half, and therefore all prices
have fallen one-half ; and similarly of every particular
commodity.

Next, suppose then that the old inventory has
remained the same as regards items and their quantities, but that relative prices have changed.   The

purchasing power of the unit at the first date would, as was shown, consist strictly of an nth part of every item where $n =$ the quantity of the national wealth measured by the standard. Similarly of the second date. If relative prices have changed, the two series cannot·be compared, but the sum totals of the series may; and the only meaning of change in the purchasing power of the unit is (quantities remaining the same) $\dfrac{w_1}{w_2}$, when w_1 is the total at old prices, and w_2 the total at the new.

But hitherto it has been assumed either that the national inventory remained the same, or else that the articles increased uniformly; but relative quantities change no less than relative prices, and in fact both changes are constantly going on. As a rule, *e.g.*, a fall in relative prices due to the improvements in manufactures leads to increased production, and a fall due to the lessened demand leads to a decrease in production, and *vice versâ*. There are, besides, changes due to a variety of special causes.

In this case the only plan seems to be, in the first place, to estimate generally the change in quantity. This can only be done strictly by reducing to some common measure, and that measure must be the standard of value. Let the total value of the new inventory (consisting of different quantities of the old items), reckoned at the old prices, be v_1, and the total value of the old inventory, also at old prices, be w_1,

then $\dfrac{v_1}{w_1}$ is the measure of the increase in the quantity

of wealth, or the m of the formula for appreciation.

But if the quantities had increased uniformly m,

then, as was shown above, $\dfrac{w_1}{w_2} \cdot m$ would give the

measure of the new purchasing power compared with

the old. Substituting for m its value $\dfrac{v_1}{w_1}$, the expres-

sion becomes $\dfrac{v_1}{w_2}$. That is to say, the change in the

purchasing power of the standard is found by dividing the value of the new inventory at the old prices
by its value at the new.

Only one other difficulty remains. It may happen
—and in progressive societies is sure to happen—
that at the second date the national inventory consists partly of new articles, and partly of different
qualities of old articles. In this case we cannot
adopt the method last described, so far as these
articles are concerned, for the old prices of undis-
covered articles cannot be obtained directly.

Let N be the total value of this part. We may
then either neglect it, and obtain the coefficient of
appreciation by considering only that part of the
new inventory for which corresponding prices may be
obtained; or the only other resource seems to be to

estimate the prices which would probably have been obtained at the former date, if the articles had been in existence.

If N is left out of consideration, and is small in amount, relatively, the coefficient thus obtained will be approximately correct. If, however, N is relatively too large to be neglected, the coefficient obtained by neglecting it will only be correct on the assumption that the articles considered are fairly representative of the whole group N included.

If the interval between the two dates is small, N will also be small; but if it is very great, and the society progressive, N will be relatively very large. N might be neglected comparing 1880 with 1881; and probably, comparing 1830 with 1880, N, though large, might be considered as represented by the other articles.

But if we compare 1880 with 1280, N would be very large, and that part of the modern national inventory which corresponds to the mediæval would not (it may be thought *primâ facie*) fairly represent the whole.

Nor does the second plan suggested—viz., that of probable estimated cost of N at the earlier period—seem even theoretically possible, when we consider the different methods of production, the cost of raw material, &c. It may however be pointed out that if between very remote periods the coefficient of appreciation cannot be found, the fact is not of much consequence, for in general, at very long intervals we only wish to compare the purchasing powers of particular kinds of income, so as to discover the relative material prosperity of various classes.

Before passing on to consider the practical uses of the formula in a simplified form, it may be convenient to re-state the general principles involved in this method of coefficients. The leading idea is this: Between any two points of time a change occurs in the aggregate value of the national wealth. This change will be due either to an increase or decrease in quantity, or to an increase or decrease in nominal value in the general level of prices—*i.e.*, the appreciation or depreciation of the standard—or to a combination of both causes. Now if we can find the increase in quantity, we can deduce the change in value. The theoretical method gives a plan by which, with sufficient statistics, the change in quantity might be computed with comparative precision. At present, however, even as regards the present century, and even in the last twenty years, sufficient statistics are not forthcoming for the application of the formula in the strict sense. It may be of use, however, as the basis of a practical method of approximation, and as leading to qualifications in the use of existing methods.

Such a method is given by taking $\frac{w_1}{w_2} . m$ as the formula, when $w_1 =$ the aggregate wealth at the first date, and w_2 at the second, whilst m is the increase in quantity, m being estimated from various independent considerations. For example, other things remaining the same, m should be proportioned to the increase in the population and to the increase in the efficiency of the labour and capital. It will be observed that we assume in this formula that N may be considered as fairly represented by the average of the articles in the old inventory: taking this method, I have worked out roughly some examples.

From calculations made in Porter's 'Progress of the Nation,' the total personal property of Great Britain was in 1821 about £1,400,000,000. In 1841 the total had risen to £2,000,000,000; thus $\frac{w_1}{w_2} = \frac{1400}{2000} = \frac{7}{10}$. Now to find m, the increase in quantity, we observe first that population increased from 14·3 to 18·7. The period also was marked by great improvements in the efficiency of labour and capital. Even in agriculture, the productive capacity of the soil had been nearly doubled, with a very small increase in the rural population. Porter calculates that 10,000 acres, cultivated as in 1801, supported 3800 as against 6000 in 1841, whilst 32 acres had been reclaimed for every 100 of population. But if in agriculture the productive power of the country was not quite doubled, there can be little doubt that with very moderate estimates in other industries it was more than doubled. This was certainly the case in the manufactures of cotton, wool, silk, linen, paper, and soap; and it is instructive to note that the tonnage of shipping, and the number of bricks and of carriages, was doubled. I think, then, we may safely say that the productive power of the nation had at any rate doubled during the period. Thus m would become, by considering population and efficiency,

$$2 \cdot \frac{18 \cdot 7}{14 \cdot 3} = \text{about } \frac{19}{7}.$$

But $\dfrac{w_1}{w_2} = \dfrac{7}{10} \therefore \dfrac{w_1}{w_2} \cdot m = \dfrac{19}{7} \cdot \dfrac{7}{10} = \dfrac{19}{10}.$

That is to say, the purchasing power of the sovereign in the period had nearly doubled, or general prices had fallen nearly 50 per cent. Roughly speaking, the personal property of the country had increased in quantity nearly three times, but in value only one and a half times.

I have been able to make the calculation only in a rough manner, but I have not exaggerated the items taken; and from other circumstances—*e.g.*, durability of many portions—we might suppose that the quantity of wealth had increased more than three times, and thus prices have fallen more than 50 per cent. I have taken only personal property, so as to use Porter's figures, but I may mention that taking also real property into account, by another calculation there is very little difference.

I have made several more calculations on the same plan, and the general result is always the same—namely, that since the end of last century down to 1850 there was a great appreciation of gold, the purchasing power of the sovereign having almost doubled even between 1821-41.

Even between 1848 and 1868—the period during which the great gold-discoveries took place, and are supposed generally to have depreciated gold to a great extent — I find that the purchasing power of the sovereign (calculated by this method) rose probably a little, and that in fact, instead of depreciation, there was on the whole appreciation.   In this calculation I have used the figures which Mr Giffen [1] adopted for his calculation by quite a different method.   The income of England assessed to income-tax at the two dates was about £230,000,000 in 1848, and £365,000,000 in 1868.

We may assume with Mr Giffen that $\frac{w_1}{.w_2}$ was also in this proportion.   Now, in finding m or the increase in quantity, we have Mr Giffen's assertion that "the population is one-quarter more numerous, and, man for man, their industry is nearly twice as productive."

If we take m as 2, we get appreciation in the proportion of 6 : 5.

[1] 'Essays on Finance,' First Series, p. 95.

In this case—

$$\frac{w_1}{w_1} = \frac{230}{365} = \frac{46}{73} = \text{roughly } \frac{3}{5}.$$

So that if we assume that $m = \frac{5}{3}$, or that the quantity of wealth was increased in the proportion of 3 to 5, there would have been neither appreciation nor depreciation.

If, again, we assume that the quantity of wealth had increased simply in proportion to the population, we should have $m = \frac{5}{4}$, and thus the coefficient of appreciation would become $\frac{3}{4}$. Thus, at the outside, the utmost depreciation of the standard by this method is 25 per cent. But when we look into the history of the times between 1848-68, we find it was a period of enormous production. The new supplies of gold in the way described by Tooke gave a tremendous stimulus to labour, and this country, more than any other, felt the effect of the stimulus. For example, between 1848 and 1858 only, the mileage of railways was doubled, the value of the exports trebled, and the tonnage of shipping increased 35 per cent. Now if we assume that the wealth per head of the community had increased in this twenty years only by 20 per cent, then by 1868 the effects of the new gold had been neutralised, and the standard had regained its former purchasing power. I am inclined to think, however, having regard to the enormous increase in the activity of production, that an actual appreciation had occurred.

It is this calculation which will probably create most surprise or doubt, as the general belief is, that the effects of the gold discoveries were much greater, and lasted much longer, and by the method of index numbers (Jevons) there seems to be a depreciation of from 26 to 30 per cent at least.

I propose, then, to make some remarks on this matter, using a more recent illustration. The most elaborate calculation recently made in this method is that by Mr Sauerbeck, formed on a list of forty-five articles of the kind mentioned, including all important food-products, minerals, raw materials of manufactures, and a number of other articles, such as hides, leather, petroleum, and timber. Now the total value of all these articles (and a certain proportion was re-exported) was on the average 1872-74, £577,000,000, and in 1883-85, £482,000,000.

Using the formula $\dfrac{w_1}{w_2} \cdot m$, we obtain m from figures quoted by him as $\dfrac{617}{525}$ (that is, for the articles in question).

Thus, $\dfrac{w_1}{w_2} \cdot m = \dfrac{617}{525} \cdot \dfrac{577}{482} =$ about $1\cdot37$ as the co-efficient of appreciation, or a fall in prices in the proportion of $137 : 100$, or a fall of about 26 per cent.

Now, when we turn to the national inventory, we find that in 1875 it was calculated by Mr Giffen as· £8,500,000,000,—land being reckoned at about £2,000,000,000, houses at about £1,400,000,000, and movable property not yielding income (furniture, &c.) at £700,000,000; these three items alone being about seven times the value of the articles used for the index numbers, which contribute about one-fifteenth only of the grand total. It must be observed, also, that Mr Giffen's calculation is only of capital, and would thus exclude, apparently, all commodities consumed within the year. This leads me to observe that one of the most important consumable commodities is the labour of the country, the amount annually spent on manual labour being reckoned at £620,000,000, and on professional labour £180,000,000. How much of this should be reckoned I shall consider later.

Now, as regards the index numbers, it is evident at once from the figures quoted that, as regards bulk, the amount is not sufficient, and therefore the measure obtained in this way can only be justified by assuming that the movement in other commodities will be fairly represented by that in raw materials.

But on analysing the causes of difference in relative values, this assumed representative character of raw materials does not seem reasonable, whether we take long periods or short intervals. Take for example the

x

rent of agricultural land and the price of agricultural produce. It is easy to show that if the yield remains the same, and there is a fall in prices, but a less fall in the expenses of working, then rent will fall more than in proportion to the fall in prices.

Then, again, as regards houses. We must dis tinguish between the building-rent and the ground-rent. Over any considerable period the rise in ground-rents in large cities has been relatively the greatest of any commodity. So far as the cost of building, however, is concerned, the movement of prices in the rate of building-rents might easily be in the opposite direction, and any change in the cost of building indirectly affects old buildings. If houses can be built cheaply, people cannot let old houses at their former rents.

It is, however, principally in articles in which machinery has taken the place of manual labour that the movement in raw material fails to be a correct measure of the fall in prices. Any economy in labour, any more effective combination or division of labour, acts in the same way as machinery. Speaking generally, over a long period the cost of production of raw materials admits of much less diminution reckoned in labour than is the case with other commodities.

This leads me to notice in passing that it is this improvement in the efficiency of labour which makes it impossible to take labour as the unit of measuring value.

If all articles were produced by unskilled labour, paid at uniform rates, then changes in these rates would be the best possible measure of change in purchasing power. Roughly speaking, if money wages doubled all prices would be doubled, and the standard would have half the purchasing power. But if the efficiency of labour has doubled, money wages might be doubled and prices remain the same. If we could allow for efficiency so as to make a quotation for wages for work done, wages would be the best possible measure of a very large group.

Now in any very short period it may be said there can be no great change in the efficiency of labour, and consequently if the hours remain the same, the average rate of wages would be a good practical measure for short periods. Between 1850 and 1856 Tooke calculated that there was a rise in the average of wages of 15 to 20 per cent in unskilled labour: the rise was in many cases 40 per cent.

But even in such a short period we find that, as regards cotton goods, the raw material was about the same, and the price of the cheaper forms of cloth the same, whilst the better cloth had fallen in price 25 per cent. Thus the rise in wages in this industry of 20 per cent must have been accompanied by more than that increase in efficiency. Still, if the rise in average wages was, as computed, 20 per cent in six years, we may assume that at first there was a depreciation of gold to about that extent.

But fascinating as this method of calculation seems at first sight, through its apparent simplicity, it is really practically of very little value. There are thousands of rates of wages for various kinds of work, and the efficiency of labour and capital is constantly changing, and the average of the change can only be roughly measured.

I give, however, one other example. Mr Giffen calculates that in fifty years the wages of skilled labourers have risen 50 per cent: in a previous calculation he supposed that between 1848 and 1868 the efficiency of labour in general was doubled, so that it does not seem unreasonable to say that in fifty years skilled labour became three times as efficient. If this is allowed, then the commodities produced by skilled labour must, on the average, have fallen at least one-half in price (for profits have also fallen). On the whole, however, it seems best to consider wages only in so far as paid for services rendered, and not to count them in the national inventory when the result of the labour appears in a material form. We should then only include the value of the wages of domestic servants and of various professional people who produce nothing material—e. g., doctors and lawyers.

This examination, however, of the rate of wages,

shows clearly enough the insufficiency of the index numbers founded on raw materials as a measure of appreciation. In the first place, the improvement in efficiency of labour has been much more marked over any considerable period in other industries than in the extractive and agricultural group. Skilled labour obtains higher nominal wages reckoned in time, but produces more cheaply. The rise in skilled labour, however, has raised proportionately the wages of un-skilled labour, in which the increase in efficiency has not been so great. Thus agricultural labour in this country costs more, and therefore the fall in produce due to foreign sources of supply has a still greater effect on the rent and the price of agricultural land.

In the same way, the relative cost in the other extractive industries has risen. Again, in America and our colonies, and in all countries in which there is a considerable element of skilled labour, the cost of unskilled labour compared with skilled, regard being paid to efficiency, has increased, and thus the relative cost of raw materials has risen. This rise will be greater still if it is assumed that in all fully peopled countries the stage of diminishing return has been reached, owing to the necessity of resorting to inferior sources of supply, and more costly methods of production and extraction. Eventually, at any rate, the tendency to a relative increase in the cost of raw material on this ground must also operate to make raw materials a still less accurate measure.

At the same time it must be allowed that at any particular time, owing to great improvements in communication, and the opening up of new countries, some kinds of food products may fall more rapidly than manufactures, in which case the fall, if general, would be less than the usual index number; and if the value of the raw material compared with the labour in manufactures is small, manufactures may fall less rapidly than the raw material (*e.g.*, fine lace).

The general method which I have described cannot at present be used with any degree of accuracy, owing to the want of statistics.   In the Unted States, when the census is taken, a careful estimate is made of the national wealth.

If the authorities were to calculate the value of the old items at the new figures, then a good approximation might be made to the general coefficient of appreciation.   It would, however, be a much more simple task in this country, where the conditions of industry are not subject to such violent changes.   As it is, all estimates of the national wealth, even for nominal value, rest on the income-tax returns, and for quantities we must resort to still vaguer measures.

Even, however, when used in this very rough manner, some very useful qualifications of the method of index numbers may be obtained.

Speaking generally, I should be inclined to say that over a long period—say, more than twenty years —the index numbers based on raw materials are likely to give too low a measure of appreciation. That is to say, if we were to take the purchasing power of the standard as regards things in general, we should find it greater than as regards raw materials. But, on the other hand, in any short period,—and the shorter it is, the more the tendency is marked,—the index numbers may make the appreciation appear greater than it is when the wider basis is taken. This is nearly equivalent to saying that raw materials, and the like, feel appreciation much more quickly than the derivative products.

If, for example, we compare 1875 with 1885, the 'Economist' index numbers give a fall of about 30 per cent, or the purchasing power of the sovereign has risen very steadily until £100 will purchase as much as £130 before.

Now, by the method of coefficients, taking the gross returns of all kinds of property and profits assessed to income-tax, and allowing for increase of population, we have (Sauerbeck) a nominal income of £17·5 in 1875 as against £17·9 in 1885 per head of population. This, it may be remarked, is an increase of 2·3 per cent, compared with an increase of 32·6 per cent in the former decade.

This great fall in the rate of increment of itself

would point to an appreciation of the standard in the second period, and this is confirmed when we endeavour to estimate m in the formula or the increase in quantities.

We find that the production and imports into the United Kingdom of all the great staples in Mr Sauerbeck's list has increased by 535 to 617, or nearly 18 per cent, and the tonnage of steamers has become doubled.

The fact that the rental of houses has increased more than 30 per cent, whilst population has only increased 11 per cent, would point to the conclusion that a great amount of building must have taken place, and that the quantity of house accommodation, regard being paid to the size and convenience of the houses, must have largely increased.

It is said the returns for the second date were taken much more strictly; but the general conclusion, after making all allowances, is that on the wide basis of national wealth the appreciation cannot at present be so great as indicated by the index numbers. Since 1880 the gross rental of lands in the United Kingdom has fallen about 5 per cent; but from 1875 the fall is only 3 per cent. In Scotland, where leases prevail, the figures are nearly the same; and in Ireland, the land of no rent, there is actually a slight increase during the last ten years. These figures show not merely the danger of trusting too much to the income-tax returns, but they show also that the gross rental of land, and thus the value of land, responds slowly to the general movements of prices. The same is probably true of houses, for unless there has been a very great change in the quality of houses, it would seem that house-rent, like land-rent, has not felt the appreciation so quickly as raw materials,—in fact, it has done so less quickly than land.

Then again, as regards Schedule D, it seems highly probable that the absolute decrease between 1876 and 1880 was due to a fall in the profits of producers owing to the fall in prices of commodities, and that the rise which has taken place since is mainly due to the increased profits of the middle-man, who is a very imperfect conductor of the fall in wholesale prices. If this view is correct, we again find that the actual appreciation, or general fall in prices, is much less than indicated by the index numbers. This view is confirmed by the slight fall in money wages.

If, however, it is true that over a long period the true appreciation is more than that marked by the index numbers, we must expect the nominal value to consumers of lands, houses, and commodities to fall much more, and although the official returns as yet hardly give evidence of this, there are abundant signs of the fall being in progress. The disturbance caused by the readjustment of rents is in full operation, the payment of the same nominal wages to the higher class of domestics is only possible by restricted employment, and any attempt at readjustment in other employments is resisted to the utmost.

The inquiry in the present paper is however purely statistical, and in the main an inquiry on the theoretical side. The only assumption made is that the price of every saleable commodity, and the prices of larger and larger groups, are the resultant of two sets of causes—one special and the other general: the wider the range and the more diversified the prices chosen, so much more do the special causes tend to neutralise one another, and to lay bare the influence of the general causes. If all kinds of raw material and simple products show a downward movement on the whole, we may presume that this is due to some very general causes; but such causes may be, although general, such as affect this large group of commodities principally. If, however, the downward movement is found in the mass of the wealth of a great country, we must go further in search of causes; and if the same tendency is observed over all countries using the same standard, still more general causes must be sought for. We can no more discover these general causes by analysing the movements of particular prices, than we can discover the velocity of the earth in its orbit by analysing the movements of the creatures upon it.   In comparing relative velocities on the earth's surface, we assume that surface to be at rest; and in analysing any number of particular prices and their relative movements, we always assume that the value of the standard remains the same.

I hope to discuss at a future time the causes and consequences of these changes in the value of the standard.

CAUSES OF MOVEMENTS IN GENERAL PRICES.

*READ BEFORE THE ROYAL SOCIETY OF
EDINBURGH, JANUARY 30, 1888.*

IT was shown in the preceding paper that if we take the total mass of purchasable commodities in any country, and allow for variations in quantity, the nominal monetary value will not vary exactly with the quantity of those commodities at different times, —in other words, that the monetary unit will at different times purchase more or less, on the whole, of all things that bear a price. From the nature of the monetary standard, this result seemed certain to ensue, and history confirms the theory, whatever method be adopted to measure the variations in the standard. In the present paper I propose to investigate what may be considered as the *veræ causæ* of such variations.

As this is probably the most difficult problem in

economics, I do not anticipate that the inquiry will be exhaustive, but I hope it may prove to be on the right lines, and thus prepare the way for a more complete solution.

The most common error is to imagine that a general movement in prices can be explained by considering the causes of changes in relative values.

The point may be made quite clear by an illustration. Suppose that a number of yachts are racing with a steady breeze,—then to explain the greater speed of some compared to others, we should look to the build, to the sails, to the seamanship, and so on: we should, in short, simply compare the sailing power of one yacht with another, and in that way explain why one was gaining and another losing.

But if the wind gradually and equally declined in force, or if the tide began to operate in a uniform way, we should, so far, simply get an increase or decrease in the absolute speed of all, and not a change in relative positions. And surely there is no need to point out that we could not discover the strength of the tide or of the wind, by examining the build of the various yachts and the seamanship of their crews; and thus that the facts which are of the utmost importance in explaining the relative speed, throw no light on the most important causes affecting the general speed of all.

Now that is precisely the way in which we must consider the effects of gold in the gold-using countries.

Gold is the wind of commerce and the tide of trade, and its abundance or scarcity raises and lowers general prices just as the wind or tide raises or lowers the speed of vessels. But we shall never discover the influence of gold simply by observing relative changes in various articles.

A concrete example may perhaps still better express the nature of this fallacy. In the fourteenth century in England, silver was the standard; and about 1300, an ounce of silver would purchase roughly the work of three common labourers for a week, or about three bushels of wheat, or a quarter of an ox, or one and a half sheep, or about a quarter of an acre of good arable land. At the present time, if we take the nominal value of silver in gold, an ounce of silver (*i.e.*, 5s.) would purchase one-ninth as much labour, half as much wheat, one twenty-fourth part as much meat, and one-fiftieth as much land as six centuries ago. Thus wheat is twice as dear, meat is twenty-four times as dear.

By considering conditions of supply, &c., we can tell why the value of meat has risen so much compared with wheat; but how in the world, without bringing in silver, can we tell the relation of both to the standard ?

It is easy to see that, taking these important commodities as samples, the value of the monetary standard has decreased very much,—in other words, that there has been a great rise in prices. But it ought to be equally plain that no account of the causes of changes in the relative values of the various commodities *inter se* would explain their average relation to silver or gold.

And yet no error is more common than to suppose that the recent fall in prices can be explained by simply showing the causes of changes in the relative demand and supply of particular commodities. We are constantly told that the fall is due to a fall in freights, which is a cause only adequate *directly* to explain the fall of sea-borne produce relatively to commodities produced at home (*e.g.*, unskilled labour); or that it is due to improvements in production by the adoption of particular processes which, as stated, is only adequate to explain directly the relative fall compared with things to which the processes do not apply. Yet no one would be so foolish, in the case of the American greenbacks and the French *assignats*, as to attempt to explain the rise in prices by shortness of supply of, or increase of demand for, commodities, or a falling off in mechanical ingenuity. Every one can see, when it is magnified, that the quantity of the circulating medium compared with the transactions to be effected is fundamental. Yet when gold and silver money are the basis of circulation, it is thought that the quantity is of no importance. Prices fall, it is said, because of the greater power of man over nature, with the fact striking us in the face that the Dakotah farmers, with prairie soil and American machinery, cannot raise wheat at so low a price as in England in the Middle Ages.

The " quantity " theory of money, after being long considered the best established proposition in political economy, has found opponents recently on two plausible grounds.

1. It may be said that, unconsciously, perhaps, but still effectively, we have in the course of time really adopted, in place of gold, a different standard of a vague composite kind.   To make this view clear, for it is difficult to grasp, an example may be taken.   Suppose next year that by law the wages for a certain type of unskilled labour are paid at so much money, no more no less, and that thus the money price of a large mass of labour is directly determined. Then, by industrial competition, other wages must be adjusted, and eventually commodities must be similarly proportioned in price.   When the process is complete, money would no longer be the real standard, but only the medium of exchange.   If there were not enough for circulation, there would be inconvenience or a use of substitutes ; and if there were too much, it would be melted and sold as old metal.

Now it seems to be imagined that custom, operating over a mass of commodities, has silently effected what this example supposes might be done by law. It is thought, apparently, that there is a customary level for very important groups of prices, that other prices are adjusted in accordance therewith, and thus that the quantity of money is simply adjusted to the level of prices, and not the converse.

A sufficient answer to this theory seems to be found in the easy manner in which the immense additions to the stock of gold, through the Australian and Californian discoveries, were put in circulation. A complete refutation would demand a restatement of the quantity theory.[1]

2. The accepted theory has also been attacked from another point. For many years it has been observed that nearly 99 per cent of the wholesale transactions in this country are effected without the actual intervention of metallic money, and from this fact it has been argued that the amount of metallic money is of the smallest importance. Now, on examination, this theory reduces either to that just noticed —namely, to the assumption of a customary level to which credit documents, just as much as gold, must be adjusted; or else it must mean that the quantity of credit, instead of the quantity of gold, determines the level of prices. But this second interpretation over-

---

[1] Compare p. 65.

looks the fundamental distinction between convertible and inconvertible paper; it implies that banking can be conducted without real reserves; and it practically assumes that the level of prices in one country is independent of the level in other countries. If it were true, there would be no limits to the rise in prices.

At the same time, it must be allowed, and indeed it has long been admitted, that within certain limits credit does influence prices in the way suggested, and the history of commercial crises confirms this view. And there is also truth in the position so well stated by Sir James Steuart, that nearly any form of wealth can be " melted down into bank money ; " and thus, by means of cheques, a circulating medium of the most elastic kind can be obtained. But it is none the less true that the quantity of metallic money, *taking the whole system of gold-using countries*, is the real basis on which the whole superstructure of credit rests.

If, then, it be granted that in gold-using countries gold is not only nominally but really the standard of value, and that it is not merely a convenient medium, directly and indirectly (through banks), for exchanging commodities the values of which are determined in relation to some other standard, it must follow that movements in general prices can only be explained by taking into account the causes which affect the demand for, and the supply of, gold.

Causes affecting the supply of gold for coinage.—The principal causes affecting the supply require little more than a bare enumeration. (1) We must consider the existing *stock in the hands of man*, and must estimate the rate of waste by wear and tear. In this respect an observation by Tooke is worth repeating— namely, that the larger the stock the greater the absolute waste. (2) It follows from this that the larger the stock, so much greater must be the annual production simply to replace the waste. Thus the *amount annually produced*, the second factor, even if all devoted to coinage, does not constitute so much positive addition to the stock in hand. (3) The supply of gold may be increased by the release of hoards ; and (4) by the melting down of plate. (5) By the *substitution* of *notes* or other *credit instruments*, the effective supply of coinage may be increased. Thus, if England were to adopt £1 notes, and were only to keep one-fifth of the gold withdrawn as a reserve, more than £70,000,000 probably could be added to the world's gold coinage in other places. Similarly, when any great country adopts inconvertible paper, a great part of its gold may be driven abroad to other gold-using countries. (6) The stock available for coinage may be *lessened* by being *hoarded*, or *converted into plate*, or *exported* for either purpose to countries with a different standard. It has been found convenient to place some elements, especially

(6) under supply, though occasionally they are treated of under demand, because a demand for gold as a commodity is directly equivalent to lessening the amount available for coinage.

Causes affecting the demand for gold as coinage.— Some of the causes affecting the demand are equally obvious; but in considering others, most of the difficulties of the subject arise. It is easy to see that (1) if a nation *substitutes gold for silver* or for *paper*, it at once increases the demand for gold. In this case, however, it might be advisable to consider the demand as tantamount to a contraction of supply, so far as the other gold-using areas are considered. (2) It is easy also to see that, as *new countries* become *more thickly peopled* and *more wealthy*, whatever economies in banking and the like they may adopt, they will, if gold is their standard, increase the demand. (3) Similarly, as *out-of-the-way districts in old countries*, in which low customary prices had been the rule, and in which the circulation had been feeble and sluggish, come under the influence of competition, they will require more gold than before, unless they happen to supply it from hoards. (4) It is also obvious that even in the *great centres of old countries*, other things remaining the same, every increase in population and trade will lead to a greater demand for gold.

In all these cases the general result is, that more

gold is required if prices are to remain at the same level; and, consequently, if an additional supply is not forthcoming in any of the modes mentioned above—*e.g.*, by the increased use of substitutes—the general level of prices must fall.

At this point the first serious difficulty arises in the question, How does the increased demand relatively to supply really operate in reducing prices? " General prices," it may well be said, is but an expression for the sum total of an infinite series of particular prices, and the meaning of the question is, How are these particular prices affected?

In the first place, it must be observed that the problem will be solved if we can show how any important group of valuables may be affected by this pressure on gold.   For it *must be admitted as fundamental and preliminary, that relative values will be adjusted when they are reckoned in money, just as they would be if money did not intervene.*   The adjustment will take time, and may be productive of real disturbances of relative values for the time being; but if one great group of things falls in price, at once there will be a tendency for the other groups to bring about again the same relation of net advantages to the respective producers as before.   In other words, all the causes embraced in industrial and commercial competition operate to make a new level of prices express the same relative values (other things remaining the same) as before. Therefore, just as we explain the emptying of a cistern by the discovery of one leak, without entering into all the causes of movement of all the particles, so we may explain a general fall in prices by the pressure of gold, if we can discover one place in which the pressure may break down the old system.

Now there appear to be two distinct modes in which a pressure on gold or a relative scarcity of supply may affect prices. In the *first* place, the pressure may make itself felt at the great commercial centres through the banking reserves; and with the present interdependence of nations, a great pressure on one bank may disturb all the rest. Every commercial crisis furnishes an example of this species of pressure. A period of buoyant credit and high prices is suddenly broken by some great failure; this failure leads to others; the banks are drawn upon; to protect themselves, they raise their rates and check their advances, and a general fall in prices ensues. The real force which brings down prices is the necessity of having a certain amount of real reserve. As prices rise through credit influences, more gold is needed for currency, and the higher level attracts imports, the payment for which may cause a foreign drain.

There is, *secondly*, the more fundamental method of reducing prices through a contraction of the cur-

rency, which, before the institution of banking, was
the only method by which a pressure on gold could
operate on prices. We find examples on a large
scale in history of this direct connection of prices
with the quantity of money; but, at present the
power of credit may seem so great as to neutralise
this influence. It is, however, a great error to suppose that this mode of action of gold upon prices can
no longer operate, simply because in great cities and
populous districts banking is highly developed.

For we must consider, also, the new and undeveloped countries in which credit has only a feeble
existence, and in which prices can only rise by an
actual increase of currency, and conversely, must fall
if the currency is contracted. Accordingly, it is
quite possible that with the reserves at the centres
of commerce increasing, with rates of interest low
and credit good, a fall in prices may occur and be
really due to a pressure on gold. For, if a contraction of currency has occurred in out-of-the-way
places, the great staples of these countries may fall
in price, and thus by commercial competition drag
down other prices. Suppose, for example, that the
old countries have in a period of prosperity advanced
large amounts of capital to more backward countries.
A commercial crisis intervenes, and it is necessary to
realise and to call in the advances, or at least further
lending is stopped. In this way a balance is due to

the old countries, and can only be met by a contraction of the currencies of the debtor States. It follows, then, that with every appearance of abundance of gold in this country, a fall in prices may take place owing to the contraction of currency in other countries.

Every one can see that foreign competition lowers prices at home in numbers of particular articles, which, again, operate indirectly on other commodities. It is strange that so much difficulty should be felt in seeing that wherever the pressure of gold operates first of all, its influence will be transmitted throughout the gold-using areas. If the pressure can be relieved from other stocks, the depression of prices due to this cause will be temporary; if, however, no relief is obtainable, the fall will be permanent, and for the future values will oscillate about a lower level.[1]

On some obscure causes affecting the value of gold compared with commodities. — There remain to be noticed some of the more obscure causes affecting the general level of prices in a system of gold-using countries. Nothing is more common than to hear the recent fall in prices in this country ascribed to *improved methods of production* of various kinds of

---

[1] The reader will observe that this argument is only a restatement of the old orthodox position. For a fuller statement, with modern instances, compare Mr Giffen's Essays on Finance.

commodities.   It is quite clear that an improvement
in the production of one thing—other things remaining the same—will cause its value to fall relatively
to other things; and in general this fall in value
will be expressed by a corresponding fall in price.
And obviously a large number of commodities may
be affected in the same way.

But the effect on the *general level* of prices of this
disturbance of relative prices is by no means so clear,
and is, in fact, indeterminate.   Let it be supposed,
for example, that there is a great improvement in
the production of all kinds of clothes, so that, relatively to other things, they fall in price.   The great
body of consumers of clothes will then have a
surplus money income, if they still use only the
same amount and quality of clothes as before.   In
this case there would probably be an increased
demand for other things, and, according to the
conditions of production of these things, they might
rise or fall in price.   If they are produced according
to the law of diminishing return,—if they can only
be increased at an increasing cost—they will rise;
but if they can be produced more cheaply on a
larger scale, they will, of course, fall in price.   Thus,
as the indirect consequence of this improvement in
production, some things may rise and others fall in
price.

But it is also possible that, attracted by the greater

cheapness, people will spend more of their income than before on clothes, and thus that there will be a lessened demand for other things, and then the converse of the effect just noticed will be observed.

In a similar manner, the effect of *improvements and reductions in freights* is also indeterminate. In fact, it is best to assume that the act of production is not complete till the commodity is in the hands of the consumer, and thus this case reduces to the former.

It is worthy of remark that, in general, any *real improvement* in production is, in the first place, accompanied by an *increase in profits*, which is, indeed, the proximate cause of the adoption of the improvement. Thus, if a large group of commodities fall in price owing to improved processes, and if, as usually happens, there is more to spend on other things, which, again, causes a fall in some things owing to the extension of division of labour, then the *apparently* general fall in prices will be characterised by an increase of profits, and a rise in the price of articles produced at an increasing cost. Conversely, it may be suspected that a so-called general fall in prices, not marked by an increase of profits, nor by such a partial rise in prices, is not due mainly to improvements in production.

Agricultural produce and the *produce of mines* follow in general the law of diminishing return. Consequently any permanent fall in the *relative value* and *price* of such produce, if the amount consumed is the same or greater, must be due to improvements in production or freight. But if there is a fall in *price* in these things, which is not merely indicative of a fall in relative value, the fall must be attributed to general currency causes, because the natural tendency is for the relative value of such produce to rise, which would, but for such a disturbance, be marked by a rise in price.

A great *increase in production generally,* or a greater addition to the chief staples than the markets can carry off, will tend to make their values, and thus their prices, fall. This fall will be accompanied by a loss of profit, and, as a consequence, production will be checked until the prices again become remunerative. *Thus a fall in prices, due simply to over-production, tends to correct itself;* and, commercial history furnishes many examples. Neither theory nor history lends support to the idea that over-production involving a loss of profit can be both general and permanent, and thus cause a general and permanent fall in prices.

A *change in the distribution of the real wealth* of the country may lead to important changes in relative values. A rise in real wages, for example, or the growth of a large middle class, founded on the splitting up of larger incomes, may lead to an increased demand for certain classes of things, and according to the conditions of production, these things will rise or fall in value; and thus there may be an effect on prices similar to that due to improved processes in production. We should in general expect some things to rise and others to fall owing to this agency. Similarly, a change in the habits of the people as regards consumption may produce effects analogous to those just described.

If we regard the whole system of gold-using countries, the various *methods of taxation* adopted in different States, and their *mutual obligations*, will affect general prices. By an extensive protective policy, a country may keep up a high level of prices compared with that in a free-trade country. But this higher level of prices will make a greater demand on the world's stock of gold.

Again, according to the state of credit, a drain of gold may be met with a much less effect on prices by some countries than by others.

If one country has a *permanent tribute* to pay to another, an adjustment of general prices will take place of the nature described by Mill,[1] *if we consider these two countries as the only countries.* But if there are more countries to be considered, it is clear that the general level of prices cannot be higher in one than in the rest, simply because it receives a tribute. Suppose A owes a tribute to B, and that there are

---

[1] 'Political Economy,' Book III., chap. xxi., § 4.

five other equally important nations trading with both of these and with one another. Obviously the level of prices in B cannot be permanently higher than in the other five countries. For these countries would increase their exports to B and diminish their imports, and thus lower the level of prices. Consequently, the effect of a tribute will be spread over a very wide area, and seeing that *general* prices must be affected, according to this theory the effect will be small.

In any actual case, since the effect on prices must be spread over the whole world, it is probably inappreciable. To take a particular example, the United Kingdom has due to it every year large sums in the shape of interest, which partly account for excess of imports over exports. But it is doubtful if the general level of prices is in consequence raised; for in all the great staples of manufacture we undersell other countries.

Thus, on the whole, it would appear that these obscure causes of variation, although *veræ causæ*, are comparatively of small magnitude—that is, compared with those formerly enumerated. Of course, if we take only a few commodities as representing the total mass, there is always a possibility that one or more of these minor influences may vitiate the result; and that was the principal reason for adopting the more elaborate and difficult method described in my former essay.

Commercial history appears to support this conclusion as to the comparative unimportance of these minor causes. During the last fifty years, for example, the methods of production and of communication have been greatly and continuously improved; but during the first part of the period prices were falling, during the second they were rising (or at least the rate of the fall declined very much), and during the third they have again fallen rapidly. There can be little doubt that the principal cause of the change in the middle division was the great gold discoveries.[1] In the same way the great silver discoveries in the sixteenth century were coincident with great improvements in industry and commerce, and yet they caused a great rise in prices. In both of these cases the rise in prices would have been probably much greater but for the great extension of trade requiring more money. Thus a disturbance of *relative values*, owing to particular improvements, seems of very small importance compared with an increase in the quantity of transactions, and the growth of trade and population.

In the same way it appears that during the last fifty years the changes in the distribution of wealth, the changes in fiscal policy, and the changes in the

[1] Compare the essay, p. 193, on "The Effects of Great Discoveries of the Precious Metals."

relation of exports to imports, have been of relatively small importance—that is to say, no general movements in prices can be mainly attributed to any of these causes.

If, then, we wish to account for the recent fall in prices in gold-using countries, we must look for more *general* causes than those connected with various changes in relative values. There remains one of much importance in addition to those already noticed.

On the interaction of gold and silver prices.—So far the argument has proceeded on the assumption that only one metal, gold, is used for standard money. If, then, we wish to examine the causes of movements of prices in silver-using countries, we have only to substitute silver for gold in the reasoning. It is, however, of course possible, and recent experience seems to afford an example, that silver prices may remain steady or rise whilst gold prices fall; and under different circumstances the converse might happen.

The explanation of the causes and consequences of such a divergence in movement is one of the most difficult problems of the present time. For we have very little actual experience which throws light on the present situation. Before the end of the eighteenth century the trade between gold- and silver-using countries was carried on under very different conditions; and from that time up to 1874 the variations in the gold price of silver were comparatively very small. A sudden depreciation of silver of the kind and extent recently experienced is a new fact, especially when coupled with the keener competition and greater sensitiveness of international markets, due to the extension of telegraphs, banking, &c.

Assume that there are two systems of countries with a considerable trade, and that in the one gold alone is the standard and silver a commodity simply, whilst in the other the converse is the case. Suppose now, that, owing to causes of the nature explained above, gold prices move downwards, whilst silver prices, being under different influences, remain the same. For example, it is possible that a rapid growth of trade and population, with diminished supplies of gold in gold-using countries, might be coincident with an extension of credit and banking in silver-using countries. At any rate, let it be assumed that a divergence takes place of the kind indicated.

If the ratio of gold to silver changes in exactly the same proportion as the general level of gold to silver prices, there will be no disturbance of trade. The exports from the gold countries will sell for the same amount of silver; but this silver, being depreciated, will be worth so much less gold than before, and thus these exports will share in the general movement of gold prices. Similarly, the exports from silver countries will obtain less gold, but it will command the same amount of silver. The only disturbance will be as to old monetary obligations.

In this case the natural course of trade would remain the same as before, a variation occurring simply in the relative values of the two metals.

It must, however, be observed, by way of qualification, that the assumption of a general movement of prices of a *perfectly uniform* character in the two systems of countries is extremely hypothetical, for some prices may move more quickly than other prices, and thus temporary disturbances of various kinds may be caused before the adjustment is completed.

But *ultimately,* as economists are too fond of saying, the price levels will leave relative values unaffected, and if the ratio has been adjusted in the precise degree supposed, international trade will take its normal course.

The question then arises—*Will the ratio be so adjusted as to correspond exactly to this divergence?* Seeing that silver is simply a commodity in the gold-using countries, we may assume that ultimately it must fall in its gold price, just as other things. If all other competing substitutes have fallen in price, the demand for silver will be lessened until it also falls to an equal degree.

z

But then, conversely, gold is simply a commodity in the silver-using countries, and thus, if general silver prices remain the same as before, the silver price of gold ought to remain the same by parity of reasoning. It is, however, quite obvious that, with inter-communication of markets, an ounce of silver cannot fetch in London (say) only one-sixth of a sovereign, whilst in India it fetches still one quarter of a sovereign.

How, then, will the adjustment be made? So long as this divergence exists, there will be a profit in exporting silver to India and exporting gold from India. An ounce of silver, bought for a sixth of a sovereign, exported to India will obtain a quarter of a sovereign; and similarly, a sovereign, exported from India, will obtain six ounces of silver instead of four. Eventually, the rate of exchange must become the same (allowing for carriage, &c.) in both countries. But this may happen, either through silver rising in price in the gold countries, or the gold rising in price in the silver countries.

Suppose now that gold, relatively to commodities, has appreciated 25 per cent, and that silver prices have remained constant. Illustrating the above argument by this figure, we should find that the gold price of silver in London had fallen 25 per cent, whilst the silver price of gold in India had remained the same; or the gold price of silver in London would

be 45d. an ounce, and in India 60d. These prices
cannot be stable, and apparently it depends simply
on the relative demands for the two metals, as commodities, what the resultant price will be. Suppose
(taking a mean) it becomes 52d. in both countries,
then general gold prices have fallen 25 per cent and
silver about 12. Then exports to India will sell for
the same silver as before, which is equivalent to 12
per cent less gold, but these same commodities in the
gold countries will only fetch 25 per cent less gold.
Conversely, exports from India will obtain 25 per
cent less gold, and this will obtain only 12 per cent
less silver. Thus exports to India increase and
from India diminish, and this condition is again unstable.

It thus appears that unless the ratio of gold to
silver is adjusted so as to correspond exactly with
the change in the levels of gold and silver prices, a
real disturbance of trade will take place, until the
levels of gold and silver prices are adjusted to the
new ratio of gold and silver.

Next, let it be supposed that there is established a
certain level of prices in gold-using countries, and a
certain level in silver countries, and that the ratio
of gold to silver is suddenly and greatly changed.
Silver is simply a commodity in the West, and if
large stocks are thrown on the market the price

(reckoned in gold) must fall. Suppose that the price of silver falls 25 per cent, and remains low for a considerable period. Then if gold prices remain the same, and also silver prices, a great stimulus would be given to exports from the silver countries, whilst exports thither would be checked. Accordingly (since this condition is not stable) the general levels of prices must be adjusted either by gold prices falling or silver prices rising.

The assumption generally made by English economists of the last generation was that, in the case supposed, silver would be exported to the East, and thus that silver prices would tend to rise, and also the gold price of silver in the West would partly recover from its fall. But it seems probable, in the light of recent history, that this theory is incorrect, and that the adjustment is more likely to take place by a fall in the gold prices proportionate to the fall in silver.

It is easy to see that to produce a rise in silver prices over the vast area of the East, where credit is still in its infancy, and custom not yet in its dotage, enormous masses of silver must be put in circulation. But if these masses of silver have first to go through Western markets, the price of silver will fall, and the state of general gold prices will be adjusted to this fall before the silver can influence the Eastern markets. The point is, that prices in silver-using countries cannot be forced up simply because gold ornaments have become dearer. Depreciated paper implies a rise of prices consequent oh excessive issues, or simply through taking gold as the real basis, but general silver prices will not move in the same easy manner according to the gold price of silver.

By the adoption of a very simple formula, a general argument may be stated, of which the above are particular cases.

It must be assumed, as before, that whatever changes take place in the general levels of prices in gold-using and silver-using countries respectively, or in the relative values of gold and silver *inter se*, after sufficient time to make the adjustment, the *relative values* of commodities generally must, so far as these changes are concerned, eventually be unaffected.

Thus, if a general fall in gold prices becomes definitely established, the articles exported to silver-using countries, and also the articles imported from those countries, must share in this fall.

Similarly, if silver prices remain steady, the exports from silver-using countries must obtain the same amount of silver, and the silver price of the imports to them also must remain steady.

Again, seeing that in actual trade the exports from gold-using countries are sold for silver, and those from silver-using countries for gold, it follows also that variations in the ratio of exchange of the metals (taken in connection with the general levels of prices) must leave relative values the same.

It will be observed that these postulates contain no more than is implied in effective industrial and commercial competition.   Suppose, for example, that owing to a sudden and extensive contraction in the supply of gold, or an increase in the demand, a general fall of prices sets in in the gold-using countries. Some commodities may not be so soon affected as others, and no doubt the fall will be irregular; but obviously those articles which happen to be exported to silver-using countries must also share in this tendency to fall—that is to say, the tendency will be for the relative *prices* of commodities to be adjusted to their former relative *values*.

Similarly it must be assumed that a mere change in the relative values of gold and silver as metals cannot neutralise the general effects of competition; although, until competition has done its work, exceptional advantages or disadvantages may ensue in particular cases.

Apart from these assumptions, however, the postulates imply that a disturbance of a general kind may arise in three distinct ways—namely, *first*, with causes primarily affecting the general level of prices in gold-using countries; *secondly*, with causes primarily affecting the general level of prices in silver-using countries ; and *thirdly,* seeing that silver in gold-using countries and gold in silver-using countries are simply commodities, with causes primarily affecting the ratio of gold to silver (as metals).

The object of the following analysis is to show the various ways in which equilibrium may be restored according to the origin of the initial disturbance, and further, to show the nature of the stimulus or the check, as the case may be, to the trade between gold-using and silver-using countries, until equilibrium is reached. It has been found convenient to take the first two cases togther.

It may further be remarked that, in any practical case, causes of the three kinds indicated may begin to operate simultaneously, or at any rate that before one has completed its effect another may come into play. Thus the recent demonetisation of silver might at the same time have tended directly to cause a disturbance in the ratio of gold to silver, and also an appreciation of gold (through greater demands upon it) relatively to commodities—that is, a fall in the general level of prices in gold-using countries. But no solution seems possible without a preliminary analysis of the effects of the various causes in isolation.

With these postulates, suppose that G_1 means the number of ounces of gold which a given mass of exports (say E_1) to silver countries will command at the rates current in the gold countries (say at English ports).

Similarly, let S_1 mean the number of ounces of silver which a given mass of exports E_2 (of equal value with E_1) to gold-using countries will command at the rates current in the silver-using countries (say at Indian ports). [The general argument, it will be plainly seen, is unaffected by the cost of carriage, which may accordingly be neglected.]

Let r_1 be the ratio of gold to silver, such that one ounce of gold is equal to r_1 ounces of silver.

Then, when trade is in equilibrium, that is to say, in the absence of any artificial impulse, $\dfrac{S_1}{G_1} = r_1$.

CASE I.—(a) Now assume that, owing to *general causes operating in gold-using countries, gold becomes definitely appreciated.* Then the mass of commodities which formerly obtained G_1 ounces of gold will now obtain less (say G_2). Therefore, for the restoration of equilibrium, either S_1 must fall proportionately (say to S_2, r_1 remaining constant), or else r_1 must rise in proportion (S_1 remaining constant), or a change in both must occur, S_1 falling and r_1 rising, until

$$\frac{S_2}{G_2} = r_2.$$

Until equilibrium is thus brought about in one or other of these ways, commodities worth G_2 in gold-using countries will be worth more gold than G_2 in silver countries, after being sold at silver prices and converted into gold; and commodities exported from silver countries will obtain less than at home. Thus there will be a stimulus to exports from gold-using countries (and the converse for silver-using countries).

(b) In a similar way it may be shown that if *gold becomes depreciated relatively to commodities*—that is, if G_2 becomes greater than G_1—then either silver prices must rise or else r_1 must fall, or both; and until equilibrium is reached, there will be a stimulus to exports from silver countries and a check on exports thither.

(c) If *silver prices rise, owing to causes operating in silver-using countries*, then equilibrium will be restored either by gold prices rising, or r_1 rising, or both—the stimulus in the mean time being to exports from the gold-using countries, and the converse for the silver-using countries.

(d) If *silver prices fall*, then either gold prices must fall or r_1 must fall, or both—the stimulus being in the mean time to exports from the silver-using countries, and the converse for the gold-using countries.

(e) If silver prices were to move one way and gold the opposite way, then the case would reduce to one of those already considered, according as $\dfrac{S_2}{G_2}$ was greater or less than $\dfrac{S_1}{G_1}$.

CASE II.—Now, let it be supposed that, *whilst S_1 and G_1 remain the same, r_1 suddenly changes and be-comes greater*—that is to say, the metal silver becomes depreciated relatively to the metal gold, whilst there is otherwise nothing to change the general levels of prices. Let r_2 be the newly established rate, then $\dfrac{S_1}{G_1}$ must become $\dfrac{S_2}{G_2}$, so that $\dfrac{S_2}{G_2} = r_2$.

(*a*) Thus, if S_1 remains the same (*i.e.*, $S_2 = S_1$), then G_2 must be less than G_1, in the proportion r_1 to r_2. In other words, if silver prices remain the same, gold prices must fall proportionately to the fall in silver. Until equilibrium is restored, under this hypothesis there will be a stimulus to exports from silver countries (and the converse for gold-using countries).

(*b*) If G_2 is equal to G_1, and S_2 becomes proportion-ately greater than S_1, so as to make $\dfrac{S_2}{G_1} = r_2$, then, until equilibrium is restored, with this kind of move-ment there will again be a stimulus to exports from the silver-using countries (and the converse for gold-using countries).

(*c*) If, on the contrary, *r_2 becomes suddenly less than r_1*—that is, as metals, gold becomes depreciated rela-tively to silver—then $\dfrac{S_1}{G_1}$ must be similarly adjusted.

If S_1 remains the same, G_1 must rise. In the

mean time, exports from the gold countries will feel the stimulus.

(d) With the same hypothesis, if S_2 becomes less, G_1 remaining the same, then, until equilibrium is reached, exports from the gold countries will again feel the stimulus.

The correctness of the general analysis is confirmed by the case (I., b) of the great gold discoveries, for there appears to have been a stimulus to exports from silver-using countries, the balance being met by the export of silver thither. (Tooke's 'History of Prices,' vol. vi. p. 718, &c.)

The use of the formula may be illustrated by the case of inconvertible paper (in place of silver) compared with gold.

In this case, substitute P for S, and let r_1 be the number by which the gold currency must be multiplied to obtain the equivalent paper, r_1 in general being a fraction greater than unity.

Then when equilibrium is established :—

$$\frac{P_1}{G_1} = r_1.$$

Case (*a*).—Suppose that, by *excessive issues* of the paper, P_1 rises in the first place. Then also, since in this case G_1 may be considered steady, r_1 must rise ; and until $\dfrac{P_2}{G_1} = r_2$, there will be a *stimulus to exports to the paper country.*   In other words, they will obtain higher prices in paper, which will command more gold until gold obtains a corresponding premium.

Case (b).—But if r_1 *rises first through the paper becoming discredited* before the general level of prices has been much affected by excessive issues, then P_1 must also rise if G_1 remains steady; and until the corresponding rise in P_1 takes place, there will be a *stimulus to exports from the paper country.*

Light may be also thrown on the problem whether the premium on gold is the *exact* measure of the depreciation of the paper relatively to commodities, by considering the possible changes in G_1, owing indirectly to the issues and depreciation of the paper.

As this analysis is of great practical importance at the present time, and also leads to a considerable modification of a well-known theory, some further explanation may be offered of the symbols used and of the assumptions implied.

The given mass of exports E_1 might be taken to mean the aggregate of exports from gold-using to silver-using countries; but for the sake of simplicity it has been found convenient to take only such an amount of E_2 (supposing E_2 is greater than E_1) as in normal conditions is equal in value to E_1.

It is also assumed in the analysis that what is true of E_1 and E_2, is also true of all the exports which, under any circumstances that arise, may be made from gold- and silver-using countries respectively. Thus, under actual conditions, any change in S_1 and G_1 implies a change of prices in groups of commodities of such magnitude that this change may be held to involve a corresponding change in other commodities.

It is easy to see, for example, if wheat falls in price, that indirectly, through the effects on agriculture, a wide range of prices will become affected, and the commodities in the aggregate of international trade between gold and silver countries are of such importance that any considerable fall in their prices must operate very widely. It should also be observed that a great rise in r_1, S_1 remaining steady, would give a proportionate profit on every exportable article from silver-using .countries unless there was a corresponding fall in the gold price.

It will be observed in every case of the formula that whenever through any change in either S or G or r the equation $\dfrac{S}{G} = r$ becomes $\dfrac{S}{G} > r$, then there is a stimulus to exports from the gold-using to the silver-using countries (and conversely a check on exports from the latter to the former); whilst if the equation becomes $\dfrac{S}{G} < r$, the stimulus and check will act in the opposite way.

For the convenience of those who are unfamiliar

with or distrust symbolical reasoning, this general conclusion may be stated as follows :—If for any reason, whether from a change in gold prices or in silver prices or in the ratio, articles exported from the gold-using to the silver-using countries obtain *relatively* more gold (on conversion) than when retained in the gold-using area, there will be a stimulus to exportation ; and similarly, if articles exported from the silver-using countries obtain *relatively* more silver than if retained in the silver area, exportation will be stimulated. And this is only a particular example of the moving principle in all international trade.

As regards the nature of the stimulus, it must be observed that the whole train of reasoning depends upon the assumption that a stimulus due to purely monetary causes will bring into play counteracting forces, and will tend to be converted into some change in silver prices, or in gold prices, or in the ratio of gold to silver. The practical difficulty is that the adjustment takes time, and that the further adjustment of contracts and customs takes still more time, so that before one disturbance has been neutralised another may begin to operate.

There will, of course, be a strong disinclination on the part of those who hold that Ricardo and Mill have said the last word on the theory of international values and the distribution of the precious metals, to admit that a mere change in the relative values of gold and silver can have such wide-reaching consequences. It is then of the utmost importance to observe that with the demonetisation of silver a new set of conditions arose, and furnished a case to which the accepted theory does not apply. In discussing the question of the effects of money on international trade, the old theory constantly takes the "precious metals" as a unit. Mill, for example, entitles his chapter: "Of the distribution of the *precious metals* throughout the commercial world;" and it is on the "*precious metals*" that the quantity of "*money*" is based.

Now, according to this view, all countries have only one monetary system (which practically was the case when Mill wrote), and, consequently, the question of the interaction of two monetary systems never comes in sight. Thus it is quite possible that Mill's theory is right under his hypotheses, and yet inapplicable to a totally different case. According to Mill's theory, the depreciation of silver can only be a mere incident of exchange, such as might occur if two trading countries had the same currency. The whole theory really implies that there is a stable par between gold and silver, whilst the present problem arises from the fact that the stability has vanished.

It is interesting to treat Case II. according to Mill's theory. Silver becomes for some reason depreciated, which in this view simply means that the exchanges become unfavourable for the silver-using countries— that is, their form of the "precious metals" obtains less than usual of the other form; or, to take a particular example, a mass of rupees or the corresponding bill obtains a less amount of sovereigns; and, conversely, sovereigns obtain more rupees. Thus there will be a stimulus to exports from the silver countries to get sovereigns wherewith to buy rupees; and, conversely, there will be a check on exports to the silver countries, because the rupees fetch less sovereigns. Consequently, the exports to the silver countries will no longer pay for the exports therefrom, and a balance of the "precious metals" will be due. When this balance arrives, it will, by the quantity theory, tend to raise prices in the silver countries, and thus to encourage exports thither, and to check exports therefrom. Then the exchange will right itself, and possibly go to the other side of the old par.

That is the pure theory; and, given a stable par between gold and silver, the theory is sound in principle, though a less direct application of the quantity theory is required with telegraphs and banks in full operation. No better proof could be given that this account of the accepted theory is correct, than the treatment of the question in Mr Goschen's standard work on the 'Foreign Exchanges.' In discussing the limits of the fluctuations in the

exchanges between gold - using and silver - using
countries, he commences by saying: " Either gold
or silver will be at what may be called the *par
value* between the two, or, as is more generally the
fact, the one will be at a premium as compared with
the other." Clearly this assumption of a par value
between the two metals must have been made under
very different conditions from the present.

The inadequacy of Mill's theory may, however, be
best shown by a somewhat startling deduction. If
England and India had the same currency (say gold),
would any one believe for a moment that a fall of
30 per cent could occur in the exchange value of the
gold rupee against a gold sovereign, or if it did occur,
that it would continue for years ? And yet those who
say that the fall in the rupee is simply *a consequence
of a readjustment of trade*, must be prepared logically
to make this admission. Hitherto such a fall in the
exchange has only taken place with depreciated paper,
and the movement in paper prices has usually re-
sponded to the premium on gold ; but to put silver
on the same footing with paper, the Governor-General
of India must be an alchemist with unlimited powers
of producing silver rupees.

The essence of the present argument is, that silver
may fall first of all in the gold-using countries, apart
from any disturbance of international trade (except
as a consequence); and those who admit that in these

countries silver is only a commodity can hardly deny this position. " Gold is simply merchandise in such countries as have a silver currency, and silver is merchandise in such countries as have a gold standard ; and according to the price of the merchandise in a given moment, so will the exchanges fluctuate." [1]

There can be no doubt that the price of silver and the exchanges fluctuate together, and that if silver falls, a sovereign or its equivalent will so far command more rupees.

And if this fall were due merely to an excess of exports from the gold-using countries, or diminution of imports from the silver-using countries, so that there was a less demand for silver than usual for export, then no doubt there would be a recovery, and the fall would only temporarily inconvenience or benefit those who had to buy or sell silver or its equivalent.

But if silver is simply merchandise in the gold-using countries, can we say that its value depends *entirely on the demand for export to the silver-using countries for trade debts,* and that no other causes can make its value fluctuate ? Obviously there are several other causes which may be of importance, as, for example, the increase of production, the release of the hoards of French peasants, the suspension of the

---

[1] Goschen's ' Foreign Exchanges,' p. 76.

Bland Act, the sale of old stocks by Germany, and further demonetisation by Western nations. And even apart from all these causes, does not the demand for export itself depend upon the general balance of indebtedness, and not only upon trade debts ?

But once let it be granted that the ratio may change apart from the course of trade,—once let it be admitted that it is not only the demand for silver for export to silver countries for *trade debts* that determines its value,—and there is no escape from the second case of the analysis. If the metal silver, for example, falls (say) 30 per cent, either silver prices must rise or gold prices must fall, or both. Hence, if silver prices remain fairly steady, the fall must be entirely in the gold prices; and to suppose that this fall in gold prices can be confined to the great staples of trade with silver countries, is to surrender all the principles of industrial and commercial competition.

It thus appears that, if we assume the *variation to occur first in the ratio,* and if silver remains depreciated, there is a stimulus to exports from silver countries, and a check on exports thither until equilibrium is restored, either by gold prices falling or silver prices rising. Reasons have been given elsewhere [1] for the belief that gold prices are more likely to fall

[1] 'Treatise on Money,' p. 115.

than silver prices to rise. The latter could only take place by large exports of silver.

If through direct causes at the same time gold prices are falling, equilibrium will be sooner attained and the stimulus neutralised.

Now, as regards recent history, we know for certain that silver has depreciated relatively to gold ; and it seems probable that silver prices have remained fairly steady, whilst gold prices have fallen. This fall in gold prices may be due partly to general causes of appreciation, and partly to the *prior* depreciation of silver. The suddenness and rapidity of the fall seems to point to the latter as, at any rate, an important factor, and the anti-silver policy of various nations accounts for the depreciation. This view also seems confirmed by the course of trade, for if the depreciation of silver were (as in Case I., *a*) simply the *effect* of the *general appreciation of gold*, it would have been accompanied by a stimulus to exports to silver-using countries and a check on exports therefrom.

It is possible that, owing to general causes, silver prices have fallen to some extent. In this case the fall in gold prices must be even greater than is indicated by the depreciation of the metal silver, if equilibrium has been restored, and part of the fall must be ascribed to general causes of appreciation.

It is worth observing that, so far as the fall in gold

prices is due to the depreciation of silver, there would
be an apparent abundance rather than a scarcity of
gold in the great commercial gold-using countries.

In order to illustrate further the practical uses of
the analysis, some possible changes in the immediate
future of gold prices may be indicated.   As soon as
the depreciation of silver as "merchandise" has
reached the limit of its fall, there may be a reaction
in gold prices which will tend also to force up silver.
So far as the fall in gold prices is due to the prior depreciation of silver, it will imply rather a superfluity
than a scarcity of gold, and with speculation wearied
with watching and ready to expand credit on the
slightest pretence, there may well be a sufficient
"quantity of money" to support a higher level of
prices.   Again, if silver were to rise owing to its increased use in America, gold prices would also tend to
rise.   And if silver were sent in large quantities to
the East, and the long-looked-for fulfilment of Mr
Bagehot's prophecy were to occur, then also a rise in
the ratio and in gold prices might take place.   The
persistent fall, however, since 1874 shows how tedious
the process may be, and so far as this fall is due to
general causes of appreciation there is no natural
tendency to recovery.

But whether the particular application is correct or
not, the bearing of this general analysis on the ques-

tion of bi-metallism is most important. If the ratio of gold to silver is left to what are termed market influences solely, then an alteration in the ratio may have as a consequence a disturbance of prices and trade, and unless the alteration is temporary such a disturbance must ensue. Silver prices being more steady than gold prices, the latter are more likely to be affected. Thus great discoveries of silver in the West, or a further demonetisation, might cause a further fall in the metal silver, and indirectly a further fall in general gold prices.

Again, if silver prices and gold prices remain subject to different influences, the metals being independent, then the ratio must be adjusted to these changes, and this change in the ratio may react on general prices, and will in any case disturb the monetary obligations of gold- and silver-using countries.

But these disturbances in the ratio, whether they are, according to circumstances, the cause or the effect of changes in the levels of gold and silver prices, can only be mischievous. It is of the smallest importance to the world at large whether the gold price of silver or the silver price of gold is much or little. If silver falls in value relatively to gold, more silver and less gold may be used in the arts; but that is only a matter of interest to jewellers and to the very small class who spend a large part of their wealth on ornaments made of the precious metals. A movement in the price of coal or iron is of much more importance to the world of *consumers* than a movement in the price of silver. But when a movement in silver has the indirect consequences indicated in this analysis, then the movement becomes of interest not only to jewellers, but to Governments—not only to a few lovers of ornament, but to nations.

If, on the other hand, gold and silver were . linked together, discoveries of either metal would act as a stimulus to trade ; both metals would replenish the general stock ; the general level of prices throughout the world, so far as the metallic currency is concerned, would be governed by the same causes, as there would be practically only one monetary system ; and instead of changes in the ratio, with the consequent disturbances of prices and contracts, the principal result would be that silver would be more largely used as the basis of note issues in the reserves of banks.

THE END.

STORMONTH'S DICTIONARY—*Continued.*

Opinions of the British and American Press—*Continued.*

Civil Service Gazette.—"We have had occasion to notice the peculiar features and merits of 'Stormonth's Dictionary,' and we need not repeat our commendations both of the judicious plan and the admirable execution. . . . This is a pre-eminently good, comprehensive, and authentic English lexicon, embracing not only all the words to be found in previous dictionaries, but all the modern words—scientific, new coined, and adopted from foreign languages, and now naturalised and legitimised."

Notes and Queries.—"The whole constitutes a work of high utility."

Dublin Irish Times.—"The book has the singular merit of being a dictionary of the highest order in every department and in every arrangement, without being cumbersome; whilst for ease of reference there is no dictionary we know of that equals it. . . . For the library table it is also, we must repeat, precisely the sort of volume required, and indispensable to every large reader or literary worker."

Liverpool Mercury.—"Every page bears the evidence of extensive scholarship and laborious research, nothing necessary to the elucidation of present-day language being omitted. . . . As a book of reference for terms in every department of English speech, this work must be accorded a high place—in fact, it is quite a library in itself. . . . It is a marvel of accuracy."

New York Tribune.—"The work exhibits all the freshness and best results of modern lexicographic scholarship, and is arranged with great care, so as to facilitate reference."

New York Mail and Express.—"Is the nearest approach to the ideal popular dictionary that has yet appeared in our language."

New York Sun.—"A well-planned and carefully-executed work, which has decided merits of its own, and for which there is a place not filled by any of its rivals."

Boston Journal.—"A critical and accurate dictionary, the embodiment of good scholarship, and the result of modern researches. . . . It holds an unrivalled place in bringing forth the result of modern philological criticism."

Boston Gazette.—"There can be but little doubt that, when completed, the work will be one of the most serviceable and most accurate that English lexicography has yet produced for general use "

Toronto Globe.—"In every respect this is one of the best works of the kind in the language."

WILLIAM BLACKWOOD & SONS, EDINBURGH AND LONDON.

CATALOGUE

OF

MESSRS BLACKWOOD & SONS'

PUBLICATIONS.

CATALOGUE

OF

MESSRS BLACKWOOD & SONS'

PUBLICATIONS.

———◆———

ALISON. History of Europe. By Sir ARCHIBALD ALISON, Bart.,
D.C.L.

1. From the Commencement of the French Revolution to the
Battle of Waterloo.
LIBRARY EDITION, 14 vols., with Portraits. Demy 8vo, £10, 10s.
ANOTHER EDITION, in 20 vols. crown 8vo, £6.
PEOPLE'S EDITION, 13 vols. crown 8vo, £2, 11s.

2. Continuation to the Accession of Louis Napoleon.
LIBRARY EDITION, 8 vols. 8vo, £6, 7s. 6d.
PEOPLE'S EDITION, 8 vols. crown 8vo, 34s.

3. Epitome of Alison's History of Europe. Twenty-ninth
Thousand, 7s. 6d.

4. Atlas to Alison's History of Europe. By A. Keith Johnston.
LIBRARY EDITION, demy 4to, £3, 3s.
PEOPLE'S EDITION, 31s. 6d.

—— Life of John Duke of Marlborough. With some Account
of his Contemporaries, and of the War of the Succession. Third Edition,
2 vols. 8vo. Portraits and Maps, 30s.

—— Essays: Historical, Political, and Miscellaneous. 3 vols.
demy 8vo, 45s.

AIRD. Poetical Works of Thomas Aird. Fifth Edition, with
Memoir of the Author by the Rev. JARDINE WALLACE, and Portrait,
Crown 8vo, 7s. 6d.

ALLARDYCE. The City of Sunshine. By ALEXANDER ALLAR-
DYCE. Three vols. post 8vo, £1, 5s. 6d.

—— Memoir of the Honourable George Keith Elphinstone,
K.B., Viscount Keith of Stonehaven Marischal, Admiral of the Red. 8vo,
with Portrait, Illustrations, and Maps, 21s.

ALMOND. Sermons by a Lay Head-master. By HELY HUTCHIN-
SON ALMOND, M.A. Oxon., Head-master of Loretto School. Crown 8vo, 5s.

ANCIENT CLASSICS FOR ENGLISH READERS. Edited by
Rev. W. LUCAS COLLINS, M.A. Complete in 28 vols., cloth, 2s. 6d. each; or in
14 vols., tastefully bound, with calf or vellum back, £3, 10s.

Contents of the Series.

HOMER: THE ILIAD, by the Editor.—HOMER: THE ODYSSEY, by the Editor.—HER-
ODOTUS, by George C. Swayne, M.A.—XENOPHON, by Sir Alexander Grant, Bart., LL.D.
EURIPIDES, by W. B. Donne—ARISTOPHANES, by the Editor.—PLATO, by Clifton W.
Collins, M.A—LUCIAN, by the Editor.—ÆSCHYLUS, by the Right Rev. the Bishop of
Colombo.—SOPHOCLES, by Clifton W. Collins, M.A —HESIOD AND THEOGNIS, by the
Rev. J. Davies, M.A.—GREEK ANTHOLOGY, by Lord Neaves.—VIRGIL, by the Editor.
—HORACE, by Sir Theodore Martin, K.C.B.—JUVENAL, by Edward Walford, M.A.—
PLAUTUS AND TERENCE, by the Editor.—THE COMMENTARIES OF CÆSAR, by Anthony
Trollope.—TACITUS, by W. B. Donne.—CICERO, by the Editor.—PLINY'S LETTERS, by
the Rev. Alfred Church, M.A., and the Rev. W. J. Brodribb, M.A.—LIVY, by the
Editor.—OVID, by the Rev. A. Church, M.A.—CATULLUS, TIBULLUS, AND PROPERTIUS,
by the Rev. Jas. Davies, M.A.—DEMOSTHENES, by the Rev. W. J. Brodribb, M.A.—
ARISTOTLE, by Sir Alexander Grant, Bart., LL.D —THUCYDIDES, by the Editor.—
LUCRETIUS, by W. H. Mallock, M.A.—PINDAR, by the Rev. F. D. Morice, M.A.

AYLWARD. The Transvaal of To-day: War, Witchcraft,
Sports, and Spoils in South Africa. By ALFRED AYLWARD, Commandant,
Transvaal Republic. Second Edition. Crown 8vo, 6s.

AYTOUN. Lays of the Scottish Cavaliers, and other Poems. By
W. EDMONDSTOUNE AYTOUN, D.C.L., Professor of Rhetoric and Belles-Lettres
in the University of Edinburgh. Cheap Edition, printed from a new type,
and tastefully bound. Fcap. 8vo, 3s. 6d.
Another Edition, being the Thirtieth. Fcap. 8vo, cloth extra, 7s. 6d.

——— An Illustrated Edition of the Lays of the Scottish Cavaliers.
From designs by Sir NOEL PATON. Small 4to, 21s., in gilt cloth.

——— Bothwell: a Poem. Third Edition. Fcap., 7s. 6d.

——— Poems and Ballads of Goethe. Translated by Professor
AYTOUN and Sir THEODORE MARTIN, K.C.B. Third Edition. Fcap., 6s.

——— Bon Gaultier's Book of Ballads. By the SAME. Fourteenth
and Cheaper Edition. With Illustrations by Doyle, Leech, and Crowquill.
Fcap. 8vo, 5s.

——— The Ballads of Scotland. Edited by Professor AYTOUN.
Fourth Edition. 2 vols. fcap. 8vo, 12s.

——— Memoir of William E. Aytoun, D.C.L. By Sir THEODORE
MARTIN, K.C.B. With Portrait. Post 8vo, 12s.

BACH. On Musical Education and Vocal Culture. By ALBERT
B. BACH. Fourth Edition. 8vo, 7s. 6d.

——— The Principles of Singing. A Practical Guide for Vocalists
and Teachers. With Course of Vocal Exercises. Crown 8vo, 6s.

——— The Art of Singing. With Musical Exercises for Young
People. Crown 8vo, 3s.

BALCH. Zorah: A Love-Tale of Modern Egypt. By ELISABETH
BALCH (D.T.S.) Post 8vo, 7s. 6d.

BALLADS AND POEMS. By MEMBERS OF THE GLASGOW
BALLAD CLUB. Crown 8vo, 7s. 6d.

BANNATYNE. Handbook of Republican Institutions in the
United States of America. Based upon Federal and State Laws, and other
reliable sources of information. By DUGALD J. BANNATYNE, Scotch Solicitor,
New York; Member of the Faculty of Procurators, Glasgow. Crown 8vo,
7s. 6d.

BEDFORD. The Regulations of the Old Hospital of the Knights
of St John at Valetta. From a Copy Printed at Rome, and preserved in the
Archives of Malta; with a Translation, Introduction, and Notes Explanatory
of the Hospital Work of the Order. By the Rev. W. K. R. BEDFORD, one of
the Chaplains of the Order of St John in England. Royal 8vo, with Frontispiece, Plans, &c., 7s. 6d.

BELLAIRS. The Transvaal War, 1880-81. Edited by Lady BEL-
LAIRS. With a Frontispiece and Map. 8vo, 15s.
—— Gossips with Girls and Maidens, Betrothed and Free.
Crown 8vo, 5s.

BESANT. The Revolt of Man. By WALTER BESANT, M.A.
Eighth Edition. Crown 8vo, 3s. 6d.
—— Readings in Rabelais. Crown 8vo, 7s. 6d.

BEVERIDGE. Culross and Tulliallan; or Perthshire on Forth. Its
History and Antiquities. With Elucidations of Scottish Life and Character
from the Burgh and Kirk-Session Records of that District. By DAVID
BEVERIDGE. 2 vols. 8vo, with Illustrations, 42s.

BLACKIE. Lays and Legends of Ancient Greece. By JOHN
STUART BLACKIE, Emeritus Professor of Greek in the University of Edin-
burgh. Second Edition. Fcap. 8vo. 5s.
—— The Wisdom of Goethe. Fcap. 8vo. Cloth, extra gilt, 6s.

BLACKWOOD'S MAGAZINE. from Commencement in 1817 to
June 1887. Nos. 1 to 860, forming 140 Volumes.
—— Index to Blackwood's Magazine. Vols. 1 to 50. 8vo, 15s.
—— Tales from Blackwood. Forming Twelve Volumes of
Interesting and Amusing Railway Reading. Price One Shilling each, in Paper
Cover. Sold separately at all Railway Bookstalls.
They may also be had bound in cloth, 18s., and in half calf, richly gilt, 30s.
Or 12 volumes in 6, Roxburghe, 21s., and half red morocco, 28s.
—— Tales from Blackwood. New Series. Complete in Twenty-
four Shilling Parts. Handsomely bound in 12 vols., cloth, 30s. In leather
back, Roxburghe style, 37s. 6d. In half calf, gilt, 52s. 6d. In half morocco, 55s.
—— Standard Novels. Uniform in size and legibly Printed.
Each Novel complete in one volume.

FLORIN SERIES, Illustrated Boards. Or in Cloth Boards, 2s. 6d.

TOM CRINGLE'S LOG. By Michael Scott.	PEN OWEN. By Dean Hook.
THE CRUISE OF THE MIDGE. By the Same.	ADAM BLAIR. By J. G. Lockhart.
CYRIL THORNTON. By Captain Hamilton.	LADY LEE'S WIDOWHOOD. By General
ANNALS OF THE PARISH. By John Galt.	Sir E. B. Hamley.
THE PROVOST, &c. By John Galt.	SALEM CHAPEL. By Mrs Oliphant.
SIR ANDREW WYLIE. By John Galt.	THE PERPETUAL CURATE. By Mrs Oli-
THE ENTAIL. By John Galt.	phant.
MISS MOLLY. By Beatrice May Butt.	MISS MARJORIBANKS. By Mrs Oliphant.
REGINALD DALTON. By J. G. Lockhart.	JOHN : A Love Story. By Mrs Oliphant.

SHILLING SERIES, Illustrated Cover. Or in Cloth Boards, 1s. 6d.

THE RECTOR, and THE DOCTOR'S FAMILY.	SIR FRIZZLE PUMPKIN, NIGHTS AT MESS,
By Mrs Oliphant.	&c.
THE LIFE OF MANSIE WAUCH. By D. M.	THE SUBALTERN.
Moir.	LIFE IN THE FAR WEST. By G. F. Ruxton.
PENINSULAR SCENES AND SKETCHES. By	VALERIUS : A Roman Story. By J. G.
F. Hardman.	Lockhart.

BLACKMORE. The Maid of Sker. By R. D. BLACKMORE, Author
of 'Lorna Doone,' &c. New Edition. Crown 8vo, 6s.

BLAIR. History of the Catholic Church of Scotland. From the
Introduction of Christianity to the Present Day. By ALPHONS BELLESHEIM,
D.D., Canon of Aix-la-Chapelle. Translated, with Notes and Additions, by
D. OSWALD HUNTER BLAIR, O.S.B., Monk of Fort Augustus. To be com-
pleted in 4 vols. 8vo. Vols. I and II. 25s.

BOSCOBEL TRACTS. Relating to the Escape of Charles the
Second after the Battle of Worcester, and his subsequent Adventures. Edited
by J. HUGHES, Esq., A.M. A New Edition, with additional Notes and Illustrations, including Communications from the Rev. R. H. BARHAM, Author of
the 'Ingoldsby Legends.' 8vo, with Engravings, 16s.

BROOKE, Life of Sir James, Rajah of Sarāwak. From his Personal
Papers and Correspondence. By SPENSER ST JOHN, H.M.'s Minister-Resident
and Consul-General Peruvian Republic ; formerly Secretary to the Rajah.
With Portrait and a Map. Post 8vo, 12s. 6d.

BROUGHAM.   Memoirs of the Life and Times of Henry Lord
Brougham. Written by HIMSELF. 3 vols. 8vo, £2, 8s. The Volumes are sold
separately, price 16s. each.

BROWN.   The Forester: A Practical Treatise on the Planting,
Rearing, and General Management of Forest-trees. By JAMES BROWN, LL.D.
Inspector of and Reporter on Woods and Forests, Benmore House, Port Elgin
Ontario. Fifth Edition, revised and enlarged. Royal 8vo, with Engravings.
36s.

BROWN.   The Ethics of George Eliot's Works. By JOHN CROMBIE
BROWN. Fourth Edition. Crown 8vo, 2s. 6d.

BROWN.   A Manual of Botany, Anatomical and Physiological.
For the Use of Students. By ROBERT BROWN, M.A., Ph.D. Crown 8vo, with
numerous Illustrations, 12s. 6d.

BUCHAN.   Introductory Text-Book of Meteorology. By ALEX-
ANDER BUCHAN, M.A., F.R.S.E., Secretary of the Scottish Meteorological
Society, &c. Crown 8vo, with 8 Coloured Charts and other Engravings,
pp. 218. 4s. 6d.

BUCHANAN.   The Shirè Highlands (East Central Africa). By
JOHN BUCHANAN, Planter at Zomba. Crown 8vo, 5s.

BURBIDGE.   Domestic Floriculture, Window Gardening, and
Floral Decorations. Being practical directions for the Propagation, Culture,
and Arrangement of Plants and Flowers as Domestic Ornaments. By F. W.
BURBIDGE. Second Edition. Crown 8vo, with numerous Illustrations,
7s. 6d.

——— Cultivated Plants: Their Propagation and Improvement.
Including Natural and Artificial Hybridisation, Raising from Seed, Cuttings,
and Layers, Grafting and Budding, as applied to the Families and Genera in
Cultivation. Crown 8vo, with numerous Illustrations, 12s. 6d.

BURTON.   The History of Scotland : From Agricola's Invasion to
the Extinction of the last Jacobite Insurrection. By JOHN HILL BURTON,
D.C.L., Historiographer-Royal for Scotland. New and Enlarged Edition,
8 vols., and Index. Crown 8vo, £3, 3s.

——— History of the British Empire during the Reign of Queen
Anne. In 3 vols. 8vo. 36s.

——— The Scot Abroad. Third Edition. Crown 8vo, 10s. 6d.

——— The Book-Hunter. New Edition. Crown 8vo, 7s. 6d.

BUTE.   The Roman Breviary : Reformed by Order of the Holy
Œcumenical Council of Trent ; Published by Order of Pope St Pius V.; and
Revised by Clement VIII. and Urban VIII.; together with the Offices since
granted. Translated out of Latin into English by JOHN, Marquess of Bute,
K.T. In 2 vols. crown 8vo, cloth boards, edges uncut. £2, 2s.

——— The Altus of St Columba. With a Prose Paraphrase and
Notes. In paper cover, 2s. 6d.

BUTLER.   Pompeii : Descriptive and Picturesque. By W.
BUTLER. Post 8vo, 5s.

BUTT.   Miss Molly. By BEATRICE MAY BUTT. Cheap Edition, 2s.

——— Alison. 3 vols. crown 8vo, 25s. 6d.

——— Lesterre Durant. 2 vols. crown 8vo, 17s.

——— Eugenie. Crown 8vo, 6s. 6d.

CAIRD.   Sermons. By JOHN CAIRD, D.D., Principal of the University of Glasgow. Sixteenth Thousand. Fcap. 8vo, 5s.

——— Religion in Common Life. A Sermon preached in Crathie
Church, October 14, 1855, before Her Majesty the Queen and Prince Albert.
Published by Her Majesty's Command. Cheap Edition, 3d.

CAMPBELL. Sermons Preached before the Queen at Balmoral. By the Rev. A. A. CAMPBELL, Minister of Crathie. Published by Command of Her Majesty. Crown 8vo, 4s. 6d.

CAMPBELL. Records of Argyll. Legends, Traditions, and Recollections of Argyllshire Highlanders, collected chiefly from the Gaelic. With Notes on the Antiquity of the Dress, Clan Colours or Tartans of the Highlanders. By LORD ARCHIBALD CAMPBELL. Illustrated with Nineteen full-page Etchings. 4to, printed on hand-made paper, £3, 3s.

CANTON. A Lost Epic, and other Poems. By WILLIAM CANTON. Crown 8vo, 5s.

CAPPON. Victor Hugo. A Memoir and a Study. By JAMES CAPPON, M.A. Post 8vo, 10s. 6d.

CARRICK. Koumiss; or, Fermented Mare's Milk: and its Uses in the Treatment and Cure of Pulmonary Consumption, and other Wasting Diseases. With an Appendix on the best Methods of Fermenting Cow's Milk. By GEORGE L. CARRICK, M.D., L.R.C.S.E. and L.R.C.P.E., Physician to the British Embassy, St Petersburg, &c. Crown 8vo, 10s. 6d.

CAUVIN. A Treasury of the English and German Languages. Compiled from the best Authors and Lexicographers in both Languages. Adapted to the Use of Schools, Students, Travellers, and Men of Business; and forming a Companion to all German-English Dictionaries. By JOSEPH CAUVIN, LL.D. & Ph.D., of the University of Göttingen, &c. Crown 8vo, 7s. 6d.

CAVE-BROWN. Lambeth Palace and its Associations. By J. CAVE-BROWN, M.A., Vicar of Detling, Kent, and for many years Curate of Lambeth Parish Church. With an Introduction by the Archbishop of Canterbury. Second Edition, containing an additional Chapter on Medieval Life in the Old Palaces. 8vo, with Illustrations, 21s.

CHARTERIS. Canonicity; or, Early Testimonies to the Existence and Use of the Books of the New Testament. Based on Kirchhoffer's 'Quellensammlung.' Edited by A. H. CHARTERIS, D.D., Professor of Biblical Criticism in the University of Edinburgh. 8vo, 18s.

CHRISTISON. Life of Sir Robert Christison, Bart., M.D., D.C.L. Oxon., Professor of Medical Jurisprudence in the University of Edinburgh. Edited by his SONS. In two vols. 8vo. Vol. I.—Autobiography. 16s. Vol. II.—Memoirs. 16s.

CHURCH SERVICE SOCIETY. A Book of Common Order: Being Forms of Worship issued by the Church Service Society. Fifth Edition. 6s.

CLOUSTON. Popular Tales and Fictions: their Migrations and Transformations. By W. A. CLOUSTON, Editor of 'Arabian Poetry for English Readers,' 'The Book of Sindibad,' &c. 2 vols. post 8vo, roxburghe binding, 25s.

COCHRAN. A Handy Text-Book of Military Law. Compiled chiefly to assist Officers preparing for Examination; also for all Officers of the Regular and Auxiliary Forces. Specially arranged according to the Syllabus of Subjects of Examination for Promotion, Queen's Regulations, 1883. Comprising also a Synopsis of part of the Army Act. By MAJOR F. COCHRAN, Hampshire Regiment, Garrison Instructor, North British District. Crown 8vo. 7s. 6d.

COLLIER. Babel. By the Hon. MARGARET COLLIER (Madame GALLETTI DI CADILHAC). Author of 'Our Home by the Adriatic.' 2 vols. post 8vo, 17s.

COLQUHOUN. The Moor and the Loch. Containing Minute Instructions in all Highland Sports, with Wanderings over Crag and Corrie, Flood and Fell. By JOHN COLQUHOUN. Seventh Edition. With Illustrations. [In preparation.

CONGREVE. Tales of Country Life in La Gruyère. From the French of Pierre Sciobéret. By L. DORA CONGREVE. Crown 8vo, 7s. 6d.

COTTERILL. Suggested Reforms in Public Schools. By C. C. COTTERILL, M.A., Assistant Master at Fettes College, Edin. Crown 8vo, 3s. 6d.

COX. The Opening of the Line: A Strange Story of Dogs and their Doings. By PONSONBY COX. Profusely Illustrated by J. H. O. BROWN. 4to, 1s.

COUNTESS IRENE. By the Author of 'Lauterdale and Caterina.' 3 vols. post 8vo. [In the press.

CRANSTOUN. The Elegies of Albius Tibullus. Translated into English Verse, with Life of the Poet, and Illustrative Notes. By JAMES CRANSTOUN, LL.D., Author of a Translation of 'Catullus.' Crown 8vo, 6s. 6d.

—— The Elegies of Sextus Propertius. Translated into English Verse, with Life of the Poet, and Illustrative Notes. Crown 8vo, 7s. 6d.

CRAWFORD. Saracinesca. By F. MARION CRAWFORD, Author of 'Mr Isaacs,' 'Dr Claudius,' 'Zoroaster,' &c. &c. Third Edition. Crown 8vo, 6s.

CRAWFORD. The Doctrine of Holy Scripture respecting the Atonement. By the late THOMAS J. CRAWFORD, D.D., Professor of Divinity in the University of Edinburgh. Fourth Edition. 8vo, 12s.

—— The Fatherhood of God, Considered in its General and Special Aspects, and particularly in relation to the Atonement, with a Review of Recent Speculations on the Subject. Third Edition, Revised and Enlarged. 8vo, 9s.

—— The Preaching of the Cross, and other Sermons. 8vo, 7s. 6d.

—— The Mysteries of Christianity. Crown 8vo, 7s. 6d.

DAVIES. Norfolk Broads and Rivers; or, The Waterways, Lagoons, and Decoys of East Anglia. By G. CHRISTOPHER DAVIES, Author of 'The Swan and her Crew.' Illustrated with Seven full-page Plates. New and Cheaper Edition. Crown 8vo, 6s.

DAYNE. In the Name of the Tzar. A Novel. By J. BELFORD DAYNE. Crown 8vo, 6s.

DESCARTES. The Method, Meditations, and Principles of Philosophy of Descartes. Translated from the Original French and Latin. With a New Introductory Essay, Historical and Critical, on the Cartesian Philosophy. By JOHN VEITCH, LL.D., Professor of Logic and Rhetoric in the University of Glasgow. A New Edition, being the Ninth. Price 6s. 6d.

DOBSON. History of the Bassandyne Bible. The First Printed in Scotland. With Notices of the Early Printers of Edinburgh. By WILLIAM T. DOBSON, Author of 'Literary Frivolities,' 'Poetical Ingenuities,' 'Royal Characters of Scott,' &c. Post 8vo, with Facsimiles and other Illustrations. 7s. 6d.

DOGS, OUR DOMESTICATED: Their Treatment in reference to Food, Diseases, Habits, Punishment, Accomplishments. By 'MAGENTA.' Crown 8vo, 2s. 6d.

DU CANE. The Odyssey of Homer, Books I.-XII. Translated into English Verse. By Sir CHARLES DU CANE, K.C.M.G. 8vo, 10s. 6d.

DUDGEON. History of the Edinburgh or Queen's Regiment Light Infantry Militia, now 3rd Battalion The Royal Scots; with an Account of the Origin and Progress of the Militia, and a Brief Sketch of the old Royal Scots. By Major R. C. DUDGEON, Adjutant 3rd Battalion The Royal Scots. Post 8vo, with Illustrations, 10s. 6d.

DUNCAN. Manual of the General Acts of Parliament relating to the Salmon Fisheries of Scotland from 1828 to 1882. By J. BARKER DUNCAN. Crown 8vo, 5s.

DUNSMORE. Manual of the Law of Scotland, as to the Relations between Agricultural Tenants and their Landlords, Servants, Merchants, and Bowers. By W. DUNSMORE. 8vo, 7s. 6d.

DUPRÉ. Thoughts on Art, and Autobiographical Memoirs of Giovanni Duprè. Translated from the Italian by E. M. PERUZZI, with the permission of the Author. New Edition. With an Introduction by W. W. Story. Crown 8vo, 10s. 6d.

ELIOT. George Eliot's Life, Related in her Letters and Journals. Arranged and Edited by her husband, J. W. CROSS. With Portrait and other Illustrations. Third Edition. 3 vols. post 8vo, 42s.

ELIOT. Works of George Eliot (Cabinet Edition). Handsomely printed in a new type, 21 volumes, crown 8vo, price £5, 5s. The Volumes are also sold separately, price 5s. each, viz.:—
Romola. 2 vols.—Silas Marner, The Lifted Veil, Brother Jacob. 1 vol.—Adam Bede. 2 vols.—Scenes of Clerical Life. 2 vols.—The Mill on the Floss. 2 vols.—Felix Holt. 2 vols.—Middlemarch. 3 vols.—Daniel Deronda. 3 vols.—The Spanish Gypsy. 1 vol.—Jubal, and other Poems, Old and New. 1 vol.—Theophrastus Such. 1 vol.—Essays. 1 vol.

———— George Eliot's Life. (Cabinet Edition.) With Portrait and other Illustrations. 3 vols. crown 8vo, 15s.

———— George Eliot's Life. (Cheap Edition.) With Portrait and other Illustrations. Crown 8vo, 7s. 6d.

———— Novels by GEORGE ELIOT. Cheap Edition. Adam Bede. Illustrated. 3s. 6d., cloth.—The Mill on the Floss. Illustrated. 3s. 6d., cloth.—Scenes of Clerical Life. Illustrated. 3s., cloth.—Silas Marner: The Weaver of Raveloe. Illustrated. 2s. 6d., cloth.—Felix Holt, the Radical. Illustrated. 3s. 6d., cloth.—Romola. With Vignette. 3s. 6d., cloth.

———— Middlemarch. Crown 8vo, 7s. 6d.

———— Daniel Deronda. Crown 8vo, 7s. 6d.

———— Essays. By GEORGE ELIOT. New Edition. Crown 8vo, 5s.

———— Impressions of Theophrastus Such. New Edition. Crown 8vo, 5s.

———— The Spanish Gypsy. Crown 8vo, 5s.

———— The Legend of Jubal, and other Poems, Old and New. New Edition. Crown 8vo, 5s., cloth.

———— Wise, Witty, and Tender Sayings, in Prose and Verse. Selected from the Works of GEORGE ELIOT. Seventh Edition. Fcap. 8vo, 6s.

———— The George Eliot Birthday Book. Printed on fine paper, with red border, and handsomely bound in cloth, gilt. Fcap. 8vo, cloth, 3s. 6d. And in French morocco or Russia, 5s.

ESSAYS ON SOCIAL SUBJECTS. Originally published in the 'Saturday Review.' A New Edition. First and Second Series. 2 vols. crown 8vo, 6s. each.

EWALD. The Crown and its Advisers; or, Queen, Ministers, Lords, and Commons. By ALEXANDER CHARLES EWALD, F.S.A. Crown 8vo, 5s.

FAITHS OF THE WORLD, The. A Concise History of the Great Religious Systems of the World. By various Authors. Being the St Giles' Lectures—Second Series. Crown 8vo, 5s.

FARRER. A Tour in Greece in 1880. By RICHARD RIDLEY FARRER. With Twenty-seven full-page Illustrations by LORD WINDSOR. Royal 8vo, with a Map, 21s.

FERRIER. Philosophical Works of the late James F. Ferrier, B.A. Oxon., Professor of Moral Philosophy and Political Economy, St Andrews. New Edition. Edited by Sir ALEX. GRANT, Bart., D.C.L., and Professor LUSHINGTON. 3 vols. crown 8vo, 34s. 6d.

———— Institutes of Metaphysic. Third Edition. 10s. 6d.

———— Lectures on the Early Greek Philosophy. Third Edition, 10s. 6d.

———— Philosophical Remains, including the Lectures on Early Greek Philosophy. 2 vols., 24s.

FLETCHER. Lectures on the Opening Clauses of the Litany, delivered in St Paul's Church, Edinburgh. By JOHN B. FLETCHER, M.A. Crown 8vo, 4s.

FLINT. The Philosophy of History in Europe. By ROBERT FLINT, D.D., LL.D., Professor of Divinity, University of Edinburgh. Vol. I. 8vo. [New Edition in preparation.

FLINT. Theism. Being the Baird Lecture for 1876. By ROBERT
FLINT, D.D., LL.D., Professor of Divinity, University of Edinburgh. Fifth
Edition. Crown 8vo, 7s. 6d.
—— Anti-Theistic Theories. Being the Baird Lecture for 1877.
Third Edition. Crown 8vo, 10s. 6d.
FORBES. Insulinde : Experiences of a Naturalist's Wife in the
Eastern Archipelago. By Mrs H. O. FORBES. Post 8vo, with a Map. 8s. 6d.
FOREIGN CLASSICS FOR ENGLISH READERS. Edited
by Mrs OLIPHANT. Price 2s. 6d. For List of Volumes published, see page 2.
GALT. Annals of the Parish. By JOHN GALT. Fcap. 8vo, 2s.
—— The Provost. Fcap. 8vo, 2s.
—— Sir Andrew Wylie. Fcap. 8vo, 2s.
—— The Entail ; or, The Laird of Grippy. Fcap. 8vo, 2s.
GENERAL ASSEMBLY OF THE CHURCH OF SCOTLAND.
—— Family Prayers. Authorised by the General Assembly of
the Church of Scotland. A New Edition, crown 8vo, in large type, 4s. 6d.
Another Edition, crown 8vo, 2s.
—— Prayers for Social and Family Worship. For the Use of
Soldiers, Sailors, Colonists, and Sojourners in India, and other Persons, at
home and abroad, who are deprived of the ordinary services of a Christian
Ministry. Cheap Edition, 1s. 6d.
—— The Scottish Hymnal. Hymns for Public Worship. Published for Use in Churches by Authority of the General Assembly. Various
sizes—viz.: 1. Large type, for Pulpit use, cloth, 3s. 6d. 2. Longprimer type,
cloth, red edges, 1s. 6d. ; French morocco, 2s. 6d. ; calf, 6s. 3. Bourgeois
type, cloth, red edges, 1s. ; French morocco, 2s. 4. Miniou type, French morocco, 1s. 6d. 5. School Edition, in paper cover, 2d. 6. Children's Hymnal,
paper cover, 1d. No. 2, bound with the Psalms and Paraphrases, cloth,
3s. ; French morocco, 4s. 6d. ; calf, 7s. 6d. No. 3, bound with the Psalms and
Paraphrases, cloth, 2s. ; French morocco, 3s.
—— The Scottish Hymnal, with Music. Selected by the Com-
mittees on Hymns and on Psalmody. The harmonies arranged by W. H. Monk.
Cloth, 1s. 6d. ; French morocco, 3s. 6d. The same in the Tonic Sol-fa Notation,
1s. 6d. and 3s. 6d.
—— The Scottish Hymnal, with Fixed Tune for each Hymn.
Longprimer type, 3s. 6d.
—— The Scottish Hymnal Appendix. 1. Longprimer type, 1s.
2. Nonpareil type, cloth limp, 4d.; paper cover, 2d.
—— Scottish Hymnal with Appendix Incorporated. Bourgeois
type, limp cloth, 1s. Large type, cloth, red edges, 2s. 6d. Nonpareil type,
paper covers, 3d. ; cloth, red edges, 6d.
GERARD. Reata : What's in a Name. By E. D. GERARD.
New Edition. Crown 8vo, 6s.
—— Beggar my Neighbour. New Edition. Crown 8vo, 6s.
—— The Waters of Hercules. New Edition. Crown 8vo, 6s.
—— The Land beyond the Forest. Facts, Figures, and
Fancies from Transylvania. By E. GERARD, Author of ' Reata,' &c. In Two
Volumes. With Maps and Illustrations. [In the press.
GERARD. Stonyhurst Latin Grammar. By Rev. JOHN GERARD.
Fcap. 8vo, 3s.
GILL. Free Trade : an Inquiry into the Nature of its Operation.
By RICHARD GILL. Crown 8vo, 7s. 6d.
GOETHE'S FAUST. Part I. Translated into English Verse by
Sir THEODORE MARTIN, K.C.B. Second Edition, post 8vo, 6s. Ninth Edi-
tion, fcap., 3s. 6d.
—— Part II. Translated into English Verse by the SAME.
Second Edition, revised. Fcap. 8vo, 6s.
GOETHE. Poems and Ballads of Goethe. Translated by Professor
AYTOUN and Sir THEODORE MARTIN, K.C.B. Third Edition, fcap. 8vo, 6s.

GORDON CUMMING. At Home in Fiji. By C. F. GORDON CUMMING, Author of 'From the Hebrides to the Himalayas.' Fourth Edition, post 8vo. With Illustrations and Map. 7s. 6d.

—— A Lady's Cruise in a French Man-of-War. New and Cheaper Edition. 8vo. With Illustrations and Map. 12s. 6d.

—— Fire-Fountains. The Kingdom of Hawaii : Its Volcanoes, and the History of its Missions. With Map and numerous Illustrations. 2 vols. 8vo, 25s.

—— Granite Crags: The Yō-semité Region of California. Illustrated with 8 Engravings. New and Cheaper Edition. 8vo, 8s. 6d.

—— Wanderings in China. New Edition. 2 vols. 8vo, with Illustrations. 25s.

GRAHAM. The Life and Work of Syed Ahmed Khan, C.S.I. By Lieut.-Colonel G. F. I. GRAHAM, B.S.C. 8vo, 14s.

GRANT. Bush-Life in Queensland. By A. C. GRANT. New Edition. Crown 8vo, 6s.

GRIFFITHS. Locked Up. By Major ARTHUR GRIFFITHS. Author of 'Chronicles of Newgate,' 'Fast and Loose,' &c. With Illustrations by C. J. STANILAND, R.I. Crown 8vo, 2s. 6d.

—— The Wrong Road ; by Hook or Crook. 3 vols. post 8vo, 25s. 6d.

HALDANE. Subtropical Cultivations and Climates. A Handy Book for Planters, Colonists, and Settlers. By R. C. HALDANE. Post 8vo, 9s.

HAMERTON. Wenderholme : A Story of Lancashire and Yorkshire Life. By PHILIP GILBERT HAMERTON, Author of 'A Painter's Camp.' A New Edition. Crown 8vo, 6s.

HAMILTON. Lectures on Metaphysics. By Sir WILLIAM HAMILTON, Bart., Professor of Logic and Metaphysics in the University of Edinburgh. Edited by the Rev. H. L. MANSEL, B.D., LL.D., Dean of St Paul's ; and JOHN VEITCH, M.A., Professor of Logic and Rhetoric, Glasgow. Seventh Edition. 2 vols. 8vo, 24s.

—— Lectures on Logic. Edited by the SAME. Third Edition. 2 vols., 24s.

—— Discussions on Philosophy and Literature, Education and University Reform. Third Edition, 8vo, 21s.

—— Memoir of Sir William Hamilton, Bart., Professor of Logic and Metaphysics in the University of Edinburgh. By Professor VEITCH of the University of Glasgow. 8vo, with Portrait, 18s.

—— Sir William Hamilton : The Man and his Philosophy. Two Lectures Delivered before the Edinburgh Philosophical Institution, January and February 1883. By the SAME. Crown 8vo, 2s.

HAMLEY. The Operations of War Explained and Illustrated. By Lieut.-General Sir EDWARD BRUCE HAMLEY, K.C.B. Fourth Edition, revised throughout. 4to, with numerous Illustrations, 30s.

—— Thomas Carlyle : An Essay. Second Edition. Crown 8vo. 2s. 6d.

—— The Story of the Campaign of Sebastopol. Written in the Camp. With Illustrations drawn in Camp by the Author. 8vo, 21s.

—— On Outposts. Second Edition. 8vo, 2s.

—— Wellington's Career ; A Military and Political Summary. Crown 8vo. 2s.

—— Lady Lee's Widowhood. Crown 8vo, 2s. 6d.

—— Our Poor Relations. A Philozoic Essay. With Illustrations, chiefly by Ernest Griset. Crown 8vo, cloth gilt, 3s. 6d.

HAMLEY. Guilty, or Not Guilty? A Tale. By Major-General W. G. HAMLEY, late of the Royal Engineers. New Edition. Crown 8vo, 3s. 6d.

—— Traseaden Hall. "When George the Third was King." New and Cheaper Edition. Crown 8vo, 6s.

HARBORD. Definitions and Diagrams in Astronomy and Navigation. By the Rev. J. B. HARBORD, M.A., Assistant Director of Education, Admiralty. 1s.

HASELL. Bible Partings. By E. J. HASELL. Crown 8vo, 6s.

—— Short Family Prayers. By Miss HASELL. Cloth, 1s.

HAY. The Works of the Right Rev. Dr George Hay, Bishop of Edinburgh. Edited under the Supervision of the Right Rev. Bishop STRAIN. With Memoir and Portrait of the Author. 5 vols. crown 8vo, bound in extra cloth, £1, 1s. Or, sold separately—viz.: The Sincere Christian Instructed in the Faith of Christ from the Written Word. 2 vols., 8s.—The Devout Christian Instructed in the Law of Christ from the Written Word. 2 vols., 8s.—The Pious Christian Instructed in the Nature and Practice of the Principal Exercises of Piety. 1 vol., 4s.

HEATLEY. The Horse-Owner's Safeguard. A Handy Medical Guide for every Man who owns a Horse. By G. S. HEATLEY, M.R.C.V.S. Crown 8vo, 5s.

—— The Stock-Owner's Guide. A Handy Medical Treatise for every Man who owns an Ox or a Cow. Crown 8vo, 4s. 6d.

HEMANS. The Poetical Works of Mrs Hemans. Copyright Editions.—One Volume, royal 8vo, 5s.—The Same, with Illustrations engraved on Steel, bound in cloth, gilt edges, 7s. 6d.—Six Volumes in Three, fcap., 12s. 6d. SELECT POEMS OF MRS HEMANS. Fcap., cloth, gilt edges, 3s.

HOLE. A Book about Roses: How to Grow and Show Them. By the Rev. Canon HOLE. Tenth Edition, revised. Crown 8vo, 3s. 6d.

HOME PRAYERS. By Ministers of the Church of Scotland and Members of the Church Service Society. Second Edition. Fcap. 8vo, 3s.

HOMER. The Odyssey. Translated into English Verse in the Spenserian Stanza. By PHILIP STANHOPE WORSLEY. Third Edition, 2 vols. fcap., 12s.

—— The Iliad. Translated by P. S. WORSLEY and Professor CONINGTON. 2 vols. crown 8vo, 21s.

HOSACK. Mary Queen of Scots and Her Accusers. Containing a Variety of Documents never before published. By JOHN HOSACK, Barrister-at-Law. A New and Enlarged Edition, with a Photograph from the Bust on the Tomb in Westminster Abbey. 2 vols. 8vo, £1, 1s.

HUTCHINSON. Hints on the Game of Golf. By HORACE G. HUTCHINSON. Third Edition. Fcap. 8vo, cloth, 1s. 6d.

HYDE. The Royal Mail; its Curiosities and Romance. By JAMES WILSON HYDE, Superintendent in the General Post Office, Edinburgh. Second Edition, enlarged. Crown 8vo, with Illustrations, 6s.

IDDESLEIGH. Lectures and Essays. By the late EARL OF IDDESLEIGH, G.C.B., D.C.L., &c. 8vo, 16s.

INDEX GEOGRAPHICUS: Being a List, alphabetically arranged, of the Principal Places on the Globe, with the Countries and Subdivisions of the Countries in which they are situated, and their Latitudes and Longitudes. Applicable to all Modern Atlases and Maps. Imperial 8vo, pp. 676, 21s.

JAMIESON. Discussions on the Atonement: Is it Vicarious? By the Rev. GEORGE JAMIESON, A.M., B.D., D.D., Author of 'Profound Problems in Philosophy and Theology.' 8vo, 16s.

JEAN JAMBON. Our Trip to Blunderland; or, Grand Excursion to Blundertown and Back. By JEAN JAMBON. With Sixty Illustrations designed by CHARLES DOYLE, engraved by DALZIEL. Fourth Thousand. Handsomely bound in cloth, gilt edges, 6s. 6d. Cheap Edition, cloth, 3s. 6d. In boards, 2s. 6d.

JENNINGS. Mr Gladstone: A Study. By LOUIS J. JENNINGS, M.P., Author of 'Republican Government in the United States,' 'The Croker Memoirs,' &c. Popular Edition. Crown 8vo, 1s.

JERNINGHAM. Reminiscences of an Attaché. By HUBERT E. H. JERNINGHAM. Second Edition. Crown 8vo, 5s.

—— Diane de Breteuille. A Love Story. Crown 8vo, 2s. 6d.

JOHNSTON. The Chemistry of Common Life. By Professor
J. F. W. JOHNSTON. New Edition, Revised, and brought down to date. By
ARTHUR HERBERT CHURCH, M.A. Oxon.; Author of 'Food: its Sonrces,
Constituents, and Uses;' 'The Laboratory Guide for Agricultural Students;'
'Plain Words about Water,' &c. Illustrated with Maps and 102 Engravings
on Wood. Complete in one volume, crown 8vo, pp. 618, 7s. 6d.

———— Elements of Agricultural Chemistry and Geology. Fourteenth Edition, Revised, and brought down to date. By Sir CHARLES A.
CAMERON, M.D., F.R.C.S.I., &c. Fcap. 8vo, 6s. 6d.

———— Catechism of Agricultural Chemistry and Geology. An
entirely New Edition, revised and enlarged, by Sir CHARLES A. CAMERON,
M.D., F.R.C.S.I.,&c. Eighty-sixth Thousand, with numerous Illustrations, 1s.

JOHNSTON. Patrick Hamilton : a Tragedy of the Reformation
in Scotland, 1528. By T. P. JOHNSTON. Crown 8vo, with Two Etchings by
the Author, 5s.

KENNEDY. Sport, Travel, and Adventures in Newfoundland
and the West Indies. By Captain W. R. KENNEDY, R.N. With Illustrations
by the Author. Post 8vo, 14s.

KING. The Metamorphoses of Ovid. Translated in English Blank
Verse. By HENRY KING, M.A., Fellow of Wadham College, Oxford, and of
the Inner Temple, Barrister-at-Law. Crown 8vo, 10s. 6d.

KINGLAKE. History of the Invasion of the Crimea. By A. W.
KINGLAKE. Cabinet Edition. Seven Volumes, illustrated with maps and
plans, crown 8vo, at 6s. each. The Volumes respectively contain :—
I. THE ORIGIN OF THE WAR between the Czar and the Sultan. II. RUSSIA
MET AND INVADED. III. THE BATTLE OF THE ALMA. IV. SEBASTOPOL
AT BAY. V. THE BATTLE OF BALACLAVA. VI. THE BATTLE OF IN-
KERMAN. VII. WINTER TROUBLES.

———— History of the Invasion of the Crimea. Vol. VI. Winter
Troubles. Demy 8vo, with a Map, 16s.

———— History of the Invasion of the Crimea. Vol. VII. From
the Morrow of Inkerman to the Fall of Canrobert. Demy 8vo, with Maps and
Plans, 14s.

———— History of the Invasion of the Crimea. Vol. VIII. From
the Opening of Pélissier's Command to the Death of Lord Raglan. With an
Index to the Whole Work. With Maps and Plans. Demy 8vo, 14s.

———— Eothen. A New Edition, uniform with the Cabinet Edition
of the 'History of the Invasion of the Crimea,' price 6s.

KNOLLYS. The Elements of Field-Artillery. Designed for the
Use of Infantry and Cavalry Officers. By HENRY KNOLLYS, Captain Royal
Artillery; Author of 'From Sedan to Saarbrück,' Editor of 'Incidents in the
Sepoy War,' &c. With Engravings. Crown 8vo, 7s. 6d.

LAING. Select Remains of the Ancient Popular and Romance
Poetry of Scotland. Originally Collected and Edited by DAVID LAING, LL.D.
Re-edited, with Memorial-Introduction, by JOHN SMALL, M.A. With a Por-
trait of Dr Laing. 4to, 25s.

LAVERGNE. The Rural Economy of England, Scotland, and Ireland. By LEONCE DE LAVERGNE. Translated from the French. With Notes
by a Scottish Farmer. 8vo, 12s.

LAWLESS. Hurrish : a Study. By the Hon. EMILY LAWLESS,
Author of 'A Chelsea Householder,' 'A Millionaire's Cousin.' Third
and cheaper Edition, crown 8vo. 6s.

LEE. A Phantom Lover : A Fantastic Story. By VERNON LEE.
Crown 8vo, 1s.

LEE. Glimpses in the Twilight. Being various Notes, Records,
and Examples of the Supernatural. By the Rev. GEORGE F. LEE, D.C.L.
Crown 8vo. 8s. 6d.

LEES. A Handbook of Sheriff Court Styles. By J. M. LEES,
M.A., LL.B., Advocate, Sheriff-Substitute of Lanarkshire. New Ed., 8vo, 21s.

———— A Handbook of the Sheriff and Justice of Peace Small
Debt Courts. 8vo, 7s. 6d.

LETTERS FROM THE HIGHLANDS.   Reprinted from 'The Times.' Fcap. 8vo, 4s. 6d.

LIGHTFOOT.   Studies in Philosophy.   By the Rev. J. LIGHTFOOT, M.A., D.Sc., Vicar of Cross Stone, Todmorden.   Crown 8vo, 5s.

LINDAU.   The Philosopher's Pendulum, and other Stories.   By RUDOLPH LINDAU.   Crown 8vo, 7s. 6d.

LITTLE.   Madagascar: Its History and People.   By the Rev HENRY W. LITTLE, some years Missionary in East Madagascar.   Post 8vo 10s. 6d.

LOCKHART.   Doubles and Quits.   By LAURENCE W. M. LOCKHART.   With Twelve Illustrations.   Fourth Edition.   Crown 8vo, 6s.

——— Fair to See : a Novel.   Eighth Edition.   Crown 8vo, 6s.

——— Mine is Thine : a Novel.   Eighth Edition.   Crown 8vo, 6s.

LORIMER.· The Institutes of Law : A Treatise of the Principles of Jurisprudence as determined by Nature.   By JAMES LORIMER, Regius Professor of Public Law and of the Law of Nature and Nations in the University of Edinburgh.   New Edition, revised throughout, and much enlarged. 8vo, 18s.

——— The Institutes of the Law of Nations.   A Treatise of the Jural Relation of Separate Political Communities.   In 2 vols. 8vo.   Volume I., price 16s.   Volume II., price 20s.

M'COMBIE.   Cattle and Cattle-Breeders.   By WILLIAM M'COMBIE, Tillyfour.   New Edition, enlarged, with Memoir of the Author.   By JAMES MACDONALD, Editor of the 'Live-Stock Journal.'   Crown 8vo, 3s. 6d.

MACRAE.   A Handbook of Deer - Stalking.   By ALEXANDER MACRAE, late Forester to Lord Henry Bentinck.   With Introduction by HORATIO ROSS, Esq.   Fcap. 8vo, with two Photographs from Life.   3s. 6d.

M'CRIE.   Works of the Rev. Thomas M'Crie, D.D.   Uniform Edition.   Four vols. crown 8vo, 24s.

——— Life of John Knox.   Containing Illustrations of the History of the Reformation in Scotland.   Crown 8vo, 6s.   Another Edition, 3s. 6d.

——— Life of Andrew Melville.   Containing Illustrations of the Ecclesiastical and Literary History of Scotland in the Sixteenth and Seventeenth Centuries.   Crown 8vo, 6s.

——— History of the Progress and Suppression of the Reformation in Italy in the Sixteenth Century.   Crown 8vo, 4s.

——— History of the Progress and Suppression of the Reformation in Spain in the Sixteenth Century.   Crown 8vo, 3s. 6d.

——— Lectures on the Book of Esther.   Fcap. 8vo, 5s.

MACDONALD.   A Manual of the Criminal Law (Scotland) Procedure Act, 1887.   By NORMAN DORAN MACDONALD.   Revised by the LORD ADVOCATE.   8vo, cloth.   10s. 6d.

M'INTOSH.   The Book of the Garden.   By CHARLES M'INTOSH, formerly Curator of the Royal Gardens of his Majesty the King of the Belgians, and lately of those of his Grace the Duke of Buccleuch, K.G., at Dalkeith Palace.   Two large vols. royal 8vo, embellished with 1350 Engravings.   £4, 7s. 6d.   Vol. I. On the Formation of Gardens and Construction of Garden Edifices.   776 pages, and 1073 Engravings, £2, 10s.   Vol. II. Practical Gardening.   868 pages, and 279 Engravings, £1, 17s. 6d.

MACKAY.   A Manual of Modern Geography; Mathematical, Physical, and Political.   By the Rev. ALEXANDER MACKAY, LL.D., F.R.G.S.   11th Thousand, revised to the present time.   Crown 8vo, pp. 688.   7s. 6d.

——— Elements of Modern Geography.   53d Thousand, revised to the present time.   Crown 8vo, pp. 300, 3s.

——— The Intermediate Geography.   Intended as an Intermediate Book between the Author's 'Outlines of Geography' and 'Elements of Geography.'   Twelfth Edition, revised.   Crown 8vo, pp. 238, 2s.

——— Outlines of Modern Geography.   176th Thousand, revised to the present time.   18mo pp. 118, 1s.

MACKAY. First Steps in Geography. 86th Thousand. 18mo, pp. 56. Sewed, 4d.; cloth, 6d.

—— Elements of Physiography and Physical Geography. With Express Reference to the Instructions recently issued by the Science and Art Department. By the Rev. ALEXANDER MACKAY, LL.D., F.R.G.S. 30th Thousand, revised. Crown 8vo, 1s. 6d.

—— Facts and Dates; or, the Leading Events in Sacred and Profane History, and the Principal Facts in the various Physical Sciences. The Memory being aided throughout by a Simple and Natural Method. For Schools and Private Reference. New Edition. Crown 8vo, 3s. 6d.

MACKAY. An Old Scots Brigade. Being the History of Mackay's Regiment, now incorporated with the Royal Scots. With an Appendix containing many Original Documents connected with the History of the Regiment. By JOHN MACKAY (late) of HERRIESDALE. Crown 8vo, 5s.

MACKAY. The Founders of the American Republic. A History of Washington, Adams, Jefferson, Franklin, and Madison. With a Supplementary Chapter on the Inherent Causes of the Ultimate Failure of American Democracy. By CHARLES MACKAY, LL.D. Post 8vo, 10s. 6d.

MACKELLAR. More Leaves from the Journal of a Life in the Highlands, from 1862 to 1882. Translated into Gaelic by Mrs MARY MACKELLAR. By command of Her Majesty the Queen. Crown 8vo, with Illustrations. 10s. 6d.

MACKENZIE. Studies in Roman Law. With Comparative Views of the Laws of France, England, and Scotland. By LORD MACKENZIE, one of the Judges of the Court of Session in Scotland. Sixth Edition. Edited by JOHN KIRKPATRICK, Esq., M.A. Cantab.; Dr Jur. Heidelb.; LL.B. Edin.; Advocate. 8vo, 12s.

MAIN. Three Hundred English Sonnets. Chosen and Edited by DAVID M. MAIN. Fcap. 8vo, 6s.

MAIR. A Digest of Laws and Decisions, Ecclesiastical and Civil, relating to the Constitution, Practice, and Affairs of the Church of Scotland. With Notes and Forms of Procedure. By the Rev. WILLIAM MAIR, D.D., Minister of the Parish of Earlston. Crown 8vo, 7s. 6d.

MAITLAND. Parva. By E. FULLER MAITLAND (E. F. M.) Fcap. 8vo. 5s.

MANNERS. Notes of an Irish Tour in 1846. By Lord JOHN MANNERS, M.P., G.C.B. New Edition. Crown 8vo, 2s. 6d.

MANNERS. Gems of German Poetry. Translated by Lady JOHN MANNERS. Small quarto, 3s. 6d.

—— Impressions of Bad-Homburg. Comprising a Short Account of the Women's Associations of Germany under the Red Cross. By Lady JOHN MANNERS. Crown 8vo, 1s. 6d.

—— Some Personal Recollections of the Later Years of the Earl of Beaconsfield, K.G. Sixth Edition, 6d.

—— Employment of Women in the Public Service. 6d.

—— Some of the Advantages of Easily Accessible Reading and Recreation Rooms, and Free Libraries. With Remarks on Starting and Maintaining Them. Second Edition, crown 8vo, 1s.

—— A Sequel to Rich Men's Dwellings, and other Occasional Papers. Crown 8vo, 2s. 6d.

—— Encouraging Experiences of Reading and Recreation Rooms. Aims of Guilds, Nottingham Social Guild, Existing Institutions, &c., &c. Crown 8vo, 1s.

MARMORNE. The Story is told by ADOLPHUS SEGRAVE, the youngest of three Brothers. Third Edition. Crown 8vo, 6s.

MARSHALL. French Home Life. By FREDERIC MARSHALL. Second Edition. 5s.

MARSHMAN. History of India. From the Earliest Period to the Close of the India Company's Government; with an Epitome of Subsequent Events. By JOHN CLARK MARSHMAN, C.S.I. Abridged from the Author's larger work. Second Edition, revised. Crown 8vo, with Map, 6s. 6d.

MARTIN. Goethe's Faust. Part I. Translated by Sir THEODORE
MARTIN, K.C.B. Second Edition, crown 8vo, 6s. Ninth Edition, fcap.
8vo, 3s. 6d.
———— Goethe's Faust. Part II. Translated into English Verse.
Second Edition, revised. Fcap. 8vo, 6s.
———— The Works of Horace. Translated into English Verse,
with Life and Notes. In 2 vols. crown 8vo, printed on hand-made
paper, 21s.
———— Poems and Ballads of Heinrich Heine. Done into Eng-
lish Verse. Second Edition. Printed on *papier vergé*, crown 8vo, 8s.
———— Catullus. With Life and Notes. Second Ed., post 8vo, 7s. 6d.
———— The Vita Nuova of Dante. With an Introduction and
Notes. Second Edition, crown 8vo, 5s.
———— Aladdin : A Dramatic Poem. By ADAM OEHLENSCHLAE-
GER. Fcap. 8vo, 5s.
———— Correggio : A Tragedy. By OEHLENSCHLAEGER. With
Notes. Fcap. 8vo, 3s.
———— King Rene's Daughter : A Danish Lyrical Drama. By
HENRIK HERTZ. Second Edition, fcap., 2s. 6d.
MARTIN. On some of Shakespeare's Female Characters. In a
Series of Letters. By HELENA FAUCIT, LADY MARTIN. Dedicated by per-
mission to Her Most Gracious Majesty the Queen. New Edition. Royal 8vo,
with Portrait. 9s.
MATHESON. Can the Old Faith Live with the New? or the
Problem of Evolution and Revelation. By the Rev. GEORGE MATHESON, D.D.
Second Edition. Crown 8vo, 7s. 6d.
———— The Psalmist and the Scientist ; or, Modern Value of the
Religious Sentiment. Crown 8vo, 7s. 6d.
MEIKLEJOHN. An Old Educational Reformer—Dr Bell. By
J. M. D. MEIKLEJOHN, M.A., Professor of the Theory, History, and Practice
of Education in the University of St Andrews. Crown 8vo, 3s. 6d.
———— The Golden Primer. With Coloured Illustrations by Wal-
ter Crane. Small 4to, boards, 5s.
———— The English Language : Its Grammar, History, and Litera-
ture. With Chapters on Versification, Paraphrasing, and Punctuation.
Second Edition. Crown 8vo, 4s. 6d.
MICHEL. A Critical Inquiry into the Scottish Language. With
the view of Illustrating the Rise and Progress of Civilisation in Scotland. By
FRANCISQUE-MICHEL, F.S.A. Lond. and Scot., Correspondant de l'Institut de
France, &c. In One handsome Quarto Volume, printed on hand-made paper,
and appropriately bound in Roxburghe style. Price 66s.
MICHIE. The Larch : Being a Practical Treatise on its Culture
and General Management. By CHRISTOPHER Y. MICHIE, Forester, Cullen House.
Crown 8vo, with Illustrations. New and Cheaper Edition, enlarged, 5s.
MILNE. The Problem of the Churchless and Poor in our Large
Towns. With special reference to the Home Mission Work of the Church
of Scotland. By the Rev. ROBT. MILNE, M.A., D.D., Ardler. Crown 8vo, 5s.
MINTO. A Manual of English Prose Literature, Biographical
and Critical : designed mainly to show Characteristics of Style. By W. MINTO,
M.A., Professor of Logic in the University of Aberdeen. Third Edition,
revised. Crown 8vo, 7s. 6d.
———— Characteristics of English Poets, from Chaucer to Shirley.
New Edition, revised. Crown 8vo, 7s. 6d.
———— The Crack of Doom. 3 vols. post 8vo, 25s. 6d.
MITCHELL. Biographies of Eminent Soldiers of the last Four
Centuries. By Major-General JOHN MITCHELL, Author of 'Life of Wallenstein.'
With a Memoir of the Author. 8vo, 9s.
MOIR. Life of Mansie Wauch, Tailor in Dalkeith. With 8
Illustrations on Steel, by the late GEORGE CRUIKSHANK. Crown 8vo, 3s. 6d.
Another Edition, fcap. 8vo, 1s. 6d.

MOMERIE. Defects of Modern Christianity, and other Sermons.
By the Rev. A. W. MOMERIE, M.A., D.Sc. Professor of Logic and Metaphysics
in King's College, London. Second Edition. Crown 8vo, 5s.
——— The Basis of Religion. Being an Examination of Natural
Religion. Second Edition. Crown 8vo, 2s. 6d.
——— The Origin of Evil, and other Sermons. Fourth Edition,
enlarged. Crown 8vo, 5s.
——— Personality. The Beginning and End of Metaphysics, and
a Necessary Assumption in all Positive Philosophy. Third Edition. Crown
8vo, 3s.
——— Agnosticism. Second Edition, Revised. Crown 8vo, 5s.
——— Preaching and Hearing; and Other Sermons. Crown
8vo, 4s. 6d.
——— Belief in God. Crown 8vo, 3s.

MONTAGUE. Campaigning in South Africa. Reminiscences of
an Officer in 1879. By Captain W. E. MONTAGUE, 94th Regiment, Author of
'Clande Meadowleigh,' &c. 8vo, 10s. 6d.

MONTALEMBERT. Memoir of Count de Montalembert. A
Chapter of Recent French History. By Mrs OLIPHANT, Author of the 'Life
of Edward Irving,' &c. 2 vols. crown 8vo, £1, 4s.

MURDOCH. Manual of the Law of Insolvency and Bankruptcy :
Comprehending a Summary of the Law of Insolvency, Notour Bankruptcy,
Composition - contracts, Trust-deeds, Cessios, and Sequestrations; and the
Winding-up of Joint-Stock Companies in Scotland; with Annotations on the
various Insolvency and Bankruptcy Statutes; and with Forms of Procedure
applicable to these Subjects. By JAMES MURDOCH, Member of the Faculty of
Procurators in Glasgow. Fifth Edition, Revised and Enlarged, 8vo, £1, 10s.

MY TRIVIAL LIFE AND MISFORTUNE : A Gossip with
no Plot in Particular. By A PLAIN WOMAN. New Edition, crown 8vo, 6s.
By the SAME AUTHOR.
POOR NELLIE. 3 vols. post 8vo, 25s. 6d.

NEAVES. Songs and Verses, Social and Scientific. By an Old
Contributor to 'Maga.' By the Hon. Lord NEAVES. Fifth Ed., fcap. 8vo, 4s.
——— The Greek Anthology. Being Vol. XX. of 'Ancient Clas-
sics for English Readers.' Crown 8vo, 2s. 6d.

NICHOLSON. A Manual of Zoology, for the Use of Students.
With a General Introduction on the Principles of Zoology. By HENRY AL-
LEYNE NICHOLSON, M.D., D.Sc., F.L.S., F.G.S., Regius Professor of Natural
History in the University of Aberdeen. Seventh Edition, rewritten and
enlarged. Post 8vo, pp. 956, with 555 Engravings on Wood, 18s.
——— Text-Book of Zoology, for the Use of Schools. Fourth Edi-
tion, enlarged. Crown 8vo, with 188 Engravings on Wood, 7s. 6d.
——— Introductory Text-Book of Zoology, for the Use of Junior
Classes. Sixth Edition, revised and enlarged, with 166 Engravings, 3s.
——— Outlines of Natural History, for Beginners ; being Descrip-
tions of a Progressive Series of Zoological Types. Third Edition, with
Engravings, 1s. 6d.
——— A Manual of Palæontology, for the Use of Students.
With a General Introduction on the Principles of Palæontology. Second
Edition. Revised and greatly enlarged. 2 vols. 8vo, with 722 Engravings,
£2, 2s.
——— The Ancient Life-History of the Earth. An Outline of
the Principles and Leading Facts of Palæontological Science. Crown 8vo,
with 276 Engravings, 10s. 6d.
——— On the "Tabulate Corals" of the Palæozoic Period,
with Critical Descriptions of Illustrative Species. Illustrated with 15
Lithograph Plates and numerous Engravings. Super-royal 8vo, 21s.

NICHOLSON. On the Structure and Affinities of the Genus Monticulipora and its Sub-Genera, with Critical Descriptions of Illustrative Species. By HENRY ALLEYNE NICHOLSON, M.D., D.Sc., F.L.S., F.G.S., Regius Professor of Natural History in the University of Aberdeen. Illustrated with numerous Engravings on wood and lithographed Plates. Superroyal 8vo, 18s.

—— Synopsis of the Classification of the Animal Kingdom. 8vo, with 106 Illustrations, 6s.

NICHOLSON. Communion with Heaven, and other Sermons. By the late MAXWELL NICHOLSON, D.D., Minister of St Stephen's, Edinburgh. Crown 8vo, 5s. 6d.

—— Rest in Jesus. Sixth Edition. Fcap. 8vo, 4s. 6d.

OLIPHANT. Masollam: a Problem of the Period. A Novel. By LAURENCE OLIPHANT. 3 vols. post 8vo, 25s. 6d.

—— Altiora Peto. Eighth Edition, Illustrated. Crown 8vo, 6s.

—— Piccadilly: A Fragment of Contemporary Biography. With Eight Illustrations by Richard Doyle. Eighth Edition, 4s. 6d. Cheap Edition, in paper cover, 2s. 6d.

—— Traits and Travesties; Social and Political. Post 8vo, 10s. 6d.

—— The Land of Gilead. With Excursions in the Lebanon. With Illustrations and Maps. Demy 8vo, 21s.

—— The Land of Khemi. Post 8vo, with Illustrations, 10s. 6d.

—— Haifa: Life in Modern Palestine. 2d Edition. 8vo, 7s. 6d.

—— Episodes in a Life of Adventure; or, Moss from a Rolling Stone. Fourth Edition. Post 8vo, 6s.

—— Fashionable Philosophy, and other Sketches. In paper cover, 1s.

—— Sympneumata: or, Evolutionary Functions now Active in Man. Edited by LAURENCE OLIPHANT. Post 8vo, 10s. 6d.

OLIPHANT. The Story of Valentine; and his Brother. By Mrs OLIPHANT. 5s., cloth.

—— Katie Stewart. 2s. 6d.

—— A House Divided against Itself. 3 vols. post 8vo, 25s. 6d.

OSBORN. Narratives of Voyage and Adventure. By Admiral SHERARD OSBORN, C.B. 3 vols. crown 8vo, 12s.

OSSIAN. The Poems of Ossian in the Original Gaelic. With a Literal Translation into English, and a Dissertation on the Authenticity of the Poems. By the Rev. ARCHIBALD CLERK. 2 vols. imperial 8vo, £1, 11s. 6d.

OSWALD. By Fell and Fjord; or, Scenes and Studies in Iceland. By E. J. OSWALD. Post 8vo, with Illustrations. 7s. 6d.

OUR OWN POMPEII. A Romance of To-morrow. 2 vols. crown 8vo, 17s.

OUTRAM. Lyrics: Legal and Miscellaneous. By the late GEORGE OUTRAM, Esq., Advocate. New Edition, with Explanatory Notes. Edited by J. H. Stoddart, LL.D.; and Illustrated by William Ralston and A. S. Boyd. Fcap. 8vo, 5s.

PAGE. Introductory Text-Book of Geology. By DAVID PAGE, LL.D., Professor of Geology in the Durham University of Physical Science, Newcastle. With Engravings on Wood and Glossarial Index. Twelfth Edition. Revised by Professor LAPWORTH of Mason Science College, Birmingham.   [In the press.

—— Advanced Text-Book of Geology, Descriptive and Industrial. With Engravings, and Glossary of Scientific Terms. Sixth Edition, revised and enlarged, 7s. 6d.

—— Introductory Text-Book of Physical Geography. With Sketch-Maps and Illustrations. Edited by CHARLES LAPWORTH, LL.D., F.G.S., &c., Professor of Geology and Mineralogy in the Mason Science College, Birmingham. 12th Edition. 2s. 6d.

PAGE. Advanced Text-Book of Physical Geography. Third
Edition, Revised and Enlarged by Prof. LAPWORTH. With Engravings. 5s.

PATON. Spindrift. By Sir J. NOEL PATON. Fcap., cloth, 5s.

—— Poems by a Painter. By Sir J. NOEL PATON. Fcap.,
cloth, 5s.

PATTERSON. Essays in History and Art. By R. HOGARTH
PATTERSON. 8vo, 12s.

—— The New Golden Age, and Influence of the Precious
Metals upon the World. 2 vols. 8vo, 31s. 6d.

PAUL. History of the Royal Company of Archers, the Queen's
Body-Guard for Scotland. By JAMES BALFOUR PAUL, Advocate of the Scottish
Bar. Crown 4to, with Portraits and other Illustrations. £2, 2s.

PEILE. Lawn Tennis as a Game of Skill. With latest revised
Laws as played by the Best Clubs. By Captain S. C. F. PEILE, B.S.C. Third
Edition, fcap. cloth, 1s. 6d.

PETTIGREW. The Handy Book of Bees, and their Profitable
Management. By A. PETTIGREW. Fourth Edition, Enlarged, with Engravings. Crown 8vo, 3s. 6d.

PHILOSOPHICAL CLASSICS FOR ENGLISH READERS.
Companion Series to Ancient and Foreign Classics for English Readers.
Edited by WILLIAM KNIGHT, LL.D., Professor of Moral Philosophy, Uni-
versity of St Andrews. In crown 8vo volumes, with portraits, price 3s. 6d.
[For list of Volumes published, see page 2.

POLLOK. The Course of Time : A Poem. By ROBERT POLLOK,
A.M. Small fcap. 8vo, cloth gilt, 2s. 6d. The Cottage Edition, 32mo, sewed,
8d. The Same, cloth, gilt edges, 1s. 6d. Another Edition, with Illustrations
by Birket Foster and others, fcap., gilt cloth, 3s. 6d., or with edges gilt, 4s.

PORT ROYAL LOGIC. Translated from the French · with Introduction, Notes, and Appendix. By THOMAS SPENCER BAYNES, LL.D., Professor in the University of St Andrews. Eighth Edition, 12mo, 4s.

POTTS AND DARNELL. Aditus Faciliores : An easy Latin Con-
struing Book, with Complete Vocabulary. By A. W. POTTS, M.A., LL.D.,
Head-Master of the Fettes College, Edinburgh, and sometime Fellow of St
John's College, Cambridge; and the Rev. C. DARNELL, M.A., Head-Master of
Cargilfield Preparatory School, Edinburgh, and late Scholar of Pembroke and
Downing Colleges, Cambridge. Ninth Edition, fcap. 8vo, 3s. 6d.

—— Aditus Faciliores Graeci. An easy Greek Construing Book,
with Complete Vocabulary. Fourth Edition, fcap. 8vo, 3s.

PRINGLE. The Live-Stock of the Farm. By ROBERT O. PRINGLE.
Third Edition. Revised and Edited by JAMES MACDONALD, Editor of the
'Live-Stock Journal,' &c. Crown 8vo, 7s. 6d.

PUBLIC GENERAL STATUTES AFFECTING SCOTLAND
from 1707 to 1847, with Chronological Table and Index. 3 vols. large 8vo, £3, 3s.

PUBLIC GENERAL STATUTES AFFECTING SCOTLAND,
COLLECTION OF. Published Annually with General Index.

RAMSAY. Rough Recollections of Military Service and Society.
By Lieut.-Col. BALCARRES D. WARDLAW RAMSAY. Two vols. post 8vo, 21s.

RAMSAY. Scotland and Scotsmen in the Eighteenth Century.
Edited from the MSS. of JOHN RAMSAY, Esq. of Ochtertyre, by ALEXANDER
ALLARDYCE, Author of 'Memoir of Admiral Lord Keith, K.B.,' &c. In two
vols. 8vo. [In the press.

RANKINE. A Treatise on the Rights and Burdens incident to
the Ownership of Lands and other Heritages in Scotland. By JOHN RANKINE
M.A., Advocate. Second Edition, Revised and Enlarged. 8vo, 45s.

RECORDS OF THE TERCENTENARY FESTIVAL OF THE
UNIVERSITY OF EDINBURGH. Celebrated in April 1884. Published
under the Sanction of the Senatus Academicus. Large 4to, £2, 12s. 6d.

RICE. Reminiscences of Abraham Lincoln. By Distinguished
Men of his Time. Collected and Edited by ALLEN THORNDIKE RICE, Editor
of the 'North American Review.' Large 8vo, with Portraits, 21s.

RIMMER. The Early Homes of Prince Albert. By ALFRED
RIMMER, Author of 'Our Old Country Towns,' &c. Beautifully Illustrated
with Tinted Plates and numerous Engravings on Wood. 8vo, 10s. 6d.

ROBERTSON. Orellana, and other Poems. By J. LOGIE ROBERT-
SON, M.A. Fcap. 8vo. Printed on hand-made paper. 6s.

—— The White Angel of the Polly Ann, and other Stories.
A Book of Fables and Fancies. Fcap. 8vo, 3s. 6d.

—— Our Holiday Among the Hills. By JAMES and JANET
LOGIE ROBERTSON. Fcap. 8vo, 3s. 6d.

ROSCOE. Rambles with a Fishing-rod. By E. S. ROSCOE. Crown
8vo, 4s. 6d.

ROSS. Old Scottish Regimental Colours. By ANDREW ROSS,
S.S.C., Hon. Secretary Old Scottish Regimental Colours Committee. Dedicated by Special Permission to Her Majesty the Queen. Folio, handsomely
bound in cloth, £2, 12s. 6d.

ROSSLYN. Love that Lasts for Ever. A Jubilee Lyric. By the
Earl of Rosslyn. Dedicated by Permission to the Queen, on the Fiftieth
Anniversary of her Accession, and published by Her Majesty's Command.
Printed on hand-made paper, with vellum cover, 1s.

RUSSELL. The Haigs of Bemersyde. A Family History. By
JOHN RUSSELL. Large 8vo, with Illustrations. 21s.

RUSTOW. The War for the Rhine Frontier, 1870 : Its Political
and Military History. By Col. W. RUSTOW. Translated from the German,
by JOHN LAYLAND NEEDHAM, Lieutenant R.M. Artillery. 3 vols. 8vo, with
Maps and Plans, £1, 11s. 6d.

ST LEGER. Under a Delusion. A Novel. By JOAN ST LEGER.
2 vols. crown 8vo, 17s.

SCHILLER. Wallenstein. A Dramatic Poem. By FREDERICK
VON SCHILLER. Translated by C. G. A. LOCKHART. Fcap. 8vo, 7s. 6d.

SCOTCH LOCH FISHING. By "Black Palmer." Crown 8vo,
interleaved with blank pages, 4s.

SCOTTISH METAPHYSICS. Reconstructed in accordance with
the Principles of Physical Science. By the Writer of 'Free Notes on Herbert
Spencer's First Principles.' Crown 8vo, 5s.

SELLER AND STEPHENS. Physiology at the Farm ; in Aid of
Rearing and Feeding the Live Stock. By WILLIAM SELLER, M.D., F.R.S.E.,
Fellow of the Royal College of Physicians, Edinburgh, formerly Lecturer on
Materia Medica and Dietetics ; and HENRY STEPHENS, F.R.S.E., Author of ' The
Book of the Farm,' &c. Post 8vo, with Engravings, 16s.

SETH. Scottish Philosophy. A Comparison of the Scottish and
German Answers to Hume. Balfour Philosophical Lectures, University of
Edinburgh. By ANDREW SETH, M.A., Professor of Logic, Rhetoric, and
Metaphysics in the University of St Andrews. Crown 8vo, 5s.

—— Hegelianism and Personality. Balfour Philosophical Lectures. Second Series. Crown 8vo, 5s.

SETON. A Budget of Anecdotes. Chiefly relating to the Current
Century. Compiled and Arranged by GEORGE SETON, Advocate, M.A. Oxon.
New and Cheaper Edition, fcap. 8vo. Boards, 1s. 6d.

SHADWELL. The Life of Colin Campbell, Lord Clyde. Illustrated by Extracts from his Diary and Correspondence. By Lieutenant-
General SHADWELL, C.B. 2 vols. 8vo. With Portrait, Maps, and Plans. 36s.

SHAND. Fortune's Wheel. By ALEX. INNES SHAND, Author of
'Against Time,' &c. 3 vols. post 8vo, 25s. 6d.

—— Half a Century ; or, Changes in Men and Manners. Second
Edition, 8vo, 12s. 6d.

—— Letters from the West of Ireland. Reprinted from the
'Times.' Crown 8vo, 5s.

SHARPE. Letters from and to Charles Kirkpatrick Sharpe.
Edited by ALEXANDER ALLARDYCE, Author of 'Memoir of Admiral Lord
Keith, K.B.,' &c. With a Memoir by the Rev. W. K. R. BEDFORD. In two
vols. 8vo. Illustrated with Etchings and other Engravings.

SIM. Margaret Sim's Cookery. With an Introduction by L. B. WALFORD, Author of 'Mr Smith: A Part of His Life,' &c. Crown 8vo, 5s.

SIMPSON. Dogs of other Days : Nelson and Puck. By EVE BLANTYRE SIMPSON. Fcap. 8vo, with Illustrations, 2s. 6d.

SKELTON. Maitland of Lethington ; and the Scotland of Mary Stuart. A History. By JOHN SKELTON, C.B., LL.D. Author of 'The Essays of Shirley.' Demy 8vo, 12s. 6d.

SMITH. Italian Irrigation : A Report on the Agricultural Canals of Piedmont and Lombardy, addressed to the Hon. the Directors of the East India Company ; with an Appendix, containing a Sketch of the Irrigation System of Northern and Central India. By Lieut.-Col. R. BAIRD SMITH, F.G.S., Bengal Engineers. Second Edition. 2 vols. 8vo, with Atlas, 30s.

SMITH. Thorndale ; or, The Conflict of Opinions. By WILLIAM SMITH, Author of 'A Discourse on Ethics,' &c. A New Edition. Crown 8vo, 10s. 6d.

——— Gravenhurst ; or, Thoughts on Good and Evil. Second Edition, with Memoir of the Author. Crown 8vo, 8s.

SMITH. Greek Testament Lessons for Colleges, Schools, and Private Students, consisting chiefly of the Sermon on the Mount and the Parables of our Lord. With Notes and Essays. By the Rev. J. HUNTER SMITH, M.A., King Edward's School, Birmingham. Crown 8vo, 6s.

SMITH. Writings by the Way. By JOHN CAMPBELL SMITH, M.A., Sheriff-Substitute. Crown 8vo, 9s.

SMITH. The Secretary for Scotland. Being a Statement of the Powers and Duties of the new Scottish Office. With a Short Historical Introduction and numerous references to important Administrative Documents. By W. C. SMITH, LL.B., Advocate. 8vo, 6s.

SOLTERA. A Lady's Ride Across Spanish Honduras. By MARIA SOLTERA. With Illustrations. Post 8vo, 12s. 6d.

SORLEY. The Ethics of Naturalism. Being the Shaw Fellowship Lectures, 1884. By W. R. Sorley, M.A., Fellow of Trinity College, Cambridge, and Examiner in Philosophy in the University of Edinburgh. Crown 8vo, 6s.

SPEEDY. Sport in the Highlands and Lowlands of Scotland with Rod and Gun. By TOM SPEEDY. Second Edition, Revised and Enlarged. With Illustrations by Lieut.-General Hope Crealocke, C.B., C.M.G., and others. 8vo, 15s.

SPROTT. The Worship and Offices of the Church of Scotland ; or, the Celebration of Public Worship, the Administration of the Sacraments, and other Divine Offices, according to the Order of the Church of Scotland. By GEORGE W. SPROTT, D.D., Minister of North Berwick. Crown 8vo, 6s.

STARFORTH. Villa Residences and Farm Architecture : A Series of Designs. By JOHN STARFORTH, Architect. 102 Engravings. Second Edition, medium 4to, £2, 17s. 6d.

STATISTICAL ACCOUNT OF SCOTLAND. Complete, with Index, 15 vols. 8vo, £16, 16s.
Each County sold separately, with Title, Index, and Map, neatly bound in cloth, forming a very valuable Manual to the Landowner, the Tenant, the Manufacturer, the Naturalist, the Tourist, &c.

STEPHENS. The Book of the Farm ; detailing the Labours of the Farmer, Farm-Steward, Ploughman, Shepherd, Hedger, Farm-Labourer, Field-Worker, and Cattleman. By HENRY STEPHENS, F.R.S.E. Illustrated with Portraits of Animals painted from the life: and with 557 Engravings on Wood, representing the principal Field Operations, Implements, and Animals treated of in the Work. A New Edition, Rewritten, and with New Illustrations.

——— The Book of Farm Buildings ; their Arrangement and Construction. By HENRY STEPHENS, F.R.S.E., Author of 'The Book of the Farm ;' and ROBERT SCOTT BURN. Illustrated with 1045 Plates and Engravings. Large 8vo, uniform with 'The Book of the Farm,' &c. £1, 11s. 6d.

——— The Book of Farm Implements and Machines. By J. SLIGHT and R. SCOTT BURN, Engineers. Edited by HENRY STEPHENS. Large 8vo, uniform with 'The Book of the Farm,' £2, 2s.

STEPHENS. Catechism of Practical Agriculture. With Engravings. 1s.

STEVENSON. British Fungi. (Hymenomycetes.) By Rev. JOHN STEVENSON, Author of 'Mycologia Scotia,' Hon. Sec. Cryptogamic Society of Scotland. 2 vols. post 8vo, with Illustrations, price 12s. 6d. each. Vol. I. AGARICUS—BOLBITIUS. Vol. II. CORTINARIUS—DACRYMYCES.

STEWART. Advice to Purchasers of Horses. By JOHN STEWART, V.S., Author of 'Stable Economy.' New Edition. 2s. 6d.

——— Stable Economy. A Treatise on the Management of Horses in relation to Stabling, Grooming, Feeding, Watering, and Working. By JOHN STEWART, V.S. Seventh Edition, fcap. 8vo, 6s. 6d.

STORMONTH. Etymological and Pronouncing Dictionary of the English Language. Including a very Copious Selection of Scientific Terms. For Use in Schools and Colleges, and as a Book of General Reference. By the Rev. JAMES STORMONTH. The Pronunciation carefully Revised by the Rev. P. H. PHELP, M.A. Cantab. Ninth Edition, Revised throughout. Crown 8vo, pp. 800. 7s. 6d.

——— Dictionary of the English Language, Pronouncing, Etymological, and Explanatory. Revised by the Rev. P. H. PHELP. Library Edition. Imperial 8vo, handsomely bound in half morocco, 31s. 6d.

——— The School Etymological Dictionary and Word-Book. Combining the advantages of an ordinary pronouncing School Dictionary and an Etymological Spelling-book. Fcap. 8vo, pp. 254. 2s.

STORY. Nero ; A Historical Play. By W. W. STORY, Author of 'Roba di Roma.' Fcap. 8vo, 6s.

——— Vallombrosa. Post 8vo, 5s.

——— He and She ; or, A Poet's Portfolio. Fcap. 8vo, in parchment, 3s. 6d.

——— Poems. 2 vols. fcap., 7s. 6d.

——— Fiammetta. A Summer Idyl. Crown 8vo, 7s. 6d.

STRICKLAND. Life of Agnes Strickland. By her SISTER. Post 8vo, with Portrait engraved on Steel, 12s. 6d.

STURGIS. John - a - Dreams. A Tale. By JULIAN STURGIS. New Edition, crown 8vo, 3s. 6d.

——— Little Comedies, Old and New. Crown 8vo, 7s. 6d.

SUTHERLAND. Handbook of Hardy Herbaceous and Alpine Flowers, for general Garden Decoration. Containing Descriptions, in Plain Language, of upwards of 1000 Species of Ornamental Hardy Perennial and Alpine Plants, adapted to all classes of Flower-Gardens, Rockwork, and Waters ; along with Concise and Plain Instructions for their Propagation and Culture. By WILLIAM SUTHERLAND, Gardener to the Earl of Minto ; formerly Manager of the Herbaceous Department at Kew. Crown 8vo, 7s. 6d.

TAYLOR. The Story of My Life. By the late Colonel MEADOWS TAYLOR, Author of 'The Confessions of a Thug,' &c. &c. Edited by his Daughter. New and cheaper Edition, being the Fourth. Crown 8vo, 6s.

TAYLOR. The City of Sarras. By U. ASHWORTH TAYLOR. Crown 8vo, 7s. 6d.

TEMPLE. Lancelot Ward, M.P. A Love-Story. By GEORGE TEMPLE. Crown 8vo. 7s. 6d.

THOLUCK. Hours of Christian Devotion. Translated from the German of A. Tholuck, D.D., Professor of Theology in the University of Halle. By the Rev. ROBERT MENZIES, D.D. With a Preface written for this Translation by the Author. Second Edition, crown 8vo, 7s. 6d.

THOMSON. Handy Book of the Flower-Garden : being Practical Directions for the Propagation, Culture, and Arrangement of Plants in Flower-Gardens all the year round. Embracing all classes of Gardens, from the largest to the smallest. With Engraved Plans, illustrative of the various systems of Grouping in Beds and Borders. By DAVID THOMSON, Gardener to his Grace the Duke of Buccleuch, K.G., at Drumlanrig. Fourth and Cheaper Edition, crown 8vo, 5s.

THOMSON. The Handy Book of Fruit-Culture under Glass : being a series of Elaborate Practical Treatises on the Cultivation and Forcing of Pines, Vines, Peaches, Figs, Melons, Strawberries, and Cucumbers. With Engravings of Hothouses, &c., most suitable for the Cultivation and Forcing of these Fruits. By DAVID THOMSON, Gardener to his Grace the Duke of Buccleuch, K.G., at Drumlanrig. Second Edition. Crown 8vo, with Engravings, 7s. 6d.

THOMSON. A Practical Treatise on the Cultivation of the Grape-Vine. By WILLIAM THOMSON, Tweed Vineyards. Ninth Edition, 8vo, 5s.

THOMSON. Cookery for the Sick and Convalescent. With Directions for the Preparation of Poultices, Fomentations, &c. By BARBARA THOMSON. Fcap. 8vo, 1s. 6d.

TOM CRINGLE'S LOG. A New Edition, with Illustrations. Crown 8vo, cloth gilt, 5s. Cheap Edition, 2s.

TRANSACTIONS OF THE HIGHLAND AND AGRICULTURAL SOCIETY OF SCOTLAND. Published annually, price 5s.

TULLOCH. Rational Theology and Christian Philosophy in England in the Seventeenth Century. By JOHN TULLOCH, D.D., Principal of St Mary's College in the University of St Andrews; and one of her Majesty's Chaplains in Ordinary in Scotland. Second Edition. 2 vols. 8vo, 16s.

—— Modern Theories in Philosophy and Religion. 8vo, 15s.

—— Theism. The Witness of Reason and Nature to an All-Wise and Beneficent Creator. 8vo. 10s. 6d.

—— Luther, and other Leaders of the Reformation. Third Edition, enlarged. Crown 8vo. 3s. 6d.

TWO STORIES OF THE SEEN AND THE UNSEEN. 'THE OPEN DOOR,' 'OLD LADY MARY.' Crown 8vo, cloth, 2s. 6d.

VEITCH. Institutes of Logic. By JOHN VEITCH, LL.D., Professor of Logic and Rhetoric in the University of Glasgow. Post 8vo, 12s. 6d.

—— The Feeling for Nature in Scottish Poetry. From the Earliest Times to the Present Day. 2 vols. fcap. 8vo, in Roxburghe binding. 15s.

VIRGIL. The Æneid of Virgil. Translated in English Blank Verse by G. K. RICKARDS, M.A., and Lord RAVENSWORTH. 2 vols. fcap. 8vo, 10s.

WALFORD. The Novels of L. B. WALFORD. New and Uniform Edition. Crown 8vo, each 5s.

MR SMITH: A PART OF HIS LIFE.	TROUBLESOME DAUGHTERS.
COUSINS.	DICK NETHERBY.
PAULINE.	THE BABY'S GRANDMOTHER.
	HISTORY OF A WEEK.

WARDEN. Poems. By FRANCIS HEYWOOD WARDEN. With a Notice by Dr Vanroth. Crown 8vo, 5s.

WARREN'S (SAMUEL) WORKS. People's Edition, 4 vols. crown 8vo, cloth, 15s. 6d. Or separately:—

Diary of a Late Physician. Cloth, 2s. 6d.; boards, 2s.

Ten Thousand A-Year. Cloth, 3s. 6d.; boards, 2s. 6d.

Now and Then. The Lily and the Bee. Intellectual and Moral Development of the Present Age. 4s. 6d.

Essays : Critical, Imaginative, and Juridical. 5s.

WARREN. The Five Books of the Psalms. With Marginal Notes. By Rev. SAMUEL L. WARREN, Rector of Esher, Surrey; late Fellow, Dean, and Divinity Lecturer, Wadham College, Oxford. Crown 8vo, 5s.

WATSON. Christ's Authority ; and other Sermons. By the late ARCHIBALD WATSON, D.D., Minister of the Parish of Dundee, and one of Her Majesty's Chaplains for Scotland. With Introduction by the Very Rev. PRINCIPAL CAIRD, Glasgow. Crown 8vo, 7s. 6d.

WEBSTER. The Angler and the Loop-Rod. By DAVID WEBSTER. Crown 8vo, with Illustrations, 7s. 6d.

WELLINGTON. Wellington Prize Essays on "the System of Field
Manœuvres best adapted for enabling our Troops to meet a Continental Army."
Edited by Lieut.-General Sir EDWARD BRUCE HAMLEY, K.C.B. 8vo, 12s. 6d.

WESTMINSTER ASSEMBLY. Minutes of the Westminster Assembly, while engaged in preparing their Directory for Church Government,
Confession of Faith, and Catechisms (November 1644 to March 1649). Edited
by the Rev. Professor ALEX. T. MITCHELL, of St Andrews, and the Rev. JOHN
STRUTHERS, LL.D. With a Historical and Critical Introduction by Professor
Mitchell. 8vo, 15s.

WHITE. The Eighteen Christian Centuries. By the Rev. JAMES
WHITE. Seventh Edition, post 8vo, with Index, 6s.

——— History of France, from the Earliest Times. Sixth Thousand, post 8vo, with Index, 6s.

WHITE. Archæological Sketches in Scotland—Kintyre and Knapdale. By Colonel T. P. WHITE, R.E., of the Ordnance Survey. With numerous Illustrations. 2 vols. folio, £4, 4s. Vol. I., Kintyre, sold separately,
£2, 2s.

——— The Ordnance Survey of the United Kingdom. A Popular
Account. Crown 8vo, 5s.

WILLS AND GREENE. Drawing-room Dramas for Children. By
W. G. WILLS and the Hon. Mrs GREENE. Crown 8vo, 6s.

WILSON. Works of Professor Wilson. Edited by his Son-in-Law,
Professor FERRIER. 12 vols. crown 8vo, £2, 8s.

——— Christopher in his Sporting-Jacket. 2 vols., 8s.

——— Isle of Palms, City of the Plague, and other Poems. 4s.

——— Lights and Shadows of Scottish Life, and other Tales. 4s.

——— Essays, Critical and Imaginative. 4 vols., 16s.

——— The Noctes Ambrosianæ. 4 vols., 16s.

——— The Comedy of the Noctes Ambrosianæ. By CHRISTOPHER
NORTH. Edited by JOHN SKELTON, Advocate. With a Portrait of Professor
Wilson and of the Ettrick Shepherd, engraved on Steel. Crown 8vo, 7s. 6d.

——— Homer and his Translators, and the Greek Drama. Crown
8vo, 4s.

WILSON. From Korti to Khartum : A Journal of the Desert
March from Korti to Gubat, and of the Ascent of the Nile in General Gordon's
Steamers. By Colonel Sir CHARLES W. WILSON, K.C.B., K.C.M.G., R.E.
Seventh Edition. Crown 8vo, 2s. 6d.

WINGATE. Annie Weir, and other Poems. By DAVID WINGATE.
Fcap. 8vo, 5s.

——— Lily Neil. A Poem. Crown 8vo, 4s. 6d.

WORDSWORTH. The Historical Plays of Shakspeare. With
Introductions and Notes. By CHARLES WORDSWORTH, D.C.L., Bishop of S.
Andrews. 3 vols. post 8vo, each price 7s. 6d.

WORSLEY. Poems and Translations. By PHILIP STANHOPE
WORSLEY, M.A. Edited by EDWARD WORSLEY. Second Edition, enlarged.
Fcap. 8vo, 6s.

YATE. England and Russia Face to Face in Asia. A Record of
Travel with the Afghan Boundary Commission. By Lieutenant A. C. YATE,
Bombay Staff Corps, Special Correspondent of the 'Pioneer,' 'Daily Telegraph,' &c., &c., with the Afghan Boundary Commission. 8vo, with Maps
and Illustrations, 21s.

YOUNG. Songs of Béranger done into English Verse. By WILLIAM
YOUNG. New Edition, revised. Fcap. 8vo, 4s. 6d.

YULE. Fortification : for the Use of Officers in the Army, and
Readers of Military History. By Col. YULE, Bengal Engineers. 8vo, with
numerous Illustrations, 10s. 6d.

ZIT AND XOE : Their Early Experiences. Reprinted from
'Blackwood's Magazine.' Crown 8vo, paper cover, 1s.

12/87.